Democratic Processes and Financial Markets: Pricing Politics

William Bernhard and David Leblang examine the conditions under which democratic events, including elections, cabinet formations, and government dissolutions, affect asset markets. Where these events have less predictable outcomes, market returns are depressed and volatility increases. In contrast, where market actors can forecast the political result, returns do not exhibit any unusual behavior. Further, political expectations condition how markets respond to the political process. When news causes market actors to update their political beliefs, market actors reallocate their portfolios, and overall market behavior changes. To measure political information, the authors employ sophisticated models of the political process. They draw on a variety of theories of market behavior, including the efficient markets hypothesis, capital asset pricing model, and arbitrage pricing theory, to trace the impact of political events on currency, stock, and bond markets. The analysis will appeal to academics, graduate students, and advanced undergraduates across political science, economics, and finance.

William Bernhard is Associate Professor of Political Science at the University of Illinois at Urbana-Champaign. His work has appeared in the *American Journal of Political Science*, the *American Political Science Review*, *International Organization*, *International Studies Quarterly*, the *Journal of Politics*, and the *Quarterly Journal of Political Science*.

David Leblang is Professor of Political Science and Research Associate at the Institute for Behavioral Sciences at the University of Colorado. He previously taught at the University of North Texas and at the College of William and Mary. His work has appeared in the *American Journal of Political Science*, the *Quarterly Journal of Political Science*, the *International Journal of Finance and Economics*, *International Organization*, and *International Studies Quarterly*.

Professors Bernhard and Leblang have jointly received the Franklin L. Burdett Pi Sigma Alpha Award from the American Political Science Association and the Robert H. Durr Award from the Midwest Political Science Association.

Democratic Processes and Financial Markets

Pricing Politics

William Bernhard
University of Illinois at Urbana-Champaign

David Leblang
University of Colorado

CAMBRIDGE UNIVERSITY PRESS
Cambridge, New York, Melbourne, Madrid, Cape Town, Singapore, São Paulo

Cambridge University Press
32 Avenue of the Americas, New York, NY 10013-2473, USA

www.cambridge.org
Information on this title: www.cambridge.org/9780521861229

First published 2006

Printed in the United States of America

A catalog record for this publication is available from the British Library.

Library of Congress Cataloging in Publication Data

Bernhard, William, 1966–
Democratic processes and financial markets: pricing politics / William
Bernhard, David Leblang.
p. cm.
Includes bibliographical references.
ISBN-13: 978-0-521-86122-9 (hardback)
ISBN-13: 978-0-521-67838-4 (pbk.)
ISBN-10: 0-521-86122-5 (hardback)
ISBN-10: 0-521-67838-2 (pbk.)
1. Capital market–Political aspects. 2. International economic relations.
3. Economics–Political aspects. I. Leblang, David. II. Title.
HG4523.B473 2006
332′.041–dc22 2006008543

ISBN-13 978-0-521-86122-9 hardback
ISBN-10 0-521-86122-5 hardback

ISBN-13 978-0-521-67838-4 paperback
ISBN-10 0-521-67838-2 paperback

For Jen, Raine, and Ezra

&

For Emily, Max, and Samantha

Contents

Acknowledgments

Authors generally express gratitude to those who provided assistance in the preparation of the manuscript. We will be no different and offer acknowledgment, appreciation, and absolution to those who helped us. Many colleagues have supported our work but two deserve special recognition for providing challenging critiques and reassuring encouragement: John Freeman and Jim Alt. John Freeman embodies the spirit of collaborative scholarship. He offered theoretical, analytical, and empirical advice on every aspect of this volume. Though we were not able to meet all of his challenges, we are extremely grateful for the time he devoted to our project. Jim Alt has been an exceptionally thoughtful discussant on more conference panels than we can count. His enthusiasm for this project was so contagious that it helped us focus on the goal of completing the book. Along with John and Jim, we also received insightful comments on our initial prospectus from Jerry Cohen, Jeff Frieden, and William Keech. Without their input, we would likely have written a very different book.

Other colleagues providing comments and advice on various elements of the manuscript include: John Aldrich, Lee Alston, Chris Anderson, Brock Blomberg, Lawrence Broz, Menzie Chinn, William Clark, Harold Clarke, Jerry Cohen, Jamie Druckman, Barry Eichengreen, Robert Franzese, Jeff Frieden, Tim Frye, Andrew Gould, Jim Granato, Clive Granger, Mark Hallerberg, Campbell Harvey, Jude Hays, Mike Herron, John Huber, Robert Jackman, William Keech, Keith Krehbiel, Nolan McCarty, Fiona McGillivray, Robert McNown, Andrew Martin, Michael Melvin, Helen Milner, Layna Mosley, Will Moore, Burt Monroe, Bumba Mukherjee, Michael Munger, Dennis Quinn, Stephen Quinn, Ron Rapaport, Dan Reiter, John Robertson, Peter Rosendorff, Brian Sala, Shanker Satyanath, Steve Shellman, Andy Sobel, Allan Stam, Scott Tarry, Michael Tomz, Michael Wallerstein, Michael Ward, Tom Willett, and Chris Zorn.

Members of our respective departments were remarkably tolerant of our attempt to integrate literatures with which we had only a basic familiarity but in which they have substantial expertise. We appreciate the help of Scott Adler, Ken Bickers, David Brown, Steve Chan, Edward Greenberg, John McIver, and Vanessa Baird at Colorado and Scott Althaus, Wendy Cho, Brian Gaines, Larry Neal, and Bob Pahre at Illinois.

We have presented parts of this book at numerous conferences and colloquia. We appreciate the comments and feedback provided by participants at the University of California at Davis, the Claremont Graduate University, Duke University, Emory University, the University of Michigan, the University of Minnesota, New York University, the University of Pittsburgh, Washington University, and the University of Wisconsin.

We are grateful to Robert Franzese for providing an opportunity for us to present our work at a day-long seminar during the 2003 EITM summer program at the University of Michigan, sponsored by the National Science Foundation. This occasion allowed us to think about the project as a unified whole rather than as a number of separate papers. Rob, Jude Hays, Jim Alt, John Aldrich, and the student participants provided extremely useful comments.

Lawrence Broz, Barry Eichengreen, and Jeff Frieden also gave us a chance to present a large portion of our work at the 2004 meeting of the Political Economy of International Finance Research Group. The interdisciplinary group of scholars participating in that meeting provided helpful suggestions from a variety of perspectives.

This book could not have been completed without a substantial amount of data. We are grateful to Heather Bell of Dow Jones, Inc.; Andre Gibson of the Chicago Mercantile Exchange; Helmut Stix of the National Bank of Austria; Jan Frazer of the Reserve Bank of New Zealand; Ashok Mody of the International Monetary Fund; Martin Boon of ICM; Andrea Volkens at the Manifesto Research Group; Dennis Quinn; Charles Franklin; Robert Erickson; and Christopher Wlezien for sharing data.

We received excellent and patient research assistance from Chad Atkinson, Rand Blimes, David Doherty, Amber Elms, Sang-Hyun Lee, Andrea Limbago, Jennifer Oats-Sargent, Dan Pemstein, Lindy van Landingham, and Kirsten Wandschneider. Financial support from the Undergraduate Research Opportunities Program at the University of Colorado and from the National Science Foundation is gratefully acknowledged.

Scott Parris and the Cambridge University Press team have provided outstanding editorial support.

We are hugely indebted to our wives and children. They were tolerant, supportive, and encouraging of a project that they suspected was merely an excuse for us to attend conferences and to tell jokes. We do not refute this. We dedicate this book to them as a token of our immense gratitude for the dedication they have extended to us.

1

Introduction

Political processes – elections, cabinet formations, referenda, legislative debates – determine a government's economic policies, which, in turn, condition the environment for investment. By anticipating the results of these processes, savvy investors can re-allocate their portfolios to meet a changed policy context. Asset owners, therefore, have a keen interest in predicting political outcomes: Which party will win the election? Who will form the government? What will be the new government's policy priorities?

The collective decisions of investors, in turn, shape how markets respond to political processes. Whether markets react to political events in a systematic manner remains an open issue. Do asset prices behave differently when left parties are in office? Will the election of a particular candidate cause a run on the currency? Does divided government – where the executive comes from a different party than a majority of legislators – cause a market downturn?

The consequences of these market responses extend far beyond questions of portfolio allocation. The investment decisions of asset owners fundamentally shape economic performance. Shifts in asset allocation can sustain an economic upswing or cut-off growth. With the technological and financial integration of asset markets, price movements can cascade across borders and markets, creating a world-wide boom or a systemic crisis.

Changes in market conditions have distributional consequences as well. Economic actors reliant on the stock market for income – firms, pensioners, etc. – are vulnerable not only to falling equity prices but also to volatility in market returns. Individuals or firms employed in export oriented and import competing industries see their fortunes rise and fall with fluctuations in the exchange rate. And changes in the market for government bonds may place public expenditures at risk if governments have to pay a higher rate to borrow.

Asset markets can also exert tremendous influence on political processes. Sharp price shifts, for instance, can threaten the approval ratings of incumbent politicians. Declining asset prices may signal government weakness. Increases in the costs of borrowing limit fiscal policy flexibility, preventing politicians from funding new policy initiatives or forcing them to cut popular programs.

Indeed, some political economists contend that the nature of capital markets threatens the quality of democracy by limiting the choices available to voters. Owners of mobile capital may react to "unfavorable" election outcomes by shifting their assets out of a market or even out of the country, punishing voters for choosing politicians unfriendly to their interests. As global markets become increasingly integrated and market actors have an ever larger range of cross-border investment options, the pressures on politicians to provide a pro-market policy environment intensify. To ensure continued investment – and continued economic growth – politicians must favor the interests of capitalists over the policy demands of other constituents. In anticipation of a potential market reaction, therefore, politicians may adopt policies and institutions to benefit asset owners. Voters, too, may expect such a market shift and alter their vote choice away from their own preferred party to one that will cater to the needs of the market. Asset owners, therefore, compel governments to adopt policies and institutions that favor their interests, even without taking any overt action.[1]

While political economists have identified the potential implications of larger, more integrated capital markets for democracy, they have not closely investigated the mechanisms that connect political events and market behavior. In fact, markets respond to political events in a variety of ways. In some instances, markets react calmly to political changes. In others, political events touch off frenetic market activity. Without a better understanding of the links between politics and asset markets, we cannot draw strong conclusions about the consequences of financial market integration for democratic governance.

In this book, we explain and empirically evaluate the conditions under which political events affect asset markets. We demonstrate that the political uncertainty created by democratic political competition can

[1] The basic outline of the argument extends back to Marx. The "classic" contemporary versions of the argument are Lindblom (1977) and Block (1977). For more recent arguments along these lines, see Garrett (1995), Goodman and Pauly (1993), Strange (1996), and Andrews (1994).

induce sharp changes in currency, bond, and equity market behavior, potentially hurting economic activity. We also draw out the political consequences of this financial market behavior. Turmoil in financial markets can have political costs, reducing public approval and increasing the costs of borrowing. Our results, therefore, can help explain recent institutional reforms in the industrial democracies. With deeper levels of financial market integration, both owners of financial assets and politicians have an incentive to support institutional reforms to (1) reduce political uncertainty and (2) limit potential financial market volatility.

INVESTMENT PORTFOLIOS AND FINANCIAL MARKETS

Financial markets, where economic actors trade financial assets such as bonds, stocks, currency, and real estate, are indispensable to a well-functioning economy.[2] These markets allow economic actors – individuals, firms, and/or governments – access to pools of capital by matching borrowers and lenders. Borrowers can forgo future consumption for present consumption by borrowing today and repaying tomorrow with interest. Lenders give up immediate consumption in the hopes that future consumption will be enhanced by making a profit on their investment.

In these markets, assets are bought and sold at different prices. Two factors condition the price behavior of these assets. First, the price is a function of the demand for and supply of capital. When little demand for (or large supply of) an asset exists, the price will be low. Strong demand and limited supply, on the other hand, result in higher prices.

Prices also reflect the risk associated with the holding of an asset. The pay-off from owning an asset often occurs in the future. Consequently, the expected return may not be realized. Risk is a relative, rather than absolute, concept: we can only compare the risk of two assets at a single point in time or the risk of a single asset across two points in time. Typically, investors require compensation for holding a risky asset. For instance, a stock of a start-up company may pay a slightly higher rate of return than a blue-chip stock because the risk of the company going bankrupt is higher.

The variety of financial markets provides economic actors with the ability to transfer wealth and risk across time and space. They also allow

[2] We do not examine issues related to the origin, transformation, and regulation of markets across countries and over time. The literature on financial development is voluminous: for example, Rajan and Zingales (2003), North (1981), Neal (1990), Bernstein (2004), and Smith (2003).

investors to hold a diversified portfolio of assets. Diversification permits investors to spread or reduce the overall risk associated with delaying consumption and investing. Understanding how individual investors balance risk and return should, in theory, yield clues about overall market performance. Indeed, the major models of finance, the capital asset pricing model, arbitrage pricing theory, etc., begin with assumptions about the micro-behavior of individual investors to generate predictions about aggregate market behavior. We discuss these models in subsequent chapters.

Investors can diversify across a variety of assets and markets. We focus on three in this book: bonds, stocks, and foreign exchange. Bonds represent promises made by the borrower to the lender that a fixed amount of capital, with interest, will be repaid at the time of maturity. Some bonds also periodically pay a fixed amount of interest between the time of issue and the time of maturity. Both corporations and governments issue debt instruments in the form of bonds to finance long-and short-term expenditures and to counteract shortfalls in revenue.

Corporations and firms can raise funds by issuing stock or equity. For investors, equity instruments provide an ownership interest in the firm and the promise of a share of the company's profits if there are any to be had. Ownership and profits are proportional to the amount of the firm's stock owned by the investor.

Economic actors may also trade in foreign exchange markets. These markets allow individuals and firms to diversify risk by purchasing and holding currency issued by foreign governments. Foreign exchange is traded largely in two different types of markets: spot and forward markets. In spot markets, currency is bought and sold today for immediate delivery. Forward markets, on the other hand, allow a contract to be signed today at a given price for delivery of the currency at some point in the future. Forward currency markets are especially important to firms engaged in cross-border transactions as they provide an opportunity to hedge their currency risk/exposure when future changes in the spot rate of a currency are unknown.

Stock, bond, and currency markets are broadly accessible to individuals, firms, and governments. And they are deep: trading in these assets reaches well over one hundred billion dollars *a day*. Most importantly, we can observe changing behavior in these markets on a daily – and in some cases on an even more disaggregated – basis, making them the perfect laboratory within which to evaluate the impact of democratic politics.

EXPLAINING MARKET REACTIONS TO POLITICAL EVENTS

A small interdisciplinary literature explicitly examines how democratic political processes – elections, cabinet negotiations, etc. – affect financial markets.[3] These studies reveal considerable variation in how markets respond to political events. Attempts to explain this variation have, for the most part, centered on institutions and partisanship.

Some political economists argue that the configuration of political and economic institutions conditions how investors will perceive the impact of a potential political change.[4] Institutional commitments that insulate economic policy from the direct control of elected politicians enhance policy stability, reassuring market actors that policy will not drastically change in the event of a partisan shift in the composition of the government. Therefore, institutions that limit policy discretion, like an independent central bank or an exchange rate commitment, should diminish market reactions to political events. Others argue that institutions that produce policy continuity will reduce market volatility. Some contend that proportional representation electoral systems, where legislative seats are distributed to parties in proportion to their vote totals, are more likely to limit policy fluctuations than winner-take-all majoritarian systems and, therefore, will dampen price shifts.

A second set of explanations centers on partisanship.[5] These arguments assume that parties differ in their policy priorities, based on the interests of their constituents. Right parties appeal to middle-and upper class voters and emphasize price stability and fiscal balance. Left parties, drawing support from the working classes, place more weight on employment and redistribution. These policy objectives suggest that asset owners prefer right parties to left parties. Political economists have evaluated whether the partisanship of the incumbent, a change in the partisan composition of the government, and the direction of partisan change systematically move markets.

Attempts to link institutions and partisanship to variations in market behavior have had, at best, mixed empirical support. For every paper

[3] See, among others, Bachman (1992), Bernhard and Leblang (2002), Blomberg and Hess (1996), Christodoulakis and Kalyvitis (1997), Eichengreen, Rose, and Wyplosz (1995), Freeman, Hays, and Stix (2000), Leblang and Bernhard (2000, 2001), Leblang and Mukherjee (2004), Lobo and Tufte (1998).

[4] For example, Bachman (1992), Blomberg and Hess (1997), Freeman, Hays, and Stix (2000).

[5] For example, Alesina and Rosenthal (1995), Alesina, Roubini, and Cohen (1993), Alt and Crystal (1983), Franzese (2002), Fiorina (1991), Hibbs (1987), and Leblang and Mukherjee (1994).

finding that, say, an independent central bank limits exchange rate volatility or that right parties strengthen stock market performance, there is another paper showing that the independence of the central bank is irrelevant to currency market behavior and that stock markets rally when left parties are in power.[6] Surveying the literature on market behavior surrounding political events, few consistent patterns emerge.

The failure of simple hypotheses underscores the need for more theoretical development about the conditions under which democratic politics affect market behavior. We argue that previous explanations fail to model adequately the information available to market actors. While institutions and partisan cues provide a context for the information available to market actors, they do not capture the dynamic flow of information during a political process. Thus, these studies are unable to capture how market actors form and update their expectations in response to political developments.

POLITICAL INFORMATION AND MARKET BEHAVIOR

Given the mixed findings of previous research, it is tempting to conclude that political events have little systematic effect on market behavior. But the strong intuition that politics matters for markets remains. The widespread reporting of political events in the business-related news media implies that markets do respond to politics. Sharp shifts in market behavior during several electoral campaigns provide anecdotal support. Why, then, are the results of academic research so inconsistent?

We contend that the mixed results reflect the difficulties of mastering different disciplines. Too often, political scientists investigate asset markets without taking advantage of the extensive research in economics and finance on the behavior of these markets. (Indeed, our first paper on the topic came back from the review process with a rather unsubtle suggestion that we learn something about how markets actually work before putting anything in writing.) On the other hand, financial economists often come at the problem with a naïve and under-developed understanding of political phenomena. Only by combining the two sets of research can we evaluate how markets respond to politics. This book, therefore, takes an interdisciplinary approach, drawing theoretical insights and empirical strategies from political science, finance, and economics. Using

[6] To explain these latter results, political economists speculate that investors shift to stocks as a hedge against the potentially inflationary consequences of a left government.

sophisticated models from both political science and finance, we hope to introduce more rigor and precision to how political economists study capital markets.

As with many analyses of asset market behavior, we build from the assumption that market actors engage in economic activity in efficient markets.[7] The efficient markets hypothesis (EMH), simply defined, states that asset prices immediately and fully reflect all available and relevant information (Fama 1991).[8] As soon as information hits the market, it is incorporated into asset prices. Market actors, therefore, cannot make excess profits (relative to the risk(s) they have undertaken) by utilizing trading strategies based exclusively on publicly available information.

Economists distinguish different types of market efficiency based on the information sets available to market actors. The weak form of efficiency assumes that past prices cannot be used to make abnormal returns (profits). That is, current prices are a function of information related to past prices and trading volumes. The semistrong form of efficiency means that public information cannot be used to make abnormal profits – in other words, prices reflect all publicly available and relevant information. Finally, the strong form of efficiency presupposes that prices reflect all relevant information at all times, including private information (e.g., insider trading).[9]

The idea of market efficiency is closely related to the statistical model of a "random walk." A variable follows a random walk if changes from the present value of the variable occur randomly, although these random changes are drawn from a known distribution. The efficient markets

[7] Recently, some scholars have argued that, given certain conditions, market actors can deviate from pure rational behavior. Models in the "behavioral finance" literature propose that market equilibria can be understood in terms of "sunspots" or with reference to "fads" or "herd" behavior. Most importantly, this literature identifies the importance of non-economic information in providing focal points to economic actors. From this perspective, the theoretical arguments and empirical evidence presented in this book are consistent with the behavioral finance approach to financial market behavior. See Thaler (1992), Barberis and Thaler (2002), and Shleifer (2000) for surveys.

[8] This view, it should be noted, reflects an evolution in thought regarding efficient markets. When introduced into the economic literature thirty five years ago an efficient market was defined as one which "adjusts rapidly to new information" (Fama, Jensen, and Roll 1969).

[9] Malkiel (2003) puts it nicely: "A capital market is said to be efficient if it fully and correctly reflects all relevant information in determining security prices. Formally, the market is said to be efficient with respect to some information set . . . if security prices would be unaffected by revealing that information to all participants. Moreover, efficiency with respect to an information set . . . implies that it is impossible to make economic profits by trading on the basis of [that information set]."

hypothesis implies that asset price changes follow a random walk – that is, changes in asset prices will occur randomly since asset prices already reflect the relevant information available to traders. Publicly available and predictable information, therefore, cannot systematically influence an asset's price.

This does not mean that information never affects asset prices. News – that is, the arrival of unanticipated information – may influence the trading behavior of economic agents. The publication of earnings reports, macroeconomic announcements, and interest rate changes may cause buyers and sellers to reevaluate their trading priorities if the information comes as a surprise. Although asset owners may know when the information will be announced and are likely to have a guess about substance of the announcement, as long as they do not know for certain the actual content, then the release of that information can change prices.

These arguments apply to political information as well. Information about political processes is widely available. The news media regularly report the activities of political leaders, offer public opinion surveys, and speculate on eventual policy outcomes. Party labels and endorsements provide other sources of information. The profusion of political information allows asset owners to form expectations about the likelihood of different political outcomes: who will win election, whether the bill will pass, or whether the country will go to war. Investors use this information to shift their portfolios to balance risk and return. This information about political processes will be quickly incorporated into asset prices.[10]

In the short-term, democratic political outcomes are often predictable. It is usually possible to forecast when the prime minister will call for elections, who will be elected, and how cabinet portfolios will be allocated, etc. before the event actually occurs. The predictability of political events allows asset owners to shift their portfolios in anticipation of the eventual outcome. Consequently, markets may not react to the actual resolution of the political event since economic actors had already anticipated the outcome. Instead, market adjustment may have occurred prior to the event when the likely outcome became apparent. The predictability of so many political processes, therefore, helps explain why there is often little market reaction to political events.

[10] Even if an investor pays attention only to price movements, she will respond to the changes in the behavior of other traders who shift their assets based on political information. Only a relatively few traders, therefore, need to be informed about political processes in order for the market to move in response to political events.

In situations where political outcomes are less predictable, however, we are more likely to observe markets responding to political events. If the eventual outcome remains unpredictable throughout the process, market actors will shift their assets only once the event has occurred. Consequently, market reactions are likely to be sharper in response to the conclusion of an unpredictable process than when market actors can anticipate the outcome.

But markets are also likely to behave differently *during* unpredictable political processes, not just at their conclusion, as traders shift their assets in response to new information. During these periods, investors may shift their portfolios toward assets that are insulated from the policy consequences of a political change, producing a drop in the price of assets that are more vulnerable to political influence and an increase in the price of the more insulated asset. For instance, asset holders may shift from bonds into equities (or vice versa) or substitute foreign assets for domestic ones.

One way to observe the market response to political events is to evaluate whether asset returns are "abnormal." The idea of an abnormal return reflects that, in the absence of a shock like an earnings announcement or a political event, forecasts of asset returns are usually fairly accurate. By comparing the actual return with the forecast return, it is possible to evaluate how market actors shifted their assets in response to an event.

Political processes, however, may not necessarily generate changes in the mean behavior of asset prices. The unpredictability of political outcomes may instead contribute to increased market volatility – a measure of the predictability of asset prices. Higher volatility indicates that price forecasts are less certain.[11] The variation in expectations surrounding the eventual political outcome may cause higher volatility, where prices jump around more than in periods where political outcomes are more predictable.

We develop these arguments and empirically evaluate their implications for a variety of markets. The importance of political information in shaping market behavior demands careful consideration of measurement issues. Unfortunately, current work in political economy tends to operate at a high level of institutional aggregation, employing simple indicators of electoral systems, partisanship, or policy institutions. These indicators are unlikely to capture the flow of information available to market actors.

[11] One way to conceptualize the concept of volatility is as a confidence interval surrounding price forecasts. Assuming efficient markets, today's asset price change is the best predictor of tomorrow's price change, but the confidence interval surrounding the forecast estimate may be wide – indicating high volatility – or small – indicating low volatility. This idea is discussed in Chapter 7.

Moreover, these institutional indicators are static. Markets learn about politics. We need to be able to update the information available to market actors during a political process. To examine the impact of politics on market behavior, therefore, we need a better understanding of (1) the type of political information that is available to market actors and (2) how that information is processed.

We contend that political science theories can provide insight into the political information available to market actors about the partisan and policy consequences of political events. Political scientists have developed models about equilibrium behavior in electoral competition (e.g., Downs 1957; Cox 1987, 1989; Shepsle 1991), cabinet formation (e.g., Laver and Shepsle 1996; Schofield 1992; Riker 1962), cabinet dissolutions (e.g., Lupia and Strom 1995; Smith 2004) and policy choice (e.g., Krehbiel 1998; Cameron 2000). Where a predictable equilibrium exists, we argue that markets should be able to anticipate that outcome and adjust accordingly. In the absence of a predictable equilibrium, however, economic actors may be less able to forecast the consequences of a political event, creating increased market volatility or abnormal returns. Using these more nuanced models of the political process helps determine the political information actually available to markets.

We also consider how political information is processed. Prior beliefs condition how the arrival of information affects the expectations of market actors. In some instances, information may simply reinforce the market's prior beliefs about the likely result of a political process, producing no shifts in asset allocation. In contrast, unexpected political developments may force market actors to update their beliefs about the eventual outcome, producing a shift in market behavior. We seek to model how market actors update information during the political process.

RESEARCH STRATEGY

We evaluate the impact of democratic political events on asset market behavior using a sample of the industrial democracies from 1980 through 2003. This choice not only reflects the availability of the political data necessary to measure market expectations – for example, polling information, party platforms, etc. – but also allows us to take advantage of advanced models of democratic politics, particularly for parliamentary systems. Further, the focus on "normal" politics in established democracies should bias our tests against finding evidence that politics influences markets. In these countries, extraordinary political events such as a coup d'etat or a major government default are rare. Asset owners, therefore, can have confidence that political events will not cause a major disruption to markets. By looking at countries where property rights are secure, we are able to isolate the role of political predictability in shaping market behavior.

Our sample period coincides with the globalization of financial capital. During this time, major changes in the regulation of domestic and international capital markets throughout the industrialized democracies, combined with technological innovations, led to an explosion in the pace and volume of asset trading.[12] The increasing integration of financial markets during this period should again make it difficult to find evidence that political events affect asset behavior.

Our concern with developing a more sophisticated understanding of the information available to markets also implies an empirical strategy. In order to capture the political information available to market actors, we must analyze specific events. Only by investigating the arrival of political information at identifiable times can we assess the relationship between political processes and market behavior. Therefore, we complement our aggregate analyses of markets and politics across space and time with studies of particular cabinet formations and elections. While one might argue that these "case studies" lack generalizability, we view them as necessary to illustrate the mechanisms of political and market equilibration. Moreover, the case studies are carefully grounded within a larger theoretical framework, improving our ability to use them as the basis for more general inferences.

The size and integration of financial markets dictates that we work at the lowest level of temporal aggregation possible. Often, studies of asset price behavior use monthly, quarterly, or even annual data to gauge how politics affects markets. But financial markets are so integrated and responsive that any evidence of a political influence on the behavior of asset prices is likely to dissipate rapidly. This necessitates that we work with temporally disaggregated data. For the most part we employ daily or weekly political and financial data series. In some cases, we work with "tick" data, which documents each transaction in a market.

[12] The United States abandoned capital controls in 1974 and continued to ease financial market restrictions to attract foreign investors, particularly during the Reagan years. The United Kingdom abandoned capital controls in 1979 and in 1986 opened the London Stock Market to foreign securities firms, a move referred to as "The Big Bang." Later in the 1980s, both Japan and countries in the European Union removed capital controls and liberalized the trading of domestic and foreign assets. See Helleiner (1994) for details of the major changes in financial markets during this period.

We draw on a variety of models of market behavior from the finance literature, including the efficient markets hypothesis (EMH), capital asset pricing model (CAPM), and arbitrage pricing theory (APT), to trace the impact of political events on the behavior of currency, stock, and bond markets. We do not evaluate whether these models provide the best explanation of market behavior. Rather, these models provide a clear analytic benchmark against which to measure market responses to political events. In each chapter, we employ one of these models to analyze behavior of a particular market, offering a short introduction to the main assumptions and implications of the model, a characterization of the market under investigation, and a discussion of how we expect to observe the effects of political information. We also utilize a variety of empirical tests and methodological tools developed by financial economists to evaluate the arguments. Each chapter, therefore, can be read individually.

This "multiple markets, multiple tests" approach will disappoint readers looking for strict adherence to contemporary guidelines of research design in political science. But the approach allows us to gain leverage on the main research question in a variety of settings. Similar results across different markets or with different methods provide strong evidence in favor of the argument. Moreover, the approach permits us to discuss different markets, theories, and techniques. By doing so, we hope to encourage other political economists to address new ideas, adopt new tools and, most importantly, ask new questions.

OUTLINE

The next four chapters investigate the effect of political uncertainty on financial markets, arguing that political predictability leads to more stable market behavior. Chapter 2 demonstrates how democratic political events – elections and cabinet dissolutions – affect the efficiency of currency markets by focusing on the relationship between the spot and forward exchange rate. The efficient markets hypothesis implies that the forward exchange rate – the price of the currency deliverable 30 days in the future – should be an unbiased predictor of the future spot exchange rate. Using weekly data from eight countries, we demonstrate that the forward exchange rate is a biased predictor of exchange rate changes more often during periods of potential political change than when the government's tenure in office is secure. That is, these political events appear to make currency markets less efficient. Nevertheless, simple hypotheses based on incumbent partisanship, partisan change, electoral institutions, and exchange rate commitments cannot account for the variation of market reactions to different political events.

The inability of these simple hypotheses to account for variations in market behavior points to the need to develop an alternative approach to evaluate the conditions under which democratic politics affect market behavior. Chapter 3, therefore, draws on political science theory to examine the proposition that unpredictable political processes affect markets differently than events with predictable outcomes. We test the argument by examining the impact of cabinet formations in parliamentary democracies on stock and bond markets. Political scientists have developed models to predict the results of a cabinet formation process. We draw on work by Laver and Shepsle (1996) who assume that parties bargain over the distribution of cabinet portfolios, rather than over the cabinet's policy priorities. From this assumption, they develop a spatial model that predicts the outcomes of cabinet negotiations based on the distribution of legislative seats, the policy positions of the parties, and the salience of different issue dimensions in that system. Using their model, we determine whether a "strong" party exists – i.e., one party that is in an advantageous negotiation position – in over 70 cabinet formations between 1970 and 2003. When a strong party exists, coalition negotiations should be fairly predictable. In these cases, we find no evidence of abnormal stock market returns during the cabinet formation process – that is, the returns are consistent with the market's performance in the months immediately prior to the election. When a strong party does not exist, however, the outcome of coalition bargaining is less predictable. In these cases, stock returns are depressed during the negotiation period, suggesting that investors have re-allocated their portfolios and increased their holdings of assets with less risky returns.

Financial markets are increasingly integrated. Shifts in asset market behavior, therefore, are likely to spill across borders. Chapter 4 investigates how political events in foreign countries affect domestic equity and bond markets. We first estimate the size of these politically induced foreign shocks. We then examine the institutional determinants of their size, including monetary arrangements, exchange rate regimes, and electoral systems. Independent central banks, fixed exchange rates, and predictable politics inhibit the transfer of politically induced financial shocks across countries. These institutional arrangements are similar to many adopted in the industrial democracies in the past twenty years, particularly in the European Union. We return to the issue of institutional reform in the conclusion.

Chapter 5 examines how political events affect interest rates. Higher interest rates can inhibit the flexibility of fiscal policy, preventing politicians from initiating new programs or forcing them to cut popular ones. Higher interest rates may also dampen economic activity in the private sector. Incumbents may be held electorally accountable for slower growth. To investigate the impact of political processes on interest rates, we continue to focus on parliamentary systems. Drawing on political science models of cabinet durability, we estimate the probability of a cabinet coming to an end – either due to a constitutionally mandated election or a loss of parliamentary support. Using the generated probability of a cabinet end as a proxy for market expectations, we show that the possibility of a cabinet coming to an end increases the costs of borrowing in both the public and private sectors.

The impact of information about political events on markets will vary according to whether market actors anticipate the event. In Chapters 6–8, we analyze how prior beliefs and expectations condition the influence of political events on market behavior. To do this, we focus on specific episodes of the political process: cabinet formations and elections. This allows us to estimate how the arrival of political information at particular times affects market behavior.

In Chapter 6, we examine bond market reactions to the *process of cabinet negotiations.* Cabinet negotiations are media events. Journalists cover the process closely, reporting on which parties are negotiating, what portfolios and policies are on the table, and what the likely outcome will be. To measure the dynamic process of cabinet bargaining, we perform content analysis of major newspapers during two instances of coalition bargaining: the surprising People's Party (ÖVP)–Freedom Party (FPO) coalition in Austria (1999–2000) and the National–New Zealand First coalition in New Zealand (1996). Using a Bayesian transformation of the information generated by the content analysis, we generate a proxy for market beliefs about which coalition is likely to form. We then test whether the bargaining process affects daily changes in government bond returns. We show that the impact of information about the bargaining process is conditioned by the prior beliefs of market actors about which coalition will form. Without an understanding of how markets update and process political information, however, we would not have been able to assess the market reaction to the cabinet negotiation process accurately.

Chapter 7 uses the case of the 2000 U.S. Presidential election to explore how the arrival of political information shapes market behavior. This analysis tracks the overnight movements of two major futures prices, the NASDAQ 100 Index and the S&P 500 Index, and the U.S. dollar–Japanese Yen exchange rate on election night. To measure the arrival of political information, we first calculate the probability of a Gore electoral college victory using state public opinion polls. When CNN called states for either candidate, we update this probability, providing a minute-by-minute estimate of the probability of a Gore victory throughout the night. Statistical analysis indicates that this updated probability affects both the price and the volatility (conditional variance) of these assets, again illustrating how the beliefs of market actors about political outcomes influence market volatility. By examining only the night of the election, the experimental design of this chapter limits the influence of earnings reports, unemployment or inflation announcements, or changes in interest rates. As a result, we are able to isolate the effect of political expectations on market behavior.

In Chapter 8, we show how excessive exchange rate movements can hurt an incumbent government's approval ratings by looking at the relationship between government popularity and exchange rate movements in Britain between 1987 and 2001. To generate an accurate measure of the short-term political costs of exchange rate fluctuations, however, we must account for the possibility that exchange rate behavior may also be a product of changes in the government's public standing. Indeed, the analyses in Chapter 3 imply that where public opinion shocks make political outcomes less certain, exchange rate volatility will increase. To deal with this endogencity issue, we estimate separate models of exchange rate behavior and government voting intention iteratively and recursively. At each iteration, we use estimates from each model to generate measures of exchange rate and public opinion shocks. We then employ these generated variables in the next iteration of the estimates, including measures of political shocks in the model of exchange rates and measures of exchange rate behavior in the model of voting intention. We are able, therefore, to measure the political costs (in terms of government popularity) of exchange rate shocks and the exchange rate consequences (in terms of exchange rate behavior) of political competition.

IMPLICATIONS FOR DEMOCRATIC POLITICS

The results of our analysis establish (1) political uncertainty can affect financial market performance, and (2) financial market turbulence can negatively affect the ability of politicians to retain office. With a better understanding of the mechanisms that link democratic politics and market behavior, more informed discussion of the impact of larger more integrated financial markets on democratic politics becomes possible.

In particular, the results suggest that the market and political reforms in the industrial democracies over the past twenty years may be designed to break the linkages between financial market behavior and democratic political outcomes. These reforms include changes in the regulation of financial markets, monetary reforms (central bank independence, exchange rate commitments, the single currency in the European Union), and political reforms designed to reduce political uncertainty (electoral reform, devolution).

With the growth of capital markets over the past twenty years, political uncertainty carries greater economic costs. High levels of democratic political uncertainty may simply have become too costly from an economic perspective. Consequently, owners of assets are likely to demand political institutions that will produce predictable political outcomes and reduce their exposure to politically-induced financial market volatility.

In turn, politicians have found themselves increasingly vulnerable to financial market fluctuations. Politicians, therefore, have incentives to supply institutional reforms that limit their susceptibility to the negative political consequences of financial market shocks and increase political predictability to prevent financial market volatility.

The intersection of interests between the demanders of institutional reform (i.e., asset owners) and the suppliers of reform (i.e., politicians) provides an important background condition for the patterns of reform.

2

Democratic Processes and Political Risk: Evidence from Foreign Exchange Markets

Foreign exchange markets are among the deepest and widest financial markets in the world. Technological innovations and market liberalization have made currency markets enormous – by 1992, the volume of transactions topped over one trillion dollars *each day*. Moreover, economic agents can trade currencies with shocking speed – during the September 1992 EMS crisis, British monetary authorities expended over two billion dollars to support the pegged value of the pound in only a few *hours*. The behavior of currency markets can affect not only trade flows and international investment, key determinants of economic performance, but also political outcomes. With increasing capital mobility, political disputes over exchange rates have become highly salient, both at the domestic and international level. Indeed, some political economists assert that rapidly adjusting international markets may overwhelm the ability of policymakers to control policy, and, according to the most extreme view, thwart any meaningful democracy. Understanding how currency markets behave, therefore, is a fundamental step to assess accurately how the internationalization of economic activity affects democratic politics.

We investigate how democratic political events influence currency markets, focusing on the relationship between the spot and forward exchange rate markets. The efficient markets hypothesis implies that the forward exchange rate – the price of the currency deliverable 30 days in the future – should be an unbiased predictor of the future spot exchange rate. That is, today's 30-day forward rate should, on average, accurately predict the spot exchange rate one month from today. Empirical studies, however, conclude that the forward rate is often a biased predictor of future exchange rate changes. Many economic models attribute this bias to a risk premium. That is, currency traders will demand a higher return for holding the currency.

We argue that democratic political processes contribute to the existence of risk premia by making it more difficult for economic agents to forecast exchange rate movements. During periods of potential political change, economic agents must infer the government's commitment to the exchange rate by processing information about the policy priorities of different parties, potential election results, and possible cabinets. The possibility of opportunistic policy behavior and the contingent nature of democratic politics complicate the inference problem. Democratic processes, therefore, are likely to increase the variation of expectations about the government's commitment to the exchange rate. Because of this variation, traders will demand compensation for taking a forward position in the market. Consequently, we expect the forward rate to be a biased predictor of exchange rate changes more often during periods of potential political change than when the government's tenure in office is secure.

FORWARD EXCHANGE RATES AND THE EFFICIENT MARKETS HYPOTHESIS

Economic agents can trade two types of contracts on the foreign exchange market: spot contracts and forward contracts.[1] The spot exchange rate is the price for a quantity of foreign currency that will be delivered within two days. Typically, economic agents use the spot market for foreign travel, foreign investment (stocks, bonds, real estate), or the purchase of foreign imports. Spot prices reflect the exchange rate arrangement chosen by the government. With a fixed exchange rate, a government fixes the value of its currency and maintains that value through the purchase and sale of local currency on the foreign exchange market. Under a floating exchange rate, supply and demand on the foreign exchange markets determine the currency's value.

Forward contracts specify a price today for delivery of a foreign currency at some point in the future – usually 30, 60, or 90 days ahead. Economic agents purchase forward contracts in order to hedge against a rise in the price of foreign currency, to profit via interest arbitrage, or to speculate against future currency movements.

One of the fundamental ideas about the relationship between spot and forward exchange rates follows from the efficient markets hypothesis (EMH). Fama (1970) defines an asset market as efficient if the price of an asset "fully reflects" all information available within that market.

[1] Economic agents can also purchase foreign currency futures.

Since traders utilize all past and present information, only "news" or new information can cause a change in the price of an asset. Therefore, profit via speculation or arbitrage should be impossible (assuming that risk-neutral actors populate the markets).

When applied to foreign exchange markets, the EMH implies that the forward rate should be a perfect predictor of the future spot exchange rate. That is (with all variables expressed as logs) the forward exchange rate (f) at time t for delivery at time $t+k$ should equal the expected spot exchange rate (s) at time $t+k$:

$$f_{t,t+k} = \mathrm{E}_t(s_{t+k}) \tag{2.1}$$

where E(•) is the expectations operator given the information set available to actors at time t.

THE FORWARD EXCHANGE RATE BIAS

A large number of scholars have tested efficiency in forward exchange rate markets (Engel 1996 and Lewis 1995 provide reviews). These tests examine whether the expected exchange rate at time $t+k$ is an unbiased predictor of the actual exchange rate at time $t+k$:

$$s_{t+k} = \alpha + \beta[E_t(s_{t+k})] + \varepsilon_{t+k} \tag{2.2}$$

where ε_t is a random error which is orthogonal (uncorrelated) to the information set at time t and α and β are parameters to be estimated. Substituting Eq. (2.1) into Eq. (2.2) yields:

$$S_{t+k} = \alpha + \beta f_{t,t+k} + \varepsilon_{t+k}. \tag{2.3}$$

Typically, both the spot and the forward exchange rates are expressed as first differences to avoid problems associated with non-stationary variables:

$$S_{t+k} - S_t = \alpha + \beta\left[f_{t,t+k} - S_t\right] + \varepsilon_{t+k}. \tag{2.4}$$

Given the assumption of risk neutral actors and perfectly competitive markets, the EMH implies the following joint hypothesis for Eq. (2.4): $(\alpha,\ \beta) = (0,\ 1)$. According to the literature, the assumption of rational expectations implies that $\alpha = 0$. Additionally, if the forward premium, $(f_{t,\ t+k} - s_t)$, is an unbiased predictor of future changes in the spot rate ($s_{t+k}-s_t$) – that is, if the equilibrium condition between forward and spot rates (Eq. (2.1)) holds – then estimates of β should not be significantly different from one.

Empirical studies of efficiency in the forward exchange market typically estimate Eq. (2.4) and treat $(\alpha, \beta) = (0, 1)$ as the null hypothesis. With few exceptions, the findings soundly reject the null hypothesis, indicating that the forward rate is a biased predictor of the future spot rate (Engel 1996; Lewis 1995).

While financial economists have offered a variety of explanations for the forward exchange rate bias,[2] one of the most prevalent arguments attributes the bias to the existence of a risk premium. That is, currency traders will demand compensation for taking a forward position in the market (e.g., MacDonald and Taylor 1991; Domowitz and Hakkio 1985; Frankel and Engle 1984; Mark 1985; Froot and Frankel 1989). Interestingly, many of these studies informally point to politics as a source of exchange rate risk. MacDonald and Taylor (1991), for example, argue that the bias in the forward rate of the French franc during the interwar period reflected uncertainty about the government's commitment to the gold standard. Frequent government turnover exacerbated concern that the government would not maintain the franc's value. In a study of the Greek drachma, Christodoulakis and Kalyvitis (1997) demonstrate that the forward bias increased (i.e., the estimated β became more negative) around the April 1992 election. Few studies, however, have explicitly incorporated political factors to explain the forward bias.[3]

[2] Some scholars view the forward exchange rate bias as primarily an econometric issue (e.g., Roll and Yan 1998). The properties of exchange rate data make it difficult to estimate market efficiency accurately. The forward premium, for instance, tends to be more volatile than the actual change in the spot exchange rates. Additionally, exchange rates may enter into periods of high and low volatility, which can last for many years. Finally, foreign exchange data may trend over significant lengths of time, creating inferential problems associated with non-stationary data.

Others argue that the bias exists because economic actors' expectations are not realized (Krasker 1980). Currency traders may expect a policy change that affects the exchange rate, but policymakers may not alter policy for an extended period. This explanation, referred to as the "peso problem," takes its name from studies of the Mexican peso. In the early 1970s, currency traders anticipated that the Mexican currency would be devalued, but policymakers remained committed to maintaining the peso's value. Consequently, the peso sold at a forward discount for a prolonged period. In general, economists contend that peso problems exist because data samples are not sufficiently long for all possible "states of the world" to be observed.

[3] Bachman (1992) is an exception. He tests whether elections change the short-term accuracy of the forward premium. Using monthly exchange rate data in a sample of 13 elections from four countries, he demonstrates that the accuracy of the forward

POLITICAL PROCESSES AND EXCHANGE RATE RISK

We argue that periods of potential political change contribute to the existence of a risk premium. Democratic political events may raise doubts about the government's commitment to the exchange rate, increasing the variation of expectations about future exchange rate movements. Because of this variation, traders will demand a higher return for taking a forward position in the market. As a result, the forward rate will be a less accurate predictor of future exchange rate movements during these events.

Economic actors incorporate information from a variety of sources into their expectations about the government's commitment to the level of the exchange rate. This information may be economic (e.g., data regarding unemployment or inflation) or political (e.g., the timing of elections or the policy preferences of governing parties). For instance, the government's partisanship serves as an informational cue for economic actors, giving them a sense of the government's policy objectives. The partisanship literature traditionally assumes that right parties are more concerned with controlling inflation while left parties place more emphasis on employment and wealth redistribution (Alesina and Sachs 1988). Economic actors, therefore, may expect that left governments are less committed to maintaining the exchange rate than right governments and adjust their behavior. The forward rate will reflect this information.

Democratic political processes, however, make it more difficult for economic actors to predict the government's commitment to the exchange rate. During elections, cabinet negotiations, and cabinet dissolutions, economic actors are bombarded with information about potential policy choices. Competing parties announce their policy objectives and programs. Opposition parties may win election or new individuals may be selected to occupy leadership positions, changing the composition of the government. Since politicians do not usually discuss the exchange rate directly, economic actors must use this information to infer the consequences of these events for the exchange rate.

Further, economic actors recognize that these periods are often associated with policy modifications that may affect the government's commitment to the exchange rate. Political parties may attempt to enhance

premium changed significantly from before to after the election in six cases. (Bachman does not indicate whether the null hypothesis of market efficiency $(\alpha, \beta) = (0, 1)$ was rejected or accepted before or after each election.) Following his methodology but using higher frequency data (weekly observations), we were not able to replicate his findings (results available upon request).

their electoral popularity by announcing policy goals and programs that will not be consistent with the maintenance of the exchange rate. The incumbent government may even resort to manipulating policy to produce short-term expansions in economic activity. Moreover, incoming governments sometimes devalue the exchange rate immediately upon entering office, while they can still blame the preceding government's economic policies (Stein and Streb 1998).

During periods of potential political change, therefore, economic actors must process a large amount of information about the government's commitment to the exchange rate – information about the policy priorities of different parties, potential election results, and possible cabinets. The contingent nature of democratic political processes exacerbates this problem. Opinion polls may not accurately predict election winners. Politicians may renege on policy promises. Policymakers may surprise economic agents with their policy choices.

As a result, democratic political events can increase the variation of expectations about the government's commitment to the exchange rate. Some currency traders may anticipate a change in the exchange rate. Other economic actors may guess that the policies of the new government will not alter the exchange rate. The variation in expectations associated with political events will contribute to a risk premium in forward markets. In turn, we expect the forward rate to be a biased predictor of future exchange rates more often during periods of potential political change than during periods when the government's tenure in office is secure.

POLITICAL INFORMATION AND EVENTS

In parliamentary systems, we identify four distinct event-periods when political news is likely to affect currency markets: campaigns, post-election negotiations, cabinet dissolutions, and the immediate month after government formation.

In parliamentary systems, elections determine the distribution of legislative seats, which shapes the composition of the cabinet and, in turn, the policy priorities of the new government. The campaign immediately prior to the election, therefore, represents an important period for economic agents to assess the government's commitment to the exchange rate. During the campaign, parties may choose candidates or announce new policies to appeal to voters. Opinion polls will chart which parties stand to gain or lose and the likely distribution of legislative seats.

Post-election negotiations begin immediately after the election and last until the new government assumes office. If no party wins a majority of legislative seats in a parliamentary system, post-election bargaining among the represented parties determines the composition of the government, the distribution of cabinet portfolios, and the cabinet's policy objectives. As a result, economic actors must pay attention to these negotiations to gauge how the election will affect the government's commitment to the exchange rate. Even in majoritarian systems where a single party forms the government, the time immediately following the election can be a source of uncertainty if party leaders must still determine the identity of key cabinet ministers.

In parliamentary systems, elections are not the only source of political change. A cabinet may dissolve at any time. A government may lose a no-confidence vote in the legislature or a party may withdraw from the governing coalition, precipitating a cabinet dissolution. After a dissolution, parties can negotiate to form a new government without calling for new elections. As with the post-election period, bargaining between political parties determines the composition of the cabinet and its policy priorities. Information about these negotiations, therefore, shapes expectations about the government's policy program.

Finally, economic actors will learn much about the government's policy priorities during the first weeks of its tenure. Even after a new government has been sworn-in, its policy objectives and the identity of policymakers may remain unclear. Policy priorities and programs come into focus only as the new government takes action. Economic actors, therefore, will closely monitor policy announcements and decisions in the first weeks of the government's administration. These initial policy actions will provide economic actors with information about the government's commitment to the exchange rate.

OTHER POLITICAL INFORMATION

Market actors also incorporate information about incumbent partisanship, partisan change, electoral institutions, and exchange rate arrangements into their economic expectations.

Incumbent Partisanship

Currency traders have information about the partisan composition and policy priorities of the incumbent government and likely alternative governments. The traditional assumptions of the partisanship literature imply that left governments will be less likely to maintain the level of the exchange rate. If currency traders expect that an election or a cabinet dissolution may produce a leftward shift in the composition of the cabinet, then they may anticipate that the new government will have less commitment to the exchange rate (Leblang and Bernhard 2000). Consequently, traders may demand compensation for holding domestic currency. On the other hand, if markets expect the political event to maintain the partisan status quo or shift the partisan composition of the government to the right, they will be more confident about the government's commitment to the exchange rate.

Measuring the anticipated change in government partisanship is difficult – regular and frequent polling data on the popularity of different political parties simply does not exist in most countries. Economic actors, however, do know the partisanship of the incumbent government. From that, they can calculate the composition of likely alternative governments. With a left government in office, currency traders know that an election or a cabinet dissolution is likely to result in either a re-formed left government – and a continuation of the policy status quo – or a new right government and a rightward shift in economic policy. These possibilities imply that any new government is likely to maintain the exchange rate.

With a right incumbent, however, a political event is likely to produce either a continued right government or a new left government – and a leftward shift in policy. This potential leftward shift may raise doubts about the maintenance of the exchange rate. As a result, we expect a risk premium to exist more often under a right incumbent government, particularly during the pre-election, campaign, and pre-dissolution periods.

To examine how partisanship affects the risk premium, we employ a measure of left government strength based on Cameron (1984). The measure multiplies the percentage of cabinet seats held by left parties by the percentage of a legislative majority held by left parties in the legislature for each year in each country. Reflecting the bimodal distribution of the measure, we define governments as Left when the partisan measure is greater than 0.7; Right when the measure is less 0.3; and Center otherwise.

Partisan Change

The partisan consequences of these political events will also affect how economic actors perceive the government's commitment to the exchange rate. If the incumbent government is returned to office, economic agents will have a clear sense of the government's policy priorities. But if the partisan composition of the government changes, economic agents are likely to have some uncertainty about the government's economic policy and whether party programs will become policy reality. As the government makes policy choices, however, economic agents will learn about the government's priorities and have more accurate expectations about future exchange rate fluctuations. In the periods after an election or a cabinet dissolution, therefore, we expect a risk premium to exist more often if the partisanship of the government changes than in situations of partisan continuity. We define a partisan shift as a change in the partisan score of more than 0.1.

Electoral Decisiveness

The decisiveness of the electoral system conditions when economic actors receive information about the government's composition. In countries with decisive electoral systems – for instance, a first-past-the post system – the election almost always determines the composition of the government, producing a single party majority government. Post-election negotiations or cabinet dissolutions usually involve choosing cabinet ministers, rather than altering the government's partisanship. In non-decisive electoral systems, however, elections rarely result in one party holding a majority of legislative seats. Instead, post-election negotiations often determine the composition of the government. Further, when no party controls a legislative majority, cabinet dissolutions are more likely to produce a change in the composition of government. As a result, we expect a risk premium to exist in the negotiations and cabinet dissolutions periods more often under non-decisive electoral systems than under majoritarian electoral systems.

Exchange Rate Commitments

Exchange rate commitments can increase the predictability of future exchange rates. A fixed exchange rate will decrease exchange rate volatility and, consequently, should decrease exchange rate risk (Mundell 1961; McKinnon 1962). We examine the effect of participation in the European Monetary System (EMS), a multilateral exchange rate arrangement among the countries of the European Community.[4] Participation committed states to maintaining the value of their currency against member currencies, particularly the German mark. As a result, the EMS decreased exchange rate volatility between EMS countries (Gros and Thygesen 1998). Since EMS membership should increase the predictability of currency movements, we expect a risk premium to exist less often when countries participate in the EMS.[5]

MEASURING THE RISK PREMIUM

We draw on Fama (1984) to measure the existence of a risk premium.[6] He argues that risk averse speculators in the forward market will require compensation for holding a net forward position in foreign exchange. He splits the forward rate into an expected spot rate and a premium (p_t):

$$f_t = E(s_{t+1}) + p_t. \tag{2.5}$$

Under the assumption of rational expectations, the difference between the forward rate and the realized spot rate, (s_{t+1}), is a function of this risk premium:

$$f_t - s_{t+1} = p_t - \varepsilon_{t+1} \tag{2.6}$$

where $\varepsilon_{t+1} = s_{t+1} - E(s_{t+1})$, the difference between the actual and the expected spot rate at time $t+1$.

[4] The EMS was founded in 1979. Participation in the EMS was restricted to member states of the European Community, although member states were not required to join.

[5] In alternative tests, we also investigated how participation in the European Exchange Arrangement, commonly called the Snake, affected the existence of the risk premium. The Snake appeared to have little effect (results not reported.).

[6] Scholars have estimated the risk premium using a variety of approaches. First, some financial economists argue that the expected variance of the returns on an asset can account for the existence of a risk premium. Using ARCH and GARCH error specifications, these models assume that the risk premium is a function of the conditional volatility of the asset (e.g., Domowitz and Hakkio 1985; MacDonald and Taylor 1991). A second approach follows either a capital asset pricing model (CAPM) or a portfolio-balance model and examines how economic fundamentals vary or shift over time (e.g., Frankel and Engle 1984; Mark 1985). Third, some scholars have modeled the risk premium using survey data about expectations of economic actors (Froot and Frankel 1989).

Fama further assumes that the risk premium is solely a linear function of the forward premium, $(f_t - s_t)$. Therefore, the difference between the forward rate and the realized spot rate becomes:

$$f_t - s_{t+1} = \alpha^* + \beta^*(f_t - s_t) - \varepsilon_{t+1}. \quad (2.7)$$

β^* can be interpreted as capturing the component of the variance of the forward premium resulting from the variance in the risk premium. If the risk premium depends on the forward premium, then $\beta^* \neq 0$. Fama then compares Eq. (2.7) with Eq. (2.4). In Eq. (2.4), the coefficient on the forward premium, β, reflects the component of the variance in the forward premium due to expected variability in exchange rate expectations (Cuthbertson 1996). He demonstrates that the difference between the coefficients on the forward premium for the two equations, β^* and β, is equal to:

$$\beta^* - \beta = \frac{[\text{var(riskpremium)} - \text{var(expectations)}]}{\text{var(forwardpremium)}}.$$

The difference between the betas results from the relative variances of the risk premium and the expected change in the spot exchange rate: if the difference is positive ($\beta^* > \beta$), then the variance in the risk premium is greater than the variance in exchange rate expectations. Cuthbertson (1996) argues that this measure offers a "quantitative guide to the relative importance of the time variation in the risk premium."[7]

We employ $(\beta^* - \beta)$ to determine whether a risk premium in forward exchange markets exists. For each period under investigation, we calculate whether this measure is positive and statistically distinguishable from zero using a 95 percent confidence interval. (Fama shows that the standard error of $(\beta^* - \beta)$ is simply twice the standard error of either β^* or β).[8]

[7] Lewis (1995) provides a more general interpretation of this measure, arguing that it captures the relationship between the variance in predictable excess returns and the variance in exchange rate expectations. The variance in predictable excess returns could be due to either variance in the risk premium or to variance in systematic forecast errors. Fama's measure has been criticized for assuming that the risk premium is solely a function of the forward premium. Additionally, the linear function of this relationship has no justification in economic theory (Cuthbertson 1996).

[8] Equations (2.4) and (2.7) are complementary due to the inclusion of similar independent and dependent variables. As such, there is the identity: $\alpha^* = -\alpha$ and $\beta^* = 1 - \beta$. Since $\beta^* + \beta = 1$, the standard error of their difference is "twice their common standard error" (Fama 1984, p. 327).

If so, we conclude that a risk premium exists. If $(\beta^* - \beta)$ is negative or not statistically different from zero, a risk premium does not exist.

ESTIMATING THE RISK PREMIUM

To gauge how democratic political events, government partisanship, and exchange rate commitments affect the forward exchange markets, we investigate whether market behavior changes across different sub-periods of the political process. Our first step is to estimate the risk premium for each political event in the sample using weekly data for 12 months before and after each event.[9] Thus, for each election and cabinet dissolution, we observe 102–104 weeks.[10]

For each two-year electoral period, we identify five sub-periods: pre-election, the campaign, post-election negotiations, the month after government formation, and post-government formation. The pre-election period begins 12 months before the election and lasts until the start of the campaign period. The campaign period begins either the week the election was announced, the week that the government collapsed, or, if these dates were unavailable, four weeks prior to the election date. The campaign period includes the week of the election.

The post-election negotiations commence the week after the election and last until the week that new government takes office. In systems where the new government is easily identifiable from the election results (e.g., a single party holds a majority of legislative seats), this period is often too short for meaningful statistical tests. But where no party holds a legislative majority, this negotiation period can be quite lengthy.

The month after government formation includes the four-week period beginning the week after the new government takes office. Finally, the post-government formation period begins five weeks after the new government is sworn-in and lasts until 12 months after the election date.

Adding dummy variables for the different sub-periods to Eqs. (2.4) and (2.7), we estimate the following equations for each election: (where $y_t = \Delta S_t = (S_{t+k} - S_k)$, $z_t = (f_{t,t+k} - s_{t+1})$, $x_t = (f_{t,t+k} - s_t)$ and s and f

[9] We also experimented with six-month and three-month periods around each election. The results were substantively similar.

[10] The 24-month time period helps control for shifts in exchange rate volatility. Exchange rate volatility tends to cluster over time. As a result, tests covering a longer period of time might produce biased results.

are logged):

$$\begin{aligned} y_t = {} & \alpha_0 + \alpha_1 * C_t + \alpha_2 * N_t + \alpha_3 * A_t + \alpha_4 * P_t \\ & + \beta_0 * x_t + \beta_1 * x_t * C_t + \beta_2 * x_t * N_t \\ & + \beta_3 * x_t * A_t + \beta_4 * x_t * P_t + \varepsilon_{t+k} \end{aligned} \tag{2.8}$$

$$\begin{aligned} z_t = {} & \alpha_0^* + \alpha_1^* * C_t + \alpha_2^* * N_t + \alpha_3^* * A_t + \alpha_4^* * P_t \\ & + \beta_0^* * x_t + \beta_1^* * x_t * C_t + \beta_2^* * x_t * N_t \\ & + \beta_3^* * x_t * A_t + \beta_4^* * x_t * P_t + \varepsilon_{t+k} \end{aligned} \tag{2.9}$$

where C_t = campaign period; N_t = post-election negotiation period; A_t = month after formation period; and P_t = post-government formation period. In addition, we include dummy variables for other elections,[11] negotiations, and cabinet dissolutions that occur within the two-year period surrounding each election. For instance, in the model of the November 1974 British elections, we also include dummy variables for the February 1974 elections and negotiations period.

To determine whether a risk premium exists in a period j, we use the estimates from Eqs. (2.8) and (2.9) to calculate whether $(\beta^* - \beta)$ is positive and statistically distinguishable from zero. The risk premium is computed as $[(\beta_0^* + \beta_j^*) - (\beta_0 + \beta_j)]$. The standard error of the risk premium is twice the standard error of the coefficient.[12]

For each two-year cabinet dissolution period,[13] we identify four sub-periods: pre-dissolution, post-dissolution negotiations, the month after government formation, and post-government formation. As with the elections, the pre-dissolution period begins 12 months before the dissolution and lasts until the week of the cabinet dissolution. The negotiations period begins the week that the government collapses and extends until the week a new cabinet is announced. The month after government formation includes the four-week period beginning the week after the new government takes office. Finally, the post-government formation period begins five weeks after the new government is sworn-in and lasts until 12 months after the dissolution date.

[11] In the French case, we control for both parliamentary and presidential elections.

[12] See note 8.

[13] We define a cabinet dissolution to occur if there is a significant change in the partisanship of the governing coalition or a change in the identity of the Prime Minister.

Adding dummy variables for the different sub-periods to Eqs. (2.4) and (2.7), we estimate the following equations for each dissolution:

$$y_t = \alpha_0 + \alpha_1 * N_t + \alpha_2 * A_t + \alpha_3 * P_t + \beta_0 * x_t + \beta_1 * x_t * N_t + \beta_2 * x_t * A_t + \beta_3 * x_t * P_t + \varepsilon_{t+k} \tag{2.10}$$

$$z_t = \alpha_0^* + \alpha_1^* * N_t + \alpha_2^* * A_t + \alpha_3^* * P_t + \beta_0^* * x_t + \beta_1^* * x_t * N_t + \beta_2^* * x_t * A_t + \beta_3^* * x_t * P_t + \varepsilon_{t+k} \tag{2.11}$$

where N_t = negotiation period; A_t = month after formation period; and P_t = post-government formation period. Again, we control for other elections, negotiations, and cabinet dissolutions that occur within the two-year period surrounding each dissolution. Using the results from Eqs. (2.10) and (2.11), we calculate the risk premium for each period as described above.

Sample

We estimate Eqs. (2.8)–(2.11) using the local currency denominated both in U.S. dollars and in German marks. For the dollar-denominated estimates, the sample includes 47 elections and 44 cabinet dissolutions in eight countries after January 1974 and prior to January 1994: Belgium (7 elections; 6 dissolutions), Britain (6 elections; 2 dissolutions), Canada (6 elections; 2 dissolutions), France (5 parliamentary elections; 5 dissolutions), Germany (5 elections; 2 dissolutions), Italy (6 elections; 16 dissolutions), Japan (7 elections; 9 dissolutions), and the Netherlands (5 elections; 2 dissolutions). For the D-mark denominated estimates, the sample excludes German political events and includes the remaining 42 elections and 42 dissolutions.

Data

The spot and 30-day forward exchange rate data consist of weekly prices of the local currency denominated in U.S. dollars and German marks. Both spot and forward prices are from the Wednesday close to avoid problems associated with bank/national holidays and increased volatility on Mondays and Fridays (Baillie and McMahon 1989). The data are from Harris Bank's weekly review. We filled in missing observations with data from Bloomberg Online.

We collected the political data on elections and partisanship from *Keesings' Archives* and various other sources. The data on exchange rate arrangements are from the International Monetary Fund's *Annual Report on Exchange Arrangements and Exchange Restrictions* (various years), Gros and Thygesen (1998), and Cobham (1994).

Methodology

We estimate the models in Eqs. (2.8)–(2.11) using weekly data, but the forward rate is quoted for a month in advance. Consequently, we have an overlapping contract/overlapping data problem (Hansen and Hodrick 1980). Each week of the month will produce a forecast error and those errors are likely to be serially correlated.[14] As a result, estimation of the standard errors is not straightforward.

Most researchers follow Hansen's (1982) strategy of estimating the parameters in Eqs.(2.8)–(2.11) via OLS (which will be unbiased and consistent) and correct the variance–covariance matrix using the approach suggested by Newey and West (e.g., Roll and Yan 1998; Lewis 1995). The Newey–West (1987) estimator of the standard error has an asymptotically consistent covariance matrix that uses a finite number of autocorrelated lags to approximate residual dynamics. As a result, it provides standard errors that are robust to autocorrelated and heteroscedastic disturbances. With weekly data and 30-day forward contracts, we expect a four-period moving average error. Consequently, we allow the Newey–West estimator to use four lags. Increasing the number of lags does not change the results.

Results

Appendix Tables 2.1 and 2.2 report the results of estimating Eqs. (2.8) and (2.10) for all 91 political events in the sample. The columns labeled Pre-Event, Campaign, Negotiations, Month-After Formation and Post-Formation show the estimated β for each sub-period (i.e., $\beta_0 + \beta_j$). (Recall that Eqs. (2.9) and (2.11) are complementary, so $[(\beta_0^* + \beta_j^*) + (\beta_0 + \beta_j)] = 1$). A star indicates that the null hypothesis of market efficiency, $(\alpha, \beta) = (0, 1)$, was rejected for that sub-period.

[14] An example will clarify the situation. Suppose two forward contracts are quoted, one at time t and the other at $t-1$, where t denotes weeks. Although both contracts mature in one month, the former contract matures at time $t+4$ and the latter contract at time $t+3$. The forecast error for the contract signed in period t will be influenced by the forecast error for the time $t-1$ contract. Hallwood and MacDonald (1994, pp. 216–7) provide a discussion.

Consider the first row of Appendix Table 2.1. For the 1974 Belgian election, in the pre-election period, the estimated β equals −0.48 (standard error = 2.47). The risk premium is positive (1.96), but not statistically significant. Additionally, the null hypothesis of market efficiency could not be rejected. During the campaign period, the estimated β jumps to 10.94 (standard error = 2.18). For this period, the risk premium was not positive (−20.88). The null hypothesis, however, was rejected, as indicated by the star. The risk premium is positive and significant for the negotiation period, but in the month-after formation and post-formation periods, the risk premium was not statistically distinguishable from zero.

POLITICAL PROCESSES AND RISK PREMIA

We expect risk premia to exist more often during the periods of potential political change than when the government's tenure in office is secure. With estimates from Eqs. (2.8) to (2.11), we calculate the number of instances where the estimate of the risk premium is positive and statistically distinguishable from zero and tabulate them with different political conditions based on the partisanship of the incumbent government, the partisan result, electoral institutions, and EMS membership. We then determine whether the rates at which the risk premium is positive and significant in the sample are statistically different from one another using techniques common to analysis of variance (ANOVA) experiments.

The first step in this analysis is to assess whether the observations from each political period are independent from one another. That is, for each "event cycle," there may be dependence across the sub-periods. This is akin to repeated measures ANOVA where the subjects are observed for each level of one or more variables that appear in the model. When that occurs, it is likely that observations for each subject are correlated. Using *F*-tests that take into account the possibility of correlation across periods (based on the Huynh–Feldt and the Geisser–Greenhouse epsilons for repeated measures), we never find evidence of such dependence (at the 95 percent confidence level). As a result, we are able to treat the periods as statistically independent.

In order to determine if the differences in the incidence of a risk premium between different periods or across different situations are statistically significant from one another, we use an *F*-test. Since we perform multiple comparisons, we use the Bonferroni adjustment to guard against falsely rejecting each hypothesis (Kirk 1995). In Tables (2.1)

Table 2.1. *Tests of risk premium by political sub-period: elections*

	Number of times risk premium is positive and significant						
	Currency	N	Pre-election	Campaign	Negotiation	Month after formation	Post-formation
All elections	**Dollar**	**47**	**10 [21]**	**19 [40]**	**19/33 [58]**	**16 [34]**	**11 [23]**
	D-Mark	**42**	**17 [40]**	**21 [50]**	**14/28 [50]**	**15 [35]**	**14 [33]**
Left incumbent	Dollar	9	3 [33]	2 [22]	2/4 [50]	4 [44]	2 [22]
	D-Mark	7	0 [0]	3 [43]	1/2 [50]	3 [43]	2 [29]
Right incumbent	**Dollar**	**35**	**6 [17]**	**17 [49]**	**15/26 [58]**	**10 [29]**	**9 [26]**
	D-Mark	32	17 [53]	17 [53]	12/23 [52]	11 [34]	11 [34]
Center incumbent	Dollar	3	1 [33]	0 [0]	2/3 [67]	2 [67]	0 [0]
	D-Mark	3	0 [0]	1 [33]	1/3 [33]	1 [33]	1 [33]
Part. change right	Dollar	11	3 [27]	1 [9]	3/6 [50]	5 [45]	2 [18]
	D-Mark	10	1 [10]	5 [50]	1/5 [20]	4 [40]	4 [40]
Part. change left	Dollar	7	2 [29]	2 [29]	2/4 [50]	1 [14]	1 [14]
	D-Mark	7	5 [71]	3 [43]	4/5 [80]	1 [14]	2 [29]
No part. change	**Dollar**	**29**	**5 [17]**	**16 [55]**	**14/23 [61]**	**10 [34]**	**8 [28]**
	D-Mark	25	11 [44]	13 [52]	9/18 [50]	10 [40]	8 [32]
Majoritarian	**Dollar**	**17**	**5 [29]**	**5 [29]**	**4/5 [80]**	**6 [35]**	**6 [35]**
	D-Mark	**17**	**6 [35]**	**8 [47]**	**5/6 [83]**	**6 [35]**	**4 [23]**
Proportional representation	**Dollar**	**30**	**5 [17]**	**14 [47]**	**15/28 [54]**	**10 [33]**	**5 [17]**
	D-Mark	25	11 [44]	13 [52]	9/22 [41]	19 [36]	10 [40]
EMS member	Dollar	18	3 [17]	5 [28]	6/12 [50]	7 [39]	3 [17]
	D-Mark	18	9 [50]	6 [33]	6/13 [46]	6 [33]	6 [33]
Not EMS member	Dollar	29	7 [24]	14 [48]	13/21 [62]	9 [31]	8 [28]
	D-Mark	24	8 [33]	15 [63]	8/15 [53]	9 [38]	8 [33]

Note: Cell entries are the number of times the risk premium is positive and statistically distinguishable from zero. Numbers are raw frequencies; entries in square brackets are row percentages. See text for details on the construction of the risk premium measure.
Rows in bold indicate a statistically significant difference in the number of times the risk premium is positive and significant across periods based on an F-test (Prob(F) < 0.01).

and (2.2), we bold those rows where the rates of a positive and significant risk premium across political periods are not equal. We also indicate in the text which individual political periods are different from one another. In all cases, we use a 95 percent confidence level.

Table 2.2. *Tests of risk premium by political sub-period: dissolutions*

	Number of times risk premium is positive and significant					
	Currency	N	Pre-Election	Negotiation	Month after formation	Post-formation
All dissolutions	**Dollar**	**44**	**7 [16]**	**16/28 [57]**	**15 [34]**	**10 [23]**
	D-Mark	**42**	**19 [45]**	**15/25 [60]**	**10 [24]**	**15 [35]**
Left incumbent	**Dollar**	**8**	**2 [25]**	**3/3 [100]**	**4 [50]**	**2 [25]**
	D-Mark	**6**	**1 [16]**	**2/2 [100]**	**2 [22]**	**1 [17]**
Right incumbent	**Dollar**	**35**	**5 [14]**	**13/24 [54]**	**11 [31]**	**8 [22]**
	D-Mark	**35**	**17 [49]**	**13/22 [59]**	**7 [20]**	**14 [40]**
Center incumbent	Dollar	1	0 [0]	0/1 [0]	0 [0]	0 [0]
	D-Mark	1	1 [100]	0/1 [0]	1 [100]	0 [0]
Part. change right	Dollar	1	0 [0]	.	1 [100]	1 [100]
	D-Mark	.	.	.	.	.
Part. change left	Dollar	4	0 [0]	0/1 [0]	0 [0]	1 [25]
	D-Mark	4	1 [25]	0/1 [0]	2 [50]	2 [50]
No part. change	**Dollar**	**39**	**7 [18]**	**16/27 [60]**	**14 [36]**	**8 [20]**
	D-Mark	**38**	**18 [47]**	**15/24 [63]**	**8 [21]**	**13 [34]**
Majoritarian	**Dollar**	**9**	**3 [33]**	**3/4 [75]**	**3 [33]**	**7 [77]**
	D-Mark	**9**	**3 [33]**	**3/4 [75]**	**3 [33]**	**4 [44]**
Proportional	**Dollar**	**35**	**4 [11]**	**13/24 [54]**	**12 [34]**	**10 [29]**
representation	**D-Mark**	**33**	**16 [48]**	**12/21 [57]**	**7 [21]**	**11 [33]**
EMS Member	**Dollar**	**22**	**3 [14]**	**7/15 [47]**	**7 [32]**	**4 [18]**
	D-Mark	22	10 [45]	7/14 [50]	8 [37]	11 [50]
Not EMS	**Dollar**	**22**	**4 [18]**	**9/13 [69]**	**8 [37]**	**6 [27]**
	D-Mark	**20**	**9 [45]**	**8/11 [73]**	**2 [10]**	**4 [20]**

Cell entries are the number of times the risk premium is positive and statistically distinguishable from zero. Numbers are raw frequencies; entries in square brackets are row percentages. See text for details on the construction of the risk premium measure.
Rows in bold indicate a statistically significant difference in the number of times the risk premium is positive and significant across periods based on an F-test ($\text{Prob}(F) < 0.01$).

Analysis

Table 2.1 reports number of times that the risk premium was positive and statistically significant in different political periods for the 47 elections in the sample. Looking at the results for the U.S. dollar in the pre-election period, the risk premium is positive and significant 10 times – about 21 percent of the sample. For the campaign period, the number of times the risk premium is positive and significant increases to 19 – about 40 percent of the sample. In the negotiation period, the risk premium is positive and significant 19 out of 33 times (recall that some of these periods were too short for meaningful statistical tests) or in about 58 percent of the sample. In the month-after period, the risk premium is positive and significant in about 34 percent of the sample (16/47 cases).[15] Finally, in the post-formation period, the risk premium is positive and significant 11 times or in 23 percent of the sample. An *F*-test indicates that the frequency of a positive and significant risk premium between different sub-periods cannot be attributed to chance. As predicted, the occurrence of a positive and significant risk premium in the "political" periods – the campaign, negotiations, and month after-formation – is statistically higher than the non-political periods. The results from the D-mark reveal a similar pattern. Although the differences between the political and non-political periods are not as pronounced, they are statistically significant ($p = 0.041$).

We next divide the sample into three categories based on the partisanship of the incumbent. Consider first the pre-election period. For the results based on exchange rates denominated in the U.S. dollar, the risk premium is positive slightly more often under left governments (3/9 cases) than right governments (6/35 cases), although this difference is not statistically significant. For the estimates based on the German mark denominator, however, the occurrence of a risk premium is much higher and statistically significant for right governments (17/32 cases) than for left governments (0/7 cases) ($p = 0.033$). For the campaign period, however, the results between the two sets of estimates are consistent. Here, the risk premium is positive more often for right governments, but these differences are not significant. The most conservative conclusion is that the partisanship of the incumbent does not affect the risk premium.

We also classify elections based on the outcome – whether there was a partisan shift to the left, to the right, or no substantive change. In the event of a partisan change, we expected that the risk premium would be positive and significant more often in the negotiations, month-after, and post-formation periods than if the election resulted in partisan continuity. These

[15] The risk premium measure was negative and significant in only a handful of cases across the periods, except for the month-after formation. For this period, the risk premium was negative and significant about one-third of the time.

predictions, however, are not supported. For the negotiation, month-after, and post-formation periods, the rate of the risk premium being positive and significant is essentially the same whether the government was returned in the election or not.

The third comparison divides the sample according to the electoral system, distinguishing between majoritarian and proportional representation electoral systems.[16] We expected the risk premium to be positive and significant more often during the campaign period in majoritarian systems, and positive and significant more often during post-election negotiations in proportional representation systems. This distinction based on electoral systems produced results directly contrary to our expectations. During the campaign period, the risk premium was positive and significant for proportional representation systems more often than for majoritarian ones (Dollar-based estimates, $p=0.0004$; German mark estimates, $p=0.0032$). During the negotiation period, however, the risk premium was positive and significant more often under the majoritarian systems (Dollar-based estimates, $p=0.003$; German mark estimates, $p=0.002$).[17]

Finally, we split the sample between elections held under the EMS and those held outside the system (i.e., either in non-participating countries or before the inception of the EMS).[18] It does not appear that membership in the EMS consistently reduced the occurrence of a risk premium.

We perform similar analyses on the sample of cabinet dissolutions. Table 2.2 reports number of times that the risk premium was positive and statistically significant in different political periods for the 44 cabinet dissolutions in the sample. For the results based on the U.S. dollar, in the pre-election period, the risk premium was positive seven times or in about 16 percent of the cases. During the negotiation period, this jumps up to about 57 percent of the testable cases (16/28). In the month-after period,

[16] Majoritarian systems include Britain, Canada, and France (with the exception of the 1986 election). Belgium, Germany, Italy, Japan, and the Netherlands are classified as proportional representation systems.

[17] We further divided the proportional representation systems into two groups based on the pattern of politics. For much of the period, Belgium, Germany, and the Netherlands had pivot coalitions. Japan and Italy, on the other hand, were dominated by one party. The risk premium was positive during the negotiations period significantly more often for the Belgian, German, and Dutch group than for Italy and Japan, perhaps reflecting the uncertainty of coalition bargaining in the former set of countries ($p = 0.001$).

[18] We did not include Germany as an EMS country. Since the German mark represented the "anchor" currency of the system, German economic policy was not constrained by an external exchange rate commitment. Consequently, the EMS did not make German exchange rates any more predictable than if it had been outside the system.

the risk premium was positive and statistically significant 15 times or about 34 percent of the time.[19] Finally, the post-formation period was positive and significant in only 10 of the cases – or about 23 percent of the time. During the negotiation period, the risk premium was positive and significant more often than during the non-political periods. This difference is statistically significant for both the dollar-based and mark-based estimates (for both, $p < 0.0001$).

We again partition the sample of cabinet dissolutions based on incumbent partisanship, partisan change, electoral institutions, and EMS membership. And, as with the findings in Table 2.1, no clear patterns emerge.

POLITICAL PROCESSES AND THE FORWARD BIAS

Many scholars argue that the existence of a risk premium contributes to the bias of the forward exchange rate in predicting changes in the spot rate. Consequently, we examine how political processes affect the forward rate bias. As with the existence of risk premia, we expect the null hypothesis of market efficiency (i.e., $(\alpha, \beta) = (0, 1)$) to be rejected more often during "political" periods than when the government's tenure in office is secure. Further, in periods where the risk premium is positive and statistically significant, we expect that the forward rate will be biased (i.e., the null hypothesis of market efficiency will be rejected).

Using the results from Eqs. (2.8) and (2.10), we test each of the following joint hypotheses for every political event:

$$\begin{aligned} H_0 &: \alpha_0 = 0 \text{ and } \beta_0 = 1 \\ H_0^1 &: \alpha_0 + \alpha_1 = 0 \text{ and } \beta_0 + \beta_1 = 1 \\ H_0^2 &: \alpha_0 + \alpha_2 = 0 \text{ and } \beta_0 + \beta_2 = 1 \\ H_0^3 &: \alpha_0 + \alpha_3 = 0 \text{ and } \beta_0 + \beta_3 = 1 \\ H_0^4 &: \alpha_0 + \alpha_4 = 0 \text{ and } \beta_0 + \beta_4 = 1. \end{aligned}$$

As with the tests of the risk premium, we calculate the number of times the null hypothesis of market efficiency is rejected across political periods.

[19] Again, the risk premium measure was negative and significant in only a handful of cases across the periods, except for the month-after formation. For this period, the risk premium was negative and significant about one-third of the time.

Results

Table 2.3 reports the results of testing for market efficiency across different periods for both elections and cabinet dissolutions. Consider first the elections. Looking at the results from the U.S. dollar, during the pre-election periods the null hypothesis was rejected 24 times. That is, the forward rate was biased in just over 50 percent of the pre-election periods in the sample. In the campaign periods, however, the null hypothesis was rejected 41 times or in 87 percent of the sample. In the post-election negotiations periods, the null hypothesis was rejected 31 out of 34 times or in 91 percent of the sample. During the month after government formation, the null hypothesis was rejected in 42 cases, about 90 percent of the sample. Finally, the null hypothesis was rejected 25 times in the post-government formation periods, about 53 percent of the sample. An *F*-test indicates that the rejection rates between different sub-periods cannot be attributed to chance.[20] As predicted, the rejection rates during the "non-political" periods – the pre-election and post-formation periods – are significantly lower than during the "political" periods. The results from using the German mark as the baseline currency reveal a similar pattern: The forward rate is biased more often in the campaign, negotiation, and

Table 2.3. *Tests of market efficiency by political sub-period: elections and cabinet dissolutions*

	Number of times null hypothesis rejected (not efficient)						
	Currency	N	Pre-event	Campaign	Negotiation	Month after formation	Post-formation
Elections	**Dollar**	**47**	**24 [51]**	**41 [87]**	**31/34 [91]**	**42 [91]**	**25 [53]**
	D-Mark	**42**	**27 [64]**	**32 [76]**	**23/29 [79]**	**37 [90]**	**23 [55]**
Dissolutions	**Dollar**	**44**	**17 [39]**	–	**27/27 [100]**	**38 [88]**	**22 [50]**
	D-Mark	42	26 [62]	–	**23/26 [88]**	**40 [97]**	**31 [74]**

Cell entries are the number of times the null hypothesis $(\alpha, \beta) = (0, 1)$ was rejected. Numbers are raw frequencies; entries in square brackets are row percentages.
Rows in bold indicate a statistically significant difference in rejection rates across political periods based on an *F*-test ($\text{Prob}(F) < 0.01$).

[20] We followed the same procedure in this section as in the previous by treating these descriptive results as data for an ANOVA experiment.

month-after periods than in the pre-election and post-formation periods. These differences are also statistically significant. Finally, in every period where the risk premium was positive and significant, the null hypothesis of market efficiency was rejected (for estimates based on both currencies).

The analysis of the cabinet dissolutions provides similar results. During the pre-dissolution period, the null hypothesis was rejected 17 times or in only about 39 percent of the sample for the U.S. dollar. For the negotiations period, the forward rate was biased 100 percent of the time (27/27). The null hypothesis was rejected 38 out of 44 times during the month-after-formation period (88 percent). And, finally, the null hypothesis was rejected 50 percent of the time in the year after the cabinet dissolution. The estimates based on the German mark reveal a similar, if somewhat less distinct, pattern. For both sets of estimates, the forward rate is biased more often during the political periods – negotiations, month-after-formation – than during the non-political periods. Moreover, these differences are statistically significant. And again, in every period where the risk premium was positive and significant, the null hypothesis of market efficiency was rejected, indicating that the forward rate was biased.[21]

POLITICAL EVENTS AND EXCHANGE RATE TURMOIL

Our next step is to identify particular political events that caused turmoil in the currency markets. We base this classification on three criteria: (1) the risk premium is positive and significant in at least one "political" sub-period *and* is not positive or not significant in at least one "non-political" period, (2) the difference in the risk premium between those two periods is statistically significant, and (3) the first two conditions must hold for both estimates using the U.S. dollar as the denominator *and* the estimates based on the German mark as the currency denominator. The combination of these criteria avoids situations where there is a structural break in the risk premium across two periods, but the risk premium in both periods is statistically indistinguishable from zero – a situation where the political event does change behavior in the exchange rate markets, but this effect

[21] We also divided the results for both the elections and cabinet dissolutions according to incumbent partisanship, partisan change, electoral decisiveness, and EMS membership. In both samples, we found no strong patterns based on these distinctions. With a few exceptions, the null hypothesis was rejected at the same rate across all of these categorizations.

Table 2.4. *Elections and foreign exchange rate turmoil*

Country	Election
Belgium	November 1991
Britain	June 1983
Britain	May 1992
Canada	February 1980
Canada	September 1984
Canada	October 1993
Italy	June 1979
Italy	March 1994

Elections meet the following criteria:
1. The risk premium is positive and significant in at least one "political" sub-period *and* is not positive or not significant in at least one "non-political" period,
2. The difference in the risk premium between those two periods is statistically significant, and
3. Both conditions hold for estimates using the U.S. dollar as the currency denominator and for estimates using the German mark as the currency denominator.

does not have substantive importance. It also discounts situations where the risk premium in one period may be positive and different from zero and the risk premium in the second period may be statistically indistinguishable from zero, but there is no structural break between periods. This situation is marked only by a small shift in currency market behavior. Finally, the requirement that the findings hold for both the dollar and the mark reduces the possibility that the results are an artifact of fluctuations in the baseline currency.

Of the 42 elections in the joint dollar/mark sample, eight meet the criteria (Table 2.4). This represents about 19 percent of the sample. In other words, almost one-fifth of elections are associated with currency market turmoil – a large percentage for established democracies in a world of integrated currency markets! Nevertheless, no simple factor connects these elections. Six occurred with a right-wing incumbent – but so did most elections in the sample. Four resulted in some sort of partisan change. Three took place under the EMS. In short, these events do not appear to have much in common.

We can easily construct *post hoc* explanations about why some of these elections affected currency markets. The British election in 1992 produced an unanticipated result, with the Conservatives holding off a Labour Party that had been widely expected to win. The 1980 Canadian election came as a surprise, after the ruling Conservative party clumsily lost a vote of no confidence. The two Italian elections also represented suspenseful contests. The 1979 election occurred on the heels of the government of "non-no confidence," where the Communist Party – excluded from office throughout the post-war period – provided tacit support for a Christian Democratic minority government. It remained unclear whether this participation would hurt the Communists or propel them to office. The 1994 Italian elections were the first under new electoral rules, after the main governing parties had been discredited in bribery and corruption scandals.

But a number of other elections belie these *post hoc* theories about the "uncertainty" or "importance" of these events. Thatcher's victory in the 1983 British elections seemed almost pre-ordained, coming in the wake of the British victory in the Falkland Islands conflict and with a recovering economy. (One might argue that the fate of the Labour party provided the real drama in this election. Divided and in disarray after the defection of several key party leaders to form the Social Democratic party, the Labour party's future as one of the two leading parties seemed uncertain.) Similarly, the identity of the winning party in the 1984 and 1993 Canadian elections was never in doubt (although the margins of victory may have been somewhat surprising). The 1991 Belgium election also does not appear to be extraordinary, although the main governing parties did lose votes to extremist parties on both the left and right. Moreover, such *post-hoc* generalizations cannot account for why some "critical" elections did not cause currency market turmoil. For instance, the 1981 French elections did not meet the criteria. While the Socialist victory in the parliamentary elections may have been anticipated, the result did represent a major break in economic policy. One would have expected to discern a market reaction to the Socialist agenda.

Only one cabinet dissolution satisfies all the criteria: the 1991 dissolution in France, where Edith Cresson became Prime Minister. The fact that so few of these events appear to affect currency markets may reflect continuity in the underlying distribution of legislative seats. A new government – even of a different partisan character – must operate under the same legislative constraints. Consequently, currency traders may expect more policy stability after a dissolution than following a change in the government due to an election.

CONCLUSION

We argue that political events influence the relationship between the spot and forward exchange rates. Democratic processes increase the variation of expectations among currency traders, contributing to the existence of a risk premium. During campaigns, post-election negotiations, cabinet dissolutions, and the month-after government formation, the results indicate that the risk premium measure was positive and significant more often than when the tenure of political leaders was secure. Moreover, the forward premium was biased more often during these periods as well.

These results lend support to those who argue that democratic politics still matter in a world of global capital (e.g., Freeman, Hays, and Stix 2000). Parliamentary events – elections, cabinet changes, party bargaining – affect how economic agents evaluate the future course of economic policy. Even in well-developed foreign exchange markets, these political processes seem to create some uncertainty among economic agents about the government's commitment to the exchange rate. This uncertainty may give politicians some room to maneuver.

Less compelling, however, were the attempts to determine which specific events would affect currency markets. Hypotheses based on incumbent partisanship, partisan change, electoral institutions, and exchange rate commitments received only weak support. Clearly, these simple arguments cannot account for the variation of market reactions to different political events.

Markets are likely to incorporate far more information about political events than can be captured by a dummy variable for the electoral system or government partisanship. Economic agents, for instance, will have more knowledge about the policy priorities of specific administrations, rather than simply relying on party labels. We contend that political science theory can provide insight into the information available to market actors about the partisan and policy consequences of political events. Although one may view democratic politics as inherently chaotic and unpredictable, much recent scholarship contends that institutions provide stability and predictability to political processes. Where a predictable equilibrium exists, markets should be able to anticipate that outcome and adjust quickly. In the absence of a predictable equilibrium, however, economic actors may be less able to forecast the consequences of a political event, creating increased market volatility or abnormal returns. In the next chapter, we draw on sophisticated models of the cabinet formation process to evaluate how markets process political information.

Appendix Table 2.1. *Elections*

Country	Year	Month	Currency	Pre-event	Campaign	Negotiations	Month-After	Post Formation
Belgium	1974	3	Dollar	−0.48	10.94*	−2.32*	2.76	2.21
Belgium	1974	3	DM	1.05	1.64	−1.24*	−5.05*	−1.59*
Belgium	1977	4	Dollar	−0.03*	8.82*	1.47	29.29*	−1.03*
Belgium	1977	4	DM	−0.57*	−8.22*	2.62	−4.74*	−0.12*
Belgium	1978	12	Dollar	0.95	2.19*	−5.19*	6.23*	1.7
Belgium	1978	12	DM	−0.94*	0.98	−0.73*	−5.39*	−0.84*
Belgium	1981	11	Dollar	−3.42*	−0.34*	−2.38*	−1.71*	−7.39*
Belgium	1981	11	DM	−0.07*	0.82	−1.17*	0.59*	0.31
Belgium	1985	10	Dollar	13.08	134.56*	−69.71*	1.08*	3.99*
Belgium	1985	10	DM	−1.24*	−5.27	44.83*	−2.45*	−1.09*
Belgium	1987	12	Dollar	−1.23	−16.44*	−19.38*	−133.16*	−37.08*
Belgium	1987	12	DM	−0.92*	−2.74*	−2.41*	1.49	−0.65*
Belgium	1991	11	Dollar	1.38	19.48*	61.65*	−77.87*	−3.43
Belgium	1991	11	DM	−1.01	−51.65*	2.25	1.03*	2.39
Britain	1974	2	Dollar	−1.18	−8.47*	.	−2.13*	3.49*
Britain	1974	2	DM	−1.3	−2.57*	.	4.81*	0.15
Britain	1974	11	Dollar	−4.26*	4.81*	.	−2.72*	−3.74*
Britain	1974	11	DM	−2.5*	4.67*	.	7.68*	2.14
Britain	1979	5	Dollar	−11.19*	−3.49*	.	−8.67*	0.58
Britain	1979	5	DM	1.91*	−2.14	.	−4.89*	−10.97*
Britain	1983	6	Dollar	−0.1	−23.4*	.	−44.87*	−11.14*
Britain	1983	6	DM	−11.53	−51.52*	.	10.32*	−2.31
Britain	1987	6	Dollar	−6.46	−64.31*	.	35.96*	−33.04*
Britain	1987	6	DM	−37.06*	−36.15*	.	40.89*	−5.15*
Britain	1992	5	Dollar	27.11*	−21.89*	.	5.81*	15.02
Britain	1992	5	DM	−1.87	76*	.	−24.25*	20.98*
Canada	1974	7	Dollar	−2.4*	0.16*	6.42*	−4.7*	−0.87*
Canada	1974	7	DM	1.5	−6.18*	7.82*	−8.68*	−8.53
Canada	1979	5	Dollar	−9.8*	−23.01*	.	−21.72*	−4.21*
Canada	1979	5	DM	−7.62*	−3.02	−18.52*	−4.13*	4.19
Canada	1980	2	Dollar	−9.33	5.48	−47.67*	0.84	−1.76
Canada	1980	2	DM	−9.99*	−0.16*	−11.21*	185.91*	−1.81
Canada	1984	9	Dollar	8.83*	−2.5	−16274.5*	−6.92*	−18.68
Canada	1984	9	DM	−9.46*	−13.93*	.	−91.21*	−12.55
Canada	1988	11	Dollar	4.18	114.53*	.	51.92*	−21.97*
Canada	1988	11	DM	−29.29	92.48*	.	−56.04*	−40.26*
Canada	1993	10	Dollar	−4.53	−17.47	−342.7*	43.85*	−7.2

(*continued*)

Appendix Table 2.1. *(continued)*

Country	Year	Month	Currency	Pre-event	Campaign	Negotiations	Month-After	Post Formation
Canada	1993	10	DM	−19.62	136.86*	−128.51*	35.34*	−0.43
France	1978	3	Dollar	−1.41*	−8.52*	−31.21*	−10.42*	−6.54*
France	1978	3	DM	0.91	−5.64*	−9.42*	2.5*	−1.06
France	1981	5	Dollar	−2.36*	−1.62	.	2.39*	1.34
France	1981	5	DM	−1.6*	0.5*	.	−2.31*	1.34*
France	1986	3	Dollar	0.66*	−9.18*	.	11.81*	1.53
France	1986	3	DM	0.39*	−55.33*	.	−2.85*	−2.69*
France	1988	5	Dollar	3.24	−7.75*	.	23.42*	−32.65
France	1988	5	DM	−5.53*	−3.51*	239.21*	−10.42*	−2.85*
France	1993	3	Dollar	20.13*	2.01*	.	−19.11*	1.31
France	1993	3	DM	−0.72	−5.73*	.	−0.34*	1.02
Germany	1976	10	Dollar	−3.88	−27.9*	−6.16*	18.84*	5.16*
Germany	1980	10	Dollar	0.53	−13.14*	22.67*	11*	−3.48
Germany	1983	3	Dollar	−3.32	−7.66*	7.98*	−3.97*	−25.91*
Germany	1987	1	Dollar	4.08*	−94.02*	25.13*	15.32*	−2.25
Germany	1990	11	Dollar	13.24*	−88.17	−82.61*	206.61*	−15.96
Italy	1976	6	Dollar	−1.63*	−0.05*	−1.7*	−0.27*	0.48*
Italy	1976	6	DM	−1.77*	−1.23*	−3.57*	0.63	0.14*
Italy	1979	6	Dollar	−0.45	−10.2*	6.92*	−42.39*	−0.24
Italy	1979	6	DM	3.37	3.09	−2.47*	−16.83	−1.44*
Italy	1983	6	Dollar	−1.06	−5.26*	2.44*	1.83*	−4.8*
Italy	1983	6	DM	−0.46*	−0.35*	−1.81*	0.38*	1.44*
Italy	1987	6	Dollar	−1.63*	−11.59*	−23.62*	16.89*	−9.66
Italy	1987	6	DM	−2.88*	−11.35*	−0.13*	−1.2*	−0.66*
Italy	1992	4	Dollar	7.88	−5.86	−17.5*	7.88*	−1.97
Italy	1992	4	DM	−5.81*	−1.41	−1.54	.*	−7.03
Italy	1994	3	Dollar	−13.97	−4.77*	.	−101.39*	−17.19*
Italy	1994	3	DM	−18.66	−78.03*	.	7.87*	−8.8*
Japan	1976	12	Dollar	−0.94*	−10.15*	6.33*	13.5*	1.94*
Japan	1976	12	DM	−2.59	−4.46*	54.05*	−22.74*	−3.77
Japan	1979	10	Dollar	0.68*	−11.69*	−21.81*	−47.54*	−5.64*
Japan	1979	10	DM	0.74*	−8.1*	−10.25*	0.78*	−3.47*
Japan	1980	6	Dollar	−9.37*	5.62*	32.61*	13.94*	−2.56*
Japan	1980	6	DM	−3.56	2.44	−44.39*	−7.16*	−4.73*
Japan	1983	12	Dollar	−2.29	−19.95*	.	−43.13*	−3.19
Japan	1983	12	DM	−0.05*	−84.16*	.	58.39*	−38.27*
Japan	1986	7	Dollar	7.2*	700.5*	86.49*	12.89	−2.42
Japan	1986	7	DM	5.78*	−1436.63*	.	−26.15*	−22.29*
Japan	1990	2	Dollar	−2.8	55.6*	62.89*	50.67*	21.48*

Country	Year	Month	Currency	Pre-event	Campaign	Negotiations	Month-After	Post Formation
Japan	1990	2	DM	4.75*	.	440.37*	28.55*	4.66
Japan	1993	7	Dollar	7.25	−5645.4*	7.25*	102.31*	7.95
Japan	1993	7	DM	−23.44*	−76.22*	113.97*	112.87*	14.71
Netherlands	1977	5	Dollar	−2.2*	−5.91*	−12.45*	−11.33*	0.86
Netherlands	1977	5	DM	−0.36*	−4.32*	−0.41	−11.68*	−1.05*
Netherlands	1981	5	Dollar	−3*	−5.41*	−35.89*	44.98*	6.08*
Netherlands	1981	5	DM	−1.77*	−2.41*	1.83	−4.31*	−3.17
Netherlands	1982	9	Dollar	4.85*	3.07*	−9.71	64.98	−19.5*
Netherlands	1982	9	DM	−2.95	19.4*	−18.64*	15.21*	−3.95
Netherlands	1986	5	Dollar	−4.07*	−67.35*	−55.46*	147.72*	−179.54*
Netherlands	1986	5	DM	−2.32*	3.94*	1.7	−64.36*	60.68*
Netherlands	1989	9	Dollar	−14.12	−277.36*	11.48*	−29.23*	33.56*
Netherlands	1989	9	DM	−5.05*	−0.28	−5.64*	−1.86	−2.14*

* An $*$ indicates that the efficiency hypothesis (joint test of $\alpha = 0$ and $\beta = 1$) can be rejected at the 0.05 level.

[1] Rows represent year and month when the event occurred.

[2] Cell entries are parameter estimates of the beta coefficients from Eqs. (2.8) and (2.10). Intercepts are not reported.

[3] Cells marked with a '.' indicate that the event period in question was of insufficient length to estimate a parameter.

Appendix Table 2.2. *Cabinet dissolutions*

Country	Year	Month	Currency	Pre-Event	Negotiations	Month-After	Post Formation
Belgium	1974	3	Dollar	−0.55	.	0.21*	1.14
Belgium	1974	3	DM	−1.36*	.	1.63*	−1.28*
Belgium	1978	12	Dollar	−1.35*	.	8.17*	−1.38
Belgium	1978	12	DM	−1.18*	.	−2.47*	−1.21*
Belgium	1980	1	Dollar	−3.72	−104.7	−12.09*	−2.6*
Belgium	1980	1	DM	−0.72*	−108.98*	11.22*	−1.11*
Belgium	1980	4	Dollar	−0.64	2.17*	2.75*	−0.87*
Belgium	1980	4	DM	−1.57*	2.5*	−5.29*	−0.77*
Belgium	1980	10	Dollar	0.15*	64.61*	0.17*	1.2*
Belgium	1980	10	DM	−1.24*	4.05	−5.87*	−0.61*
Belgium	1981	3	Dollar	−1.06	.	2.35	−79.07
Belgium	1981	3	DM	−1.22*	.	−1.07*	−0.73
Britain	1976	3	Dollar	−5.35*	−6.2*	−2.62*	−1.4
Britain	1976	3	DM	1.42	−7.87*	0.07*	−1.85
Britain	1990	11	Dollar	−26.85*	−190.09*	−12.47	24.23
Britain	1990	11	DM	−19.7*	−1010.76*	−27.33*	−5.2*
Canada	1983	6	Dollar	−2.24*	10.76*	10.71*	11.61*
Canada	1983	6	DM	−7.11*	−57.93*	−21.14*	−8.08
Canada	1993	2	Dollar	−4.85	0.2*	−95.78*	−8.77*
Canada	1993	2	DM	−19.91*	−24.26	76.1*	−11.75*
France	1976	8	Dollar	0.91	.	4.49*	2.2*
France	1976	8	DM	1.01	.	0.48*	−3.71*
France	1983	3	Dollar	1.43	.	11.31*	−4.94
France	1983	3	DM	0.86	.	2.19*	−1.96*
France	1984	7	Dollar	−6.3*	.	−68.7*	−13.15
France	1984	7	DM	−0.54*	.	−7.98*	0.73*
France	1991	5	Dollar	27.49	.	−214.01*	11.16*
France	1991	5	DM	0.93	.	−4.33*	3.64
France	1992	4	Dollar	5.63	.	−14.27*	22.65*
France	1992	4	DM	0.64	.	22.76*	−1.73
Germany	1974	5	Dollar	1.18	0.41*	−13.98*	−7.44*
Germany	1982	10	Dollar	3.55*	.	−44.28*	−27.95*
Italy	1974	3	Dollar	1.35	−102*	4.05	−0.91*
Italy	1974	3	DM	1.95	8.82*	2.42*	−1.07*
Italy	1974	10	Dollar	−0.27	−1.65*	1.49*	−3.05*

Country	Year	Month	Currency	Pre-Event	Negotiations	Month-After	Post Formation
Italy	1974	10	DM	0.07	−7.86*	2.22*	0.64*
Italy	1976	1	Dollar	−3.59	−27.84*	−0.52*	−0.39*
Italy	1976	1	DM	−3.57*	−28.37*	0.33*	−1.27
Italy	1978	1	Dollar	0.16*	−4.69*	−9.93*	−0.51
Italy	1978	1	DM	−1*	−0.52*	7.51*	3.83*
Italy	1979	1	Dollar	−0.34	−3.6*	14.92	−1
Italy	1979	1	DM	3.45	10.91*	13.51*	−2.75*
Italy	1980	3	Dollar	−1.25	57.81*	1.56*	−1.56*
Italy	1980	3	DM	−2.54*	−2.71*	−0.83*	−0.95*
Italy	1980	9	Dollar	−0.09	26.64*	−0.71*	−2.89*
Italy	1980	9	DM	−0.65*	−21.4*	2.43*	0.69
Italy	1981	5	Dollar	−1.82*	2.93*	−6.55*	0.26
Italy	1981	5	DM	−0.86*	−0.2*	1.36*	1.87
Italy	1982	8	Dollar	−1.79	.	−0.85*	−0.47
Italy	1982	8	DM	1.38	.	−3.61*	−0.5*
Italy	1982	11	Dollar	−5.35*	−13.74*	−5.35*	−0.81
Italy	1982	11	DM	−3.17*	−13.89		−0.26*
Italy	1986	6	Dollar	0.56*	−24.79*	2.99*	−1.49
Italy	1986	6	DM	−0.66*	−3.08*	0.04*	−2.71*
Italy	1987	3	Dollar	5.38*	−10.39*	−31.21	−2.84
Italy	1987	3	DM	−0.14	−5.05*	−6.4*	−3.09*
Italy	1988	3	Dollar	−3.18	−15.09	−2.53*	−3.77
Italy	1988	3	DM	−3.51*	.	2.03*	−4.25*
Italy	1989	5	Dollar	−8.81	−3.13*	22.78*	3.23*
Italy	1989	5	DM	−3.51*	−6.56*	6.09*	3.73*
Italy	1991	3	Dollar	19.92*	−502.18*	−356.06*	10.24
Italy	1991	3	DM	−1.61*	79.38*	16.22*	−6.04*
Italy	1993	4	Dollar	10.66	.	−30.07*	2.85
Italy	1993	4	DM	−9.31	.	23.06*	8.41
Japan	1974	11	Dollar	−0.013	0.25*	3.03*	0.58
Japan	1974	11	DM	0.46	.	7.45*	2.33
Japan	1978	12	Dollar	−7.6	.	−8.5*	0.13*
Japan	1978	12	DM	−3.11	.	−3.39*	5.36*
Japan	1982	10	Dollar	5.4*	−58.13*	36.09*	−0.88

(*continued*)

Appendix Table 2.2. ***(continued)***

Country	Year	Month	Currency	Pre-Event	Negotiations	Month-After	Post Formation
Japan	1982	10	DM	4.98*	103.41*	21.35*	−1.83*
Japan	1984	10	Dollar	−12.82*	.	−11.1*	−36.14*
Japan	1984	10	DM	−42.7*	.	8.66*	−15.93*
Japan	1987	11	Dollar	−6.58	.	19.22*	−2.6
Japan	1987	11	DM	−23.56*	.	5.18*	−9.5*
Japan	1989	4	Dollar	−9.38*	−85.94*	−40.96*	1.67
Japan	1989	4	DM	−9.34*	−8*	31.96*	−11.69*
Japan	1989	7	Dollar	−25.12*	14.72*	−138.18*	−6.21
Japan	1989	7	DM	−8.61*	−38.42*	2.17*	−17.21*
Japan	1991	10	Dollar	−0.82	.	123.88*	1.31*
Japan	1991	10	DM	−14.05	.	19.41*	−4.21*
Japan	1992	12	Dollar	15.81	.	−93.75*	−55.62*
Japan	1992	12	DM	−1.53	.	10.92*	40.17
Netherlands	1981	10	Dollar	−3.34*	9.35*	8.07*	6.96*
Netherlands	1981	10	DM	−1.36*	4.29*	−1.01*	−4.36*
Netherlands	1982	5	Dollar	5.9	48.92*	63.27*	−10.29*
Netherlands	1982	5	DM	−3.23	−32.55*	0.65	−5.08

* An $*$ indicates that the efficiency hypothesis (joint test of $\alpha = 0$ and $\beta = 1$) can be rejected at the 0.05 level.

[1] Rows represent year and month when the event occurred.

[2] Cell entries are parameter estimates of the beta coefficients from Eqs. (2.8) and (2.10). Intercepts are not reported.

[3] Cells marked with a '.' indicate that the event period in question was of insufficient length to estimate a parameter.

3

When Markets Party: Stocks, Bonds, and Cabinet Formations

The outcomes of democratic political events – which party will win the election, which parties will form the cabinet, who will become Prime Minister – are often predictable. When market actors can easily forecast the political outcome, we expect market behavior to remain relatively stable. On the other hand, when political outcomes are less predictable, market actors will shift their portfolios out of assets whose value is vulnerable to alternative government policies toward assets offering returns that are better insulated. Therefore, we expect returns to be relatively lower in these vulnerable markets during periods of pronounced political uncertainty.

In this chapter, we assess this proposition more systematically. We continue to examine parliamentary politics. But we go beyond the simple periodization of campaigns, elections, and cabinet negotiations to discuss the predictability of coalition formations. To do so, we exploit a highly developed political science literature on cabinet government. This literature has produced models that, given the distribution of legislative seats and the policy positions of the different parties, predict which parties will form the cabinet, which policies the new government will pursue, and how long the new cabinet is likely to last. We draw on these models to develop proxy measures for the predictability of coalition formation events.

To evaluate how the predictability of cabinet formations affects asset markets, we focus on stock and government bond markets rather than currency markets. Foreign exchange trades on intermediated and disintermediated markets around the globe. In contrast, equities and bonds trade on a small number of well defined (mostly national) markets. Therefore, traders are more likely to be aware of the detailed information associated with national political events. Additionally, domestic stocks and bonds are easily comparable assets (unlike comparing equities and foreign exchange). According to a large literature in finance, government bonds represent a less risky asset than stocks (Mehra and Prescott 1985; Campbell 2002). This is particularly true for our sample of countries where the risk of a government default is minimal.

For our empirical analysis, we draw on two workhorse models from the finance literature: the Capital Asset Pricing Model and Arbitrage Pricing Theory. Using their predictions to provide analytical benchmarks, we perform three empirical tests to evaluate market performance during coalition formations. First, we compare the median abnormal return of national stock and bond markets during periods of potential political change with periods when the government's position in office is secure. This test is similar to the previous chapter in that we find differences in returns between the two periods, but we do not provide an explanation of their variation. The second test evaluates the impact of political predictability on average abnormal returns during cabinet formation periods in both stock and bond markets. Finally, we use a panel regression to show that simple returns during cabinet formation periods are lower when coalition negotiations are less predictable.

The results consistently indicate that stock market returns during the cabinet formation period are lower when the outcome of coalition bargaining is less predictable. When market actors are better able to predict the outcome of cabinet negotiations, stock returns are unaffected. The results for the bond markets are less conclusive. Overall, the results imply that, during periods when political outcomes are not predictable, asset owners shift out of stocks to assets that are better insulated from the policy consequences of a potential political change.

THE PREDICTABILITY OF POLITICAL CHANGE IN PARLIAMENTARY SYSTEMS

Political scientists have developed increasingly sophisticated models to predict the results of a cabinet formation process (Laver and Schofield 1998 and Lijphart 1999 provide reviews). Laver and Shepsle (1996) present one of the most complete theories of cabinet formation. They assume that parties bargain over the distribution of cabinet portfolios, rather than over the cabinet's policy priorities.[1] From this assumption, they develop

[1] In contrast, Schofield (1992) assumes that parties bargain over policy. Instead of dividing the policy space into single dimensions or "jurisdictions," he views the bargaining space between parties as continuous. Relying on the game-theoretic concept of the core, he classifies parties as strong core parties, weak core parties, anti-core parties, and peripheral parties. He argues that the existence of different party types determines the outcome of coalition bargaining.

a spatial model that predicts the outcomes of cabinet negotiations based on the distribution of legislative seats among the parties, the policy positions of the parties, and the salience of different issue dimensions.

The logic of their argument is best grasped with a simple example. Fig. 3.1A shows a two-dimensional policy space. Each dimension corresponds to a cabinet portfolio, say, finance and foreign policy. Each of three parties, A, B, and C, has an ideal point in the policy space, labeled in bold at AA, BB, and CC, respectively. (For simplicity, assume that each party controls enough seats in the legislature so that any two can form a majority coalition.) Laver and Shepsle argue that, once a party holds a specific cabinet portfolio, it will seek to implement its most preferred policy on that dimension. During bargaining, therefore, parties cannot credibly offer any policy except its own ideal point. This means that parties can only bargain along two lines, parallel to each dimension. This restriction creates a lattice of nine possible bargaining points where these lines intersect. Point AC, for instance, represents the government where party A holds the finance ministry and party C controls foreign policy. Point CA, on the other hand, represents the government where party C controls finance and party A holds the foreign ministry.

Figure 3.1B shows each party's indifference curve for a cabinet composed of BA. Each party prefers potential coalition combinations that lie within its indifference curve through BA. The intersection of those indifference curves represent the "win set" of the BA cabinet – that is, the set of positions preferred by at least two parties. If one of the lattice points

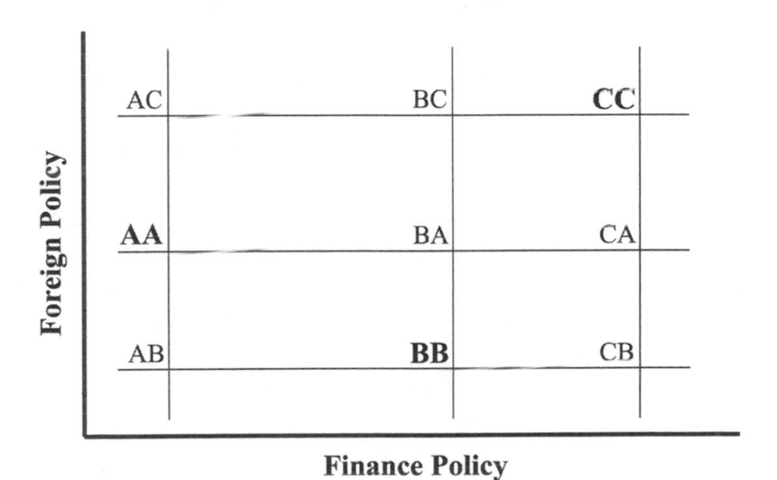

Figure 3.1A. A lattice of potential coalitions.

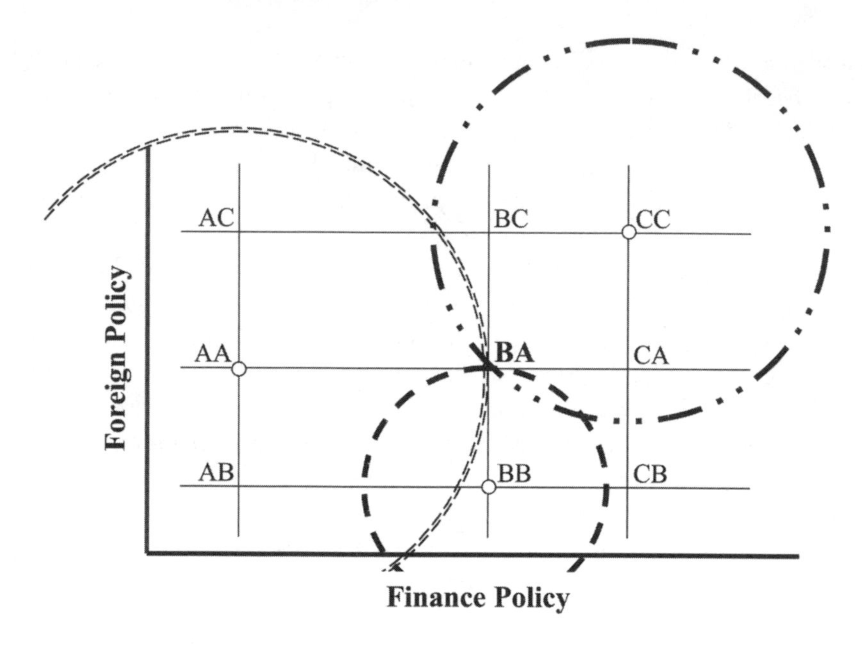

Figure 3.1B. An equilibrium cabinet.

(that is, a potential alternative cabinet) lies within the win set, parties have an incentive to pursue that cabinet combination rather than BA. On the other hand, if no potential cabinet lies in the win set – as in our example – then that cabinet combination is an equilibrium cabinet. That cabinet, therefore, should be stable as no parties have an incentive to defect from it.

Laver and Shepsle show that, under certain conditions, a specific party will enjoy a privileged position in the negotiation process – what they call a "strong" party. Specifically, a strong party participates in every potential cabinet preferred by a majority of legislators to a cabinet in which the strong party assumes all of the portfolios (that is, a minority government controlled by the strong party). These strong parties, therefore, have veto power over the partisan identity of the cabinet government.

Again, a simple example clarifies the definition. Figure 3.2 again shows a simple two-dimensional space with three parties, A, B, and C. To see if party B is a strong party, consider the win set formed by party A's and party C's indifference curves drawn through point BB – the lattice point where party B controls both the finance and foreign policy portfolios. That win set is not empty. Both A and C prefer two potential cabinets over the BB combination: BA, where B controls finance and A controls foreign policy, and BC, where B controls finance and C controls foreign policy.

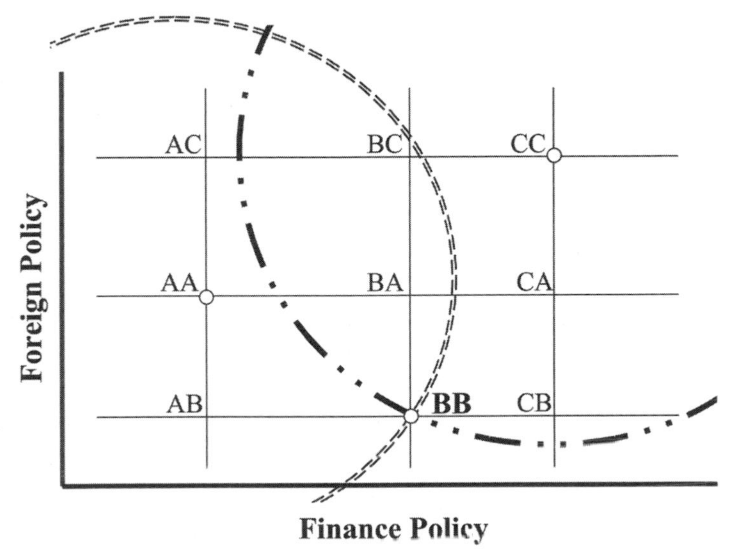

Figure 3.2. A strong party.

What is interesting is that party B must participate in both these alternatives. That is, party B has the ability to determine which cabinet will be selected. Party B, therefore, is a strong party.

Laver and Shepsle demonstrate that there can be at most one strong party for a particular configuration of party ideal points and legislative seats. Further, Laver and Shepsle show theoretically and empirically that strong parties are likely to participate in a governing coalition and, as such, structure the cabinet negotiations. Where a strong party does not exist, however, the outcome of cabinet negotiations is less predictable.

We employ their conception of a strong party to provide a measure of the predictability of cabinet negotiations.[2] When a strong party exists, coalition negotiations should be fairly predictable and, as a result, we expect markets prices to remain relatively stable. When a strong party does not exist, the outcome of coalition bargaining is less predictable and, in turn, we expect market returns to be depressed during the negotiation period.

Because of the complexity of the strong party concept, Laver and Shepsle develop a computer program that calculates the existence of a strong party.[3] The "winset" program requires information about the distribution of seats

[2] Laver and Shepsle distinguish between a very strong party and a merely strong party. We collapse the two categories since we found no systematic differences between our results.

[3] The winset program is available at http://homepage.tinet.ie/~doylep/Winset/ws_index.htm.

and party positions to compute whether a strong party exists – i.e., one party that is in an advantageous negotiation position. We calculate the existence of a strong party in 73 post-election cabinet formations between 1970 and 2003 in 10 parliamentary democracies with proportional representation electoral systems: Austria, Belgium, Denmark, Germany, Ireland, Italy, Netherlands, New Zealand (post-1996), Norway, and Sweden.

While the distribution of legislative seats for each post-election bargaining period is trivial to obtain, each party's policy position needs to be calculated. Although political scientists have developed a number of scales to indicate relative policy positions of parties (e.g., Castles and Mair 1984; Laver and Budge 1991; Laver 2001; Huber and Gabel 2000), these scales tend to be unidimensional and static. Laver and Shepsle's model of cabinet formation, however, demands multidimensional measures of party positions. Additionally, we want to capture changes in party positions from election to election.

To do so, we use data from the party manifesto project (Budge et al. 2001). At each election, parties issue manifestos that outline policy priorities and set the tone for the campaign. (In the United States, these are referred to as party platforms.) The Manifestos data project performs content analysis on party programmes for over twenty democracies from 1945–2003. For each manifesto, the data set codes the proportion of sentences (or quasi-sentences) devoted to a particular issue in six sets of policy domains: external relations, freedom and democracy, political system, economy, welfare and quality of life, fabric of society, and social groups. Within these policy domains, the manifestos are coded for more specific topics. For example, within the freedom and democracy domain, there are variables for mentions of freedom and human rights, democracy, constitutionalism: positive, and constitutionalism: negative. A party receiving a score of five on the issue of "constitutionalism: negative" devoted five percent of their manifesto to negative mentions of constitutionalism.

To convert the manifestos data to party positions on an economic dimension and a social dimension, we first chose variables related to each dimension. Following Budge and Klingemann 2001, we selected a number of relevant questions for each dimension and then subtracted the number of negative mentions from the number of positive mentions. Table 3.1 shows the exact questions used to construct the indices.

Laver and Shepsle's winset program requires that party positions fall between 0 and 1. Therefore, we normalized the party position data on country-by-country basis. For each dimension, we calculated the largest

Table 3.1. *Construction of policy positions*

Two dimensional mapping		
	Economic dimension	
Pro-market		Pro-state intervention
Free enterprise (401)		Market regulation (403)
Incentives (402)	minus	Economic planning (404)
Protectionism negative (407)		Protectionism positive (406)
Economic orthodoxy (414)		Controlled economy (412)
Welfare state limitation (505)		Nationalization (413)
		Welfare state expansion (504)
		Labor groups: positive (701)
	Social dimension	
Authoritarian		Not authoritarian
Military: positive (104)		Anti-imperialism (103)
Freedom and human rights (201)		Military: negative (105)
Constitutionalism: positive (203)		Peace (106)
Political authority (305)	minus	Internationalism: negative (109)
National way of life: positive (601)		Democracy (202)
Traditional morality: positive (603)		Education expansion (506)
Law and order (605)		
Social harmony (606)		

Numbers in parentheses are variable numbers from Budge et al. 2001.

difference in party scores between all parties running for election at any time during the post-war period. We then divided each party's score by this maximum value to standardize the party scores.

To illustrate these party system maps, Figs. 3.3 and 3.4 show the 2002 Austrian party system and the 1998 Dutch party system, respectively. Each map shows the location of each party based on its party manifesto. In the Austrian party system, the Socialist Party (SPO) is the most left on the economic dimension while the People's Party (ÖVP) is furthest to the right. On the social dimension, however, the SPO and the ÖVP are in relative agreement. Instead, the Freedom Party (FPO) puts forward the most conservative social policies. After the 2002 election, the incumbent ÖVP–FPO coalition eventually decided to re-form.

The two-dimensional representation of the Dutch party system also comports well with conventional understandings of how the parties line-up.

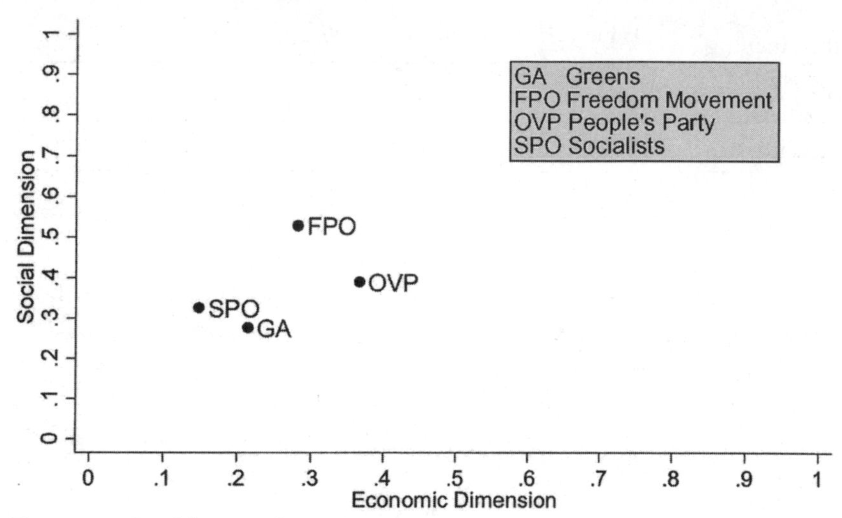

Figure 3.3. Spatial map of Austrian party system in 2002.

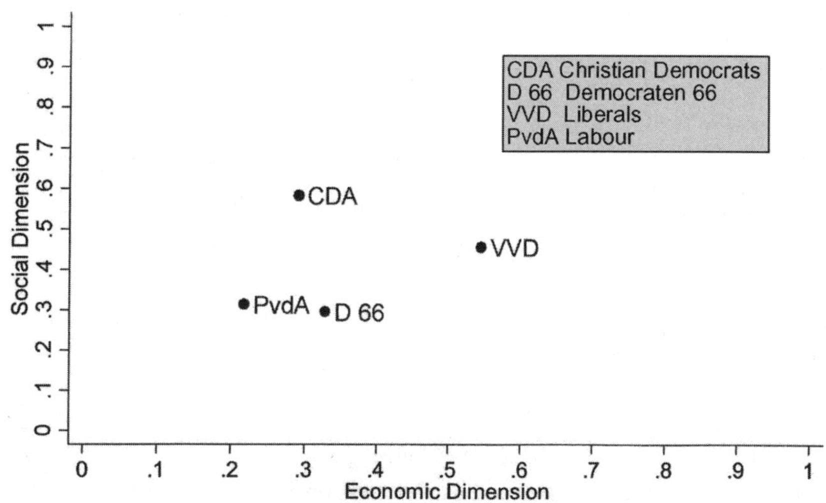

Figure 3.4. Spatial map of Dutch party system in 1998.

(We omit a number of smaller Left parties for ease of presentation.) The Labour party (PvdA) is the most left on economic issues, while the Liberal party (VVD) possesses the most free market orientation. The Christian Democratic party (CDA) is moderate on economic issues, but distinguishes itself with a more conservative social appeal. In this case, the incumbent PvdA–VVD coalition decided to continue in office, focusing on their relative proximity on social issues to cement their partnership.

With these maps of party positions and the distribution of legislative seats for each country-election, we then calculated the existence of a strong party using the winset program.[4] Table 3.2 indicates whether a strong party exists for each negotiation period. Strong parties exist in 53 of 73 cases.

We know, however, that our estimates of party positions contain measurement error. The winset program allows us to investigate the possibility that measurement error affects the existence of a strong party. For each cabinet, we ran a simulation of 1000 runs that varied each party's position on each dimension with a shock drawn from a normal distribution with a standard deviation of 0.05. The results of the simulation exercise indicate the number of times out of 1000 that each party was a strong party and the number of times that no strong party existed. Table 3.2 reports the number of runs in which no strong party existed and the number of runs that the party with the most number of times as a strong party was a strong party. These results provide continuous variables that tap into the "certainty" of the strong party prediction and, hence, the predictability of cabinet bargaining.

The existence of a strong party, the number of times that no strong party exists in the simulations, and the number of runs that the leading party is a strong party provide three measures of the predictability of coalition formation processes.[5] We use these variables to evaluate how markets react – we expect that the less predictable the cabinet formation, the lower stock and bond market returns will be during the negotiation period.

A BRIEF INTRODUCTION TO PORTFOLIO ALLOCATION[6]

We examine how political information influences the allocation of resources by market participants across assets. We concentrate on

[4] For all simulations, we assumed that each dimension has equal salience. We also did not exclude any parties from consideration as potential coalition partners.

[5] We report the results from using only the strong party and no strong party variables. Results using the top party variable were similar.

[6] Useful expositions include Alexander (2001), Campbell, Lo and MacKinlay (1997), Cochrane (2001), Duffie (2001), Elton et al. (2003), and Solnik (2000). A helpful critique based on experimental evidence is Bossaerts (2002).

Table 3.2. *Existence of a strong party*

Country	Date	Strong party	No strong	Top strong
Austria	4/24/1983	1	184	673
Austria	11/23/1986	1	21	976
Austria	10/7/1990	1	54	782
Austria	10/9/1994	1	281	714
Austria	12/17/1995	1	325	659
Austria	10/3/1999	1	238	631
Austria	11/24/2002	1	305	552
Belgium	11/8/1981	1	343	576
Belgium	10/13/1985	1	409	480
Belgium	12/13/1987	0	820	80
Belgium	11/24/1991	0	732	69
Belgium	5/21/1995	0	699	118
Belgium	6/13/1999	0	486	105
Denmark	12/8/1981	1	480	420
Denmark	1/10/1984	1	660	307
Denmark	9/8/1987	0	897	61
Denmark	5/10/1988	0	741	181
Denmark	12/12/1990	1	387	595
Denmark	9/21/1994	1	679	161
Denmark	3/11/1998	0	780	155
Denmark	11/20/2001	0	911	29
France	6/14/1981	1	0	1000
France	3/16/1986	1	596	346
France	6/5/1988	1	6	994
France	3/21/1993	1	164	813
France	5/25/1997	1	113	850
France	6/9/2002	1	0	1000
Germany	10/9/1980	1	0	1000
Germany	3/6/1983	1	0	1000
Germany	1/25/1987	1	423	505
Germany	12/2/1990	0	772	134
Germany	10/16/1994	0	1000	0
Germany	9/27/1998	1	3	997
Germany	9/22/2002	1	0	1000
Ireland	6/11/1981	1	0	860
Ireland	2/18/1982	1	0	997
Ireland	11/24/1982	1	319	646

Country	Date	Strong party	No strong	Top strong
Ireland	2/17/1987	1	0	954
Ireland	6/15/1989	1	53	603
Ireland	11/25/1992	1	95	882
Ireland	6/6/1997	1	0	765
Italy	6/26/1983	1	504	277
Italy	6/14/1987	0	739	139
Italy	4/6/1992	1	443	389
Italy	3/28/1994	1	240	440
Italy	4/21/1996	0	542	315
Italy	5/13/2001	1	405	242
Netherlands	5/26/1981	1	38	899
Netherlands	9/8/1982	1	263	495
Netherlands	5/21/1986	1	152	728
Netherlands	9/6/1989	1	217	651
Netherlands	5/3/1994	1	7	659
Netherlands	5/6/1998	0	425	184
Netherlands	5/15/2002	1	376	523
Netherlands	1/22/2003	0	343	502
New Zealand	10/12/1996	0	697	226
New Zealand	11/27/1999	0	395	359
New Zealand	7/27/2002	0	673	212
Norway	9/14/1981	1	380	388
Norway	9/8/1985	1	485	230
Norway	9/11/1989	0	568	204
Norway	9/13/1993	0	360	424
Norway	9/16/1997	0	504	241
Norway	9/10/2001	1	518	358
Sweden	9/19/1982	1	18	975
Sweden	9/15/1985	1	50	945
Sweden	9/18/1988	1	93	791
Sweden	9/15/1991	0	420	395
Sweden	9/18/1994	1	52	942
Sweden	9/21/1998	1	70	916
Sweden	9/15/2002	1	248	688

Strong party: Strong party exists = 1; No strong party = 0.
No strong: Number of runs out of 1000 where a strong party does not exist.
Top strong: Number of runs out of a 1000 where the top party is a strong party.

two asset markets: equity or stock markets and bond markets.[7] Both stocks and bonds can be interpreted as a promise by the issuer to pay a return at some point in the future. The prices that rational investors are willing to pay for these assets, therefore, depend on prospective evaluations of future economic performance and government policy. As with most work in finance, we assume that economic actors have rational expectations: that investors form their expectations of future prices and returns with an awareness of the factors generating those values.[8]

Following the literature in finance and economics, we assume that market participants invest their capital in a variety of instruments and choose their portfolios with the goal of balancing risk and return.[9] Each individual investor chooses a portfolio (not to exceed total initial wealth) that maximizes

$$M = M(m_{\mathrm{M}}, s^2_{\mathrm{M}})$$

where $m_{\mathrm{M}}$is the mean (or expected) return on the portfolio and $s^2_{\mathrm{M}}$is the variance (or a proxy for the overall riskiness) of the portfolio.[10] According to the framework, an investor's portfolio choices occur in two parts. The investor first constructs the portfolio frontier – the set of portfolios for which s^2_{M} is minimized and m_{M} is maximized. From this set, the investor selects a portfolio that maximizes the objective function M based on his/her preferences. The mean-variance framework, therefore, provides a theory of individual decision making regardless of whether the market is in equilibrium.

[7] Both stocks and bonds are traded on primary and secondary markets. We focus on secondary markets where the prices of both assets are driven by supply and demand and where trading is predominantly among investors without a significant involvement by the issuer. We examine the political factors leading to bond issues on the primary market in Chapter 5.

[8] A growing literature argues that traders deviate from pure rational behavior. The literature in behavioral finance traces deviations from rational expectations equilibria to fads, herding behavior, the existence of noise traders, sunspots, etc. See Barberis and Thaler (2002) for a survey.

[9] The fundamental idea motivating the tradeoff between risk and return imposes some structure on the investor's (von Neumann–Morgenstern) utility function. If we assume that utility is quadratic in wealth then expected utility can be expressed as a function of the expected value (mean) and variance (or standard deviation) of the return on an asset. The "mean-variance" approach to finance is due to Markovitz (1959). Sharpe (1970) developed the basics of portfolio theory.

[10] We follow standard practice and define the return on an asset as $R_{\mathrm{t}} = (P_{\mathrm{t}} - P_{\mathrm{t-1}})/P_{\mathrm{t-1}}$ where P refers to the price of an asset or the level of an index that measures the performance of the asset.

The Capital Asset Pricing Model

The capital asset pricing model (CAPM) extends the mean-variance approach to portfolio selection to the economy as a whole: "If all investors behave according to a mean-variance objective and if they all have the same beliefs (expressed by the means and variances of asset returns), then the CAPM determines what can be inferred about the pattern of asset returns when asset markets are in equilibrium" (Bailey 2005, p. 107). As originally developed by Sharpe (1964) and Lintner (1965), the CAPM represents a model of market equilibrium that links the return on an asset to the performance of comparable assets within the economy. If there are no arbitrage opportunities available, the difference between the return on a specific asset and the return for the market as a whole should be a function of only risk.

A (linear) representation of the CAPM can be expressed as:

$$R_t = \alpha + \beta X_t + \varepsilon_t \tag{3.1}$$

where R_t represents the return to an asset, X_t represents the return to a market index, and ε_t the asset specific return all measured at time t.[11] In this specification, as in ordinary least squares regression, the estimated value of β ($\hat{\beta}$) can be interpreted as the relationship between the return on the market index and the return on the particular asset. If $\hat{\beta} = 0$ then there is no systematic relationship between the market index and R; a value of $\hat{\beta}$ equal to one indicates that R follows the market return. Values of $\hat{\beta}$ greater (lower) than one mean that, in relation to the market return, R is riskier (safer). In Eq. (3.1) the constant (α) indicates, conditional on the estimated value of $\hat{\beta}$, the minimum (or maximum depending on sign) expected return for the asset in question. The error term (ε_t) is assumed to be distributed normally with constant variance and can be interpreted as the asset specific return. We discuss other interpretations of the error term in more detail later in this section.

Although the CAPM has proven to be useful in both theory and practice, it has significant limitations. First, as is apparent from Eq. (3.1), values of $\hat{\beta}$ are sensitive to the selection of the market index (X). If, for example, one is interested in pricing the return on shares of IBM, values for $\hat{\beta}$ may vary significantly if the Dow Jones Industrial Average or the S&P 500 index

[11] The original version of the CAPM based on mean-variance analysis derived R and X as deviations from a risk free rate. Black (1972) modified the model to allow R and X to be interpreted as real returns.

is used as the market index. Second, critics have noted that the CAPM requires an exact identification of the market portfolio which must include all possible investable assets (Roll 1977).[12]

Arbitrage Pricing Theory

To combat these problems, arbitrage pricing theory (APT) extends the CAPM to a more general linear setting (Ross 1976). The notion of arbitrage – the simultaneous purchase and sale of essentially similar assets in different markets and at different prices – is an integral component of competitive markets. Shleifer (2000) argues that arbitrage allows for theories of efficient markets where traders are not fully rational.[13] In APT, the return on an asset is determined by a number of "risk" factors that are common to all assets (within a class) plus a term specific to the asset. Factor models of asset prices state that the return on an asset can be expressed as a function of a (relatively) small number of factors. The simplest case, that of a single factor model, can be written as:

$$R_t = \alpha + \beta_1 X_t + \varepsilon_t \tag{3.2}$$

where R_t is the rate of return on an asset (or portfolio), X_t is the factor used to describe R_t, and ε_t is the asset specific return. In this model, β captures the sensitivity of X to R and is often referred to as a "factor loading." Further it is assumed that the conditional expectation of the error given the factor is zero ($E[\varepsilon_t|X_t] = 0$).

The single factor APT model is easily extended to multiple factors where the rate of return on an asset (R) depends on a number of risk factors:

$$R_t = \alpha + \beta_1 X_{1t} + \beta_2 X_{2t} + \cdots + \beta_k X_{kt} + \varepsilon_t \tag{3.2$'$}$$

where α is again the intercept and ε is the random asset specific term and is independent of the Xs. The Xs are a set of factors common to all assets and the betas represent the sensitivity or "risk exposure" of the asset to each factor.

[12] Roll argues that "(a) no correct and unambiguous test of the [CAPM] theory has appeared in the literature and (b) there is practically no possibility that such a test can be accomplished in the future" (1977, 129–30).

[13] Imagine a set of irrational traders who trade randomly. Shleifer (2000) points out that the trading strategies of a large number of these traders will cancel each other out. Arbitrage also implies, as Friedman (1953) observed, that irrational traders cannot lose money forever and in the long run will disappear from the market.

The APT model in Eq. (3.2) is identical in form to the CAPM model in Eq. (3.1). The theoretical underpinnings and empirical implementation of these two models, however, differ considerably.[14] Theoretically, APT provides a more general description of equilibria than the CAPM since prices can be determined by more than expected means and variances. Since investors attempt to take advantage of arbitrage opportunities, subsequent returns on an asset (and its relationship to various market indices) are constrained by the law of one price. Because no arbitrage opportunities remain unexploited (and thus no arbitrage opportunities exist in equilibrium), it is easier to implement an empirical APT model – it is not necessary to identify "all" risky assets or the "true" market portfolio. This generality of the APT, however, comes at a price: it is difficult to isolate the "appropriate" factors to include in an empirical model.

The identification of the appropriate factors represents one of the major issues in working with APT models. An enormous literature describes, analyzes, and evaluates the relative contribution of various factors in explaining stock and bond market returns.[15] One set of papers points to the growing importance of international factors in shaping local returns. Given (relatively) integrated markets, the expected return on a domestic stock or bond may be correlated with the world market (Karolyi and Stulz 2002 provide a review). A sizable literature on cross-economy "synchronization" examines comovement in business cycles and correlations between real variables (e.g., Kose, Otrok, and Whiteman 2003).

A second set of arguments emphasizes the role of local factors in asset pricing. Roll (1992), Heston and Rouwenhorst (1994), and Cavaglia, Brithgman, and Aked (2000) contend that differences in domestic industrial structures drive stock market returns.[16]

While much less work has been published on the factors appropriate for pricing bonds, Barr and Priestley (2002), Ilmanen (1996), and Harvey, Solnik, and Zhou (1994) find that the factors driving equity returns also play a role in generating bond market returns.[17]

[14] See Campbell, Lo, and MacKinlay (1997) and Elton et al. (2003) for a detailed discussion.

[15] Chen, Roll, and Ross (1986), Chen (1991), and Fama and French (1993) are but a few papers that employ a multi-factor approach to asset pricing.

[16] Brooks and Del Negro (2002) and Griffin and Karolyi (1998) provide a dissenting point of view.

[17] Bond markets are more segmented than equity markets due to cross-national differences in legal restrictions, tax regulations, as well as the persistent problems of home bias and asymmetric information. Jorion (1992) provides a valuable discussion.

We examine returns of both stocks and ten-year government bonds. The generic form of our APT model for stocks (bonds) is:

$$R_{it}^{S} = \alpha + \beta_1 RUS_t^S + \beta_2 \Delta Gold_t + \beta_3 \Delta Oil_t + \beta_3 \Delta Sec_t + \varepsilon_t. \quad (3.3)$$

According to Eq. (3.3), the return R_{it}^{S} on country i's stock (bond) market is a function of the rate of return on the stock (bond) market in the United States, the change in the price of gold, the change in the price of oil, the underlying performance of 14 industrial sectors, and a random error.[18]

Equation (3.3) is the fundamental model for our empirical analysis. Conditional upon the specified factors, ε_t represents the asset specific return; that is, the return on the asset that is not predicted by the factors in Eq. (3.3). We make the standard assumption (and check it empirically) that ε_t is distributed normally with mean zero and constant variance.

Sample and Economic Data

To evaluate the impact of democratic political events on asset market behavior, we employ the factor model in Eq. (3.3) on fifteen parliamentary democracies: Australia, Austria, Belgium, Canada, Demark, France, Germany, Ireland, Italy, Japan, Netherlands, New Zealand, Norway, Sweden, and the United Kingdom. (Note that some of these countries possess majoritarian electoral systems.)

Given that political information is likely to possess a short half-life, we need to work at the lowest level of temporal aggregation possible. Our data consist of daily stock and bond market returns. Working at the daily level, however, does limit the type and availability of control variables. Most of the data come from two sources: Morgan Stanley Capital International (MSCI) and DataStream. Datastream's national stock market indices are weighted to be representative of all major markets in the country. We calculate daily stock market returns based on these indices from January 1, 1972 through December 30, 2002. MSCI calculates 36 indices corresponding to different industrial sectors. Following Forbes and Chinn (2003), we run a factor analysis on fourteen of these sectoral factors to determine a single underlying factor to capture sectoral performance.

[18] This specification is similar to Forbes and Chinn (2003) with two important modifications. First, we control for the U.S. rather than a world or European index because the latter two indices are heavily influenced by the indices from countries in our sample. Second, we use principle components analysis to generate a specific factor common to the fourteen industrial sectors available from MSCI.

We employ the annualized interest rate on ten-year government bonds[19] from DataStream. The bond market data does not begin until January 1, 1985 for most of the sample. DataStream is also the source for two additional global variables: oil prices (measured as the current dollar price per barrel for Brent oil) and gold prices (measured as the price of gold bullion in $/oz in the London market).

ABNORMAL RETURNS DURING PERIODS OF POTENTIAL POLITICAL CHANGE

Our tests examine whether stock and bond returns differ during periods of potential political change, particularly during cabinet formations. We expect that stock and bond returns will be lower during these periods than in the absence of political events. When political outcomes are predictable, however, we expect stock and bond returns to be relatively unaffected. As a proxy for the predictability of a cabinet formation, we employ the presence of a strong party, as defined by Laver and Shepsle.

In this section, we present three tests. First, we compare the median abnormal return of national stock and bond markets during periods of potential political change with periods when the government's position in office is secure. The second test evaluates the impact of political predictability on average abnormal returns in both stock and bond markets. Finally, we estimate the impact of political predictability on simple returns using a straightforward panel regression framework.

Median Abnormal Returns in Political and Non-Political Periods

Financial economists commonly use a "market model" to forecast returns (Brown and Warner 1980, 1985). A market model argues that, given efficient markets, the best predictor of an individual asset's performance is the performance of the market as a whole. This argument is based on the idea that anomalous events – macroeconomic announcements, expectations of war, etc. – may influence the market as a whole. Controlling for these "market" influences allows the analyst to observe changes in the behavior of an asset that are caused by factors outside of the events.

[19] The data series for 10 year (long-term) government bonds are available for most of the sample countries for the longest periods of time. Shorter maturities are available for only a portion of the sample period. The correlations between 10 year bonds, 1-month bonds, and 3-month bonds are high. Using these shorter maturities in a sub-sample did not alter the results.

We use the market model in Eq. (3.3) as our baseline for both stock and bond market returns. The residuals ($\hat{\varepsilon}_t$) represent abnormal returns.

To determine whether returns differ during periods of potential political change, we compare the median abnormal return during a political event to a distribution of medians generated during non-political periods. For each country and asset (stock and bond), we first select a random sequence of ninety consecutive non-political days – that is, a period when there is no campaign, election, or cabinet negotiations. For each of these randomly-selected periods, we estimate the market model (Eq. 3.3) for the respective asset and calculate the abnormal returns ($\hat{\varepsilon}_t$), and then identify the median abnormal return. We repeat this process 1000 times and generate an empirical distribution of median abnormal returns. We then calculate a 90 percent confidence interval around the average median abnormal return for these non-political periods for both the equity and bond markets.

In the second step, we calculate the median abnormal return for each political period. That is, we estimate Eq. (3.3) for each campaign or coalition formation period in the sample and calculate the median abnormal return. We then compare the median abnormal return for each period of potential political change with the empirical distribution of median abnormal returns.

This research design deals with two potential problems in evaluating the impact of politics on financial markets. First, distributions of returns on financial assets are notoriously fat tailed: large observations occur more frequently than expected under a normal distribution. Since some of the political event periods are relatively short (they range between 1 and 141 days), a single outlier or short series of unusually large abnormal returns during any of these periods could distort the average abnormal return for the entire period. If the sample of financial returns contains a larger number of extreme values, then the median will be a more reliable indicator of central tendency.

A second concern reflects the possibility that any differences in abnormal returns between political and non-political periods might be driven by selection issues. It is possible that large abnormal returns occur randomly and that, by focusing only on periods of potential political change, we happen to select these periods. Any differences, therefore, might represent a function of the time periods selected, rather than the occurrence of political processes. By generating a distribution of median abnormal returns, we are able to demonstrate that these selection issues do not drive the results.

Results

Table 3.3 presents the full results. The first set of columns contains the empirical 90% confidence interval for equity and bond median abnormal returns for all the countries in our sample. In Austria, for example, ninety percent of the median abnormal stock returns fall between 0.016 and 0.0307. The column labeled year indicates the year of the political event. The Stock (Bond) Market columns indicate the median abnormal stock (bond) return for each campaign and coalition formation period. Entries marked in bold (italics) are greater (less) the average median return at the 90 percent confidence level. Again turning to Austria as an example, the 1975 campaign period and cabinet formation periods had a median abnormal stock return (−0.0004 and 0.0000, respectively) that was significantly lower than the sample distribution of median returns.

For the stock returns, the median abnormal return in campaign periods is significantly lower than the average median return in 54 of 125 political events, about 43 percent of the cases, a proportion well above what we would expect if these returns occurred by chance. During campaign periods, the median return is statistically indistinguishable from the average median in 42 cases (34 percent), and significantly higher in 29 events (23 percent). During campaign periods, therefore, stock returns are frequently lower than what the distribution of returns in "non-political" periods implies.

The pattern of stock returns changes slightly for the government formation periods. Returns are significantly lower than the average median abnormal return in 46 of 125 events, more than 37 percent of the time – still far more than what one would expect by chance. The median return during government formation periods is statistically indistinguishable from the average median in 33 cases, around 26 percent, and significantly higher in 46 of the events, about 37 percent of the cases. The shift from the campaign periods to the cabinet formation periods – fewer periods with lower returns, more periods with higher returns – may reflect the resolution of political uncertainty that often occurs with a decisive electoral result.

In bond markets, the median abnormal return also differs from the empirical distribution more than would occur by chance. During the campaign periods, the median abnormal bond return is significantly lower than the average median return in 36 of 68 cases, about 53 percent of the events. Returns are statistically indistinguishable from the empirical distribution in 24 cases, around 35 percent and significantly higher in only 8 cases (12 percent).

Table 3.3. *Median abnormal returns*

	90% Confidence interval			Campaign period		Cabinet formation period	
Country	Lower	Upper	Year	Stocks	Bonds	Stocks	Bonds
Austria							
STOCKS	0.0160	0.0307	1975	*−0.0004*		*0.0000*	
INTEREST	0.0064	0.0240	1979	*−0.0014*		*−0.0018*	
RATES			1983	*0.0011*		*−0.0015*	
			1986	*−0.0046*	*−0.0156*	*−0.0020*	*0.0004*
			1990	*−0.0074*	*−0.0108*	*−0.0039*	*0.0033*
			1994	*−0.0006*	*−0.0007*	*0.0012*	*0.0015*
			1995	*−0.0094*	*−0.0263*	*−0.0011*	*−0.0062*
			1999	0.0193	*−0.0296*	*−0.0059*	*−0.0014*
			2002	*−0.0350*	*−0.0126*	*−0.0068*	0.0156
Belgium							
STOCKS	−0.0229	−0.0095	1974	*−0.0013*		**0.0029**	
INTEREST	0.0015	0.0182	1977	*−0.0011*		**0.0006**	
RATES			1978	*0.0063*		**−0.0013**	
			1981	*−0.0013*		−0.0106	
			1985	*0.0148*		**−0.0024**	
			1987	−0.0181		**−0.0058**	
			1991	*−0.0038*	*−0.0083*	**0.0034**	*−0.0024*
			1995	*−0.0007*	*−0.0120*	**−0.0063**	0.0027
			1999	*0.0406*	**0.0184**	−0.0139	0.0086
Denmark							
STOCKS	−0.0042	0.0108	1973	0.0020		−0.0033	
INTEREST	−0.0188	−0.0007	1975	0.0025		−0.0152	
RATES			1977	0.0003		0.0088	
			1979	**0.0175**		−0.0008	
			1981	*−0.0185*		0.0062	
			1984	0.0024		**0.0137**	
			1987	**0.0426**		*−0.0555*	
			1988	0.0059		*−0.0191*	
			1990	*−0.0349*	*−0.0373*	**0.0203**	*−0.0810*
			1994	0.0031	−0.0022	0.0101	**0.0119**
			1998	*−0.0244*	−0.0066	*−0.0253*	**−0.0004**
			2001	*−0.0149*	*−0.0289*	0.0100	**0.0031**

	90% Confidence interval			Campaign period		Cabinet formation period	
Country	Lower	Upper	Year	Stocks	Bonds	Stocks	Bonds
France							
STOCKS	−0.0103	0.0068	1978	**0.0069**		**0.0106**	
INTEREST	−0.0136	−0.0008	1981	−0.0067	*−0.0323*	**0.0132**	*−0.0156*
RATES			1986	−0.0039	*−0.0157*	**0.0145**	−0.0118
			1988	**0.0155**	*−0.0188*	**0.0122**	−0.0088
			1993	0.0003	−0.0127	*−0.0134*	**0.0418**
			1997	*−0.0227*	*−0.0219*	**0.0167**	**0.0135**
			2002	**0.0251**	**0.0082**	**0.0672**	**0.0111**
Germany							
STOCKS	0.0037	0.0159	1976	*0.0031*		*−0.0007*	
INTEREST	0.0057	0.0217	1980	*−0.0072*		*−0.0048*	
RATES			1983	0.0044		0.0136	
			1987	*−0.0057*	*−0.0148*	*−0.0119*	*−0.0049*
			1990	*−0.0200*	*−0.0319*	*−0.0042*	**0.0005**
			1994	0.0040	*−0.0008*	0.0063	*−0.0069*
			1998	**0.0375**	*0.0011*	*−0.0020*	*−0.0167*
			2002	*−0.0123*	*−0.0171*	*−0.0093*	*−0.0132*
Italy							
STOCKS	−0.0230	−0.0062	1976	**0.0032**		**0.0081**	
INTEREST	−0.0180	0.0028	1979	**0.0024**		**0.0001**	
RATES			1983	**0.0046**		**0.0057**	
			1987	0.0074		**−0.0010**	
			1992	**0.0036**	−0.0047	**0.0059**	**0.0042**
			1994	**0.0004**	−0.0123	**0.0211**	−0.0102
			1996	**0.0082**	−0.0099	**0.0033**	−0.0119
			2001	−0.0116	−0.0129	−0.0125	**0.0045**
Netherlands							
STOCKS	−0.0051	0.0075	1977	0.0004		−0.0006	
INTEREST	−0.0073	0.0071	1981	−0.0026		0.0046	
RATES			1982	*−0.0121*		*−0.0105*	
			1986	0.0069		0.0032	
			1989	−0.0007	*−0.0114*	0.0028	−0.0036

(*continued*)

Table 3.3. ***(continued)***

	90% Confidence interval			Campaign period		Cabinet formation period	
Country	Lower	Upper	Year	Stocks	Bonds	Stocks	Bonds
			1994	0.0047	0.0065	*−0.0056*	0.0129
			1998	**0.0098**	−0.0005	**0.0114**	−0.0057
			2002	**0.0296**	**0.0191**	**0.0289**	**0.0406**
Norway							
STOCKS	−0.0200	−0.0002	1981	**0.0109**		**0.0055**	
INTEREST	0.0004	0.0245	1985	**0.0030**		**0.0061**	
RATES			1989	**0.0102**		−0.0022	
			1993	**0.0058**	0.0026	**0.0106**	0.0035
			1997	**0.0151**	*−0.0026*	−0.0056	*−0.0012*
			2001	**0.0158**	*−0.0038*	**0.0020**	0.0154
Sweden							
STOCKS	−0.0123	0.0075	1982	−0.0062		−0.0048	
INTEREST	0.0014	0.0191	1985	**0.0078**		0.0017	
RATES			1988	−0.0019		**0.0138**	
			1991	**0.0212**	0.0103	*−0.0139*	0.0160
			1994	−0.0060	*−0.0214*	0.0001	*−0.0052*
			1998	**0.0433**	0.0050	**0.0164**	**0.0696**
			2002	*−0.0365*	*−0.0339*	*−0.0198*	*0.0005*
Canada							
STOCKS	−0.0017	0.0074	1974	0.0000		0.0037	
INTEREST	−0.0027	0.0078	1979	0.0000		*−0.0011*	
RATES			1980	−0.0001		**0.0158**	
			1984	*−0.0045*		*−0.0062*	
			1988	*−0.0018*	*−0.0066*	0.0014	0.0014
			1993	0.0011	*−0.0151*	**0.0077**	*−0.0125*
			1997	*−0.0255*	*−0.0281*	*−0.0306*	**0.0104**
			2000	0.0000	0.0032	**0.0227**	**0.0476**
Japan							
STOCKS	−0.0257	−0.0089	1976	*−0.0035*		**0.0034**	
INTEREST	−0.0259	0.0012	1979	*0.0001*		**0.0040**	
RATES			1980	*−0.0023*		**−0.0003**	
			1983	*0.0060*		**0.0065**	

	90% Confidence interval			Campaign period		Cabinet formation period	
Country	Lower	Upper	Year	Stocks	Bonds	Stocks	Bonds
			1986	−0.0097	*−0.0121*	**0.0110**	**0.0147**
			1990	*−0.0085*	−0.0012	**−0.0047**	**0.0046**
			1993	*−0.0055*	−0.0219	**−0.0064**	*−0.0559*
			1996	−0.0120	−0.0152	**−0.0001**	**0.0159**
			2000	*0.0176*	0.0131	*−0.0587*	**0.0254**
Ireland							
STOCKS	−0.0046	0.0125	1977	*−0.0092*		−0.0041	
INTEREST	−0.0103	0.0058	1981	−0.0030		0.0067	
RATES			1982	−0.0032		0.0122	
			1982	**0.0215**		0.0055	
			1987	−0.0020	−0.0039	*−0.0086*	*−0.0131*
			1989	−0.0001	−0.0102	*−0.0103*	**0.0122**
			1992	*−0.0053*	*−0.0211*	0.0072	−0.0040
			1997	0.0099	0.0006	*−0.0166*	0.0041
			2002	**0.0483**	**0.0274**	**0.0329**	**0.0317**
Australia							
STOCKS	0.0081	0.0245	1974	*−0.0007*		*−0.0136*	
INTEREST	0.0007	0.0214	1975	0.0116		*−0.0177*	
RATES			1977	*−0.0083*		*−0.0015*	
			1980	*−0.0248*		0.0116	
			1983	*−0.0096*		0.0182	
			1984	0.0103		*0.0044*	
			1987	*−0.0036*	*−0.0125*	0.0095	*−0.0119*
			1990	*−0.0133*	*−0.0131*	*0.0027*	*−0.0019*
			1993	0.0155	*−0.0058*	0.0187	**0.0284**
			1996	−0.0118	*−0.0229*	*−0.0487*	*−0.0544*
			1998	−0.0136	*−0.0227*	*−0.0353*	0.0032
			2001	−0.0138	*−0.0118*	*−0.0079*	*−0.2146*
New Zealand							
STOCKS	−0.0235	0.0000	1990	**0.0023**		−0.0376	
INTEREST	−0.0276	−0.0040	1993	**0.0065**	−0.0090	−0.0080	**0.0033**
RATES			1996	**0.0033**	**−0.0012**	**0.0001**	**−0.0032**

(*continued*)

Table 3.3. *(continued)*

	90% Confidence interval			Campaign period		Cabinet formation period	
Country	Lower	Upper	Year	Stocks	Bonds	Stocks	Bonds
			1999	*−0.0379*	*−0.0306*	**0.0210**	**0.0027**
			2002	**0.0603**	**0.0603**	*−0.0604*	**0.1157**
UK							
STOCKS	0.0029	0.0170	1974	0.0061		*−0.0114*	
INTEREST	−0.0217	−0.0069	1974	*−0.0025*		*−0.0179*	
			1979	0.0029		**0.0447**	
			1983	0.0054	−0.0085	*−0.0217*	−0.0214
			1987	0.0064	−0.0099	*−0.0250*	**0.0165**
			1992	*−0.0018*	−0.0071	0.0069	*−0.0659*
			1997	*0.0019*	**−0.0024**	*−0.0394*	−0.0106
			2001	*−0.0047*	**−0.0066**	**0.0552**	**−0.0055**

Entries marked in bold (italics) are greater (less) than the average median return at the 90 percent confidence level.

Returns in bond markets shift across the cabinet formation period in a manner similar to stock markets. The frequency of significantly lower returns decreases – only 23 cases (34 percent). In contrast, the proportion of significantly higher returns increases substantially, up to 27 cases (40 percent). Finally, during cabinet formation periods, the median abnormal returns for bonds are statistically indistinguishable from the empirical distribution in 18 cases (26 percent).

Overall, the results confirm that stock and bond returns during periods of potential political change regularly differ from the empirical distribution of abnormal returns. Lower abnormal returns occur relatively often during the campaign period. Once the election occurs, the frequency of lower abnormal returns decreases during the government formation period and the proportion of significantly higher abnormal returns increases. At the same time, many political events do not appear to affect market behavior. What explains this variation? We turn to this question in the next test. In particular, we evaluate whether political predictability affects market behavior during periods of potential political change by focusing on the coalition formation process in parliamentary democracies.

Average Abnormal Returns and Political Predictability

To examine how political information affects market returns, our second test uses an event study approach.[20] Event studies examine the effect of some event (or set of events) on the value of an asset (or set of assets) during a particular period of time. For example, event studies in finance examine whether the return on a particular stock differs after a stock split, an earnings announcement, a merger or takeover announcement, and/or a regulatory change. The idea is to compare the performance of an asset during a period of relative stability prior to the event (the estimation window) to a period after the event (the event window). If asset returns are different after the event – if the returns are higher or lower than expected based on the estimation window – then the event is said to have an effect on the asset in question.

We want to estimate whether campaigns, elections, and cabinet formation affect stock and bond market performance in a systematic fashion. Our first step is to identify the event window. For each election, we define the campaign period as the day when an election was called until the day prior to the election.[21] Once the election has occurred, parties that have won seats in parliament engage in a period of negotiation during which cabinet offices are distributed. This period provides market participants with information about which party – and politician – will control specific areas of the policymaking process. The formation period extends from the day after the election until the day the new cabinet is installed. These two periods combined – the campaign and election/negotiation period – are the event window: the period of time when we expect market behavior to be influenced by the (un)predictability of cabinet formation (Figure 3.5).

In order to demonstrate whether market performance is unusual due to political events, we next need to identify a baseline – a period when no political (or other unusual) event is taking place. For this baseline

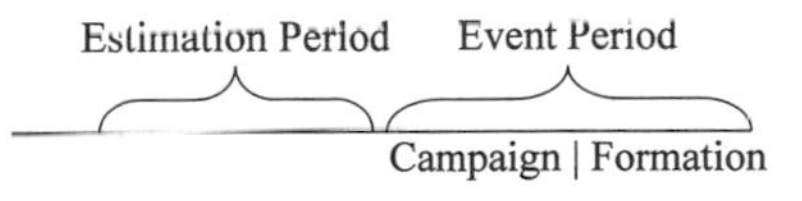

Figure 3.5. An event study model.

[20] Campbell, Lo, and MacKinlay (1997) contain a particularly lucid treatment of event studies.

[21] We relied on *Keesing's Contemporary Archive* for this information. In the rare cases when we could not find the date when an election was called we coded the election period as sixty days prior to the election date.

estimation window, we employ a sample of 150 trading days prior to the beginning of the campaign period.[22]

Having identified the event and estimation windows, the next task is to develop a statistical model that can be used to predict market returns during the event window. We again use the market model in Eq. (3.3) as our baseline for both stock and bond market returns. Equation (3.3) is estimated for the estimation window; the residuals ($\hat{\varepsilon}_t$), or abnormal returns, are then generated for the event window.

A standard event study would then calculate the cumulative abnormal returns (CAR) by summing the residuals during the event window and would test the null hypothesis that the CAR is no different from zero. Our approach differs slightly. Because we compare the behavior of abnormal returns across political periods where the event window is of differing lengths we calculate the average abnormal return (AAR) rather than the cumulative abnormal return.

Next we use ordinary least squares regression to test whether the predictability of cabinet formation influences the returns on stock and bond markets. As a proxy for the predictability of cabinet negotiations, we employ measures of the presence of a strong party. Since the existence of a strong party will generate clearer expectations about the identity of policymakers, we expect that average abnormal returns during the coalition formation period will be larger in the presence of a strong party than if a strong party does not exist.

We regress the average abnormal returns during the cabinet formation period on a dummy variable representing the presence of a strong party (or one of the other strong party measures). We also include a variable measuring the average abnormal returns during the campaign periods. Inclusion of this variable not only controls for possible unmeasured factors that influence a market during a period of potential political change, but also acts as an independent test of whether a structural break in returns between the campaign and negotiation periods exists. Because the data represent repeated observations within countries, we calculate robust standard errors with clustering across countries.

Finally, we present results from two samples. The first sample is limited to parliamentary systems with proportional representation electoral rules. In these systems, it is rare for one party to control a majority of legislative seats, so the formation of the cabinet is almost always subject to party bargaining. The presence of a strong party will shape the predictability

[22] The results do not change if we use 100 or 200 days for the estimation period.

of those negotiations. The second sample includes parliamentary systems with both proportional representation and majoritarian electoral rules. In this specification, we include a dummy variable for coalition formation periods where a strong party exists in the proportional representation electoral systems and a dummy variable for majoritarian systems. The omitted category is proportional representation systems with no strong party. In majoritarian systems, one party almost always controls a majority of legislative seats after an election and quickly forms a new government. (In a trivial sense, that party is a strong party.) There is rarely any doubt about which party will form the government in a majoritarian system. Therefore, if both the dummy variable for the presence of a strong party and the dummy variable for majoritarian systems have a similar parameter estimate, we can be confident that the strong party is a good measure of the reduction of political uncertainty.

Results

Column 1 of Table 3.4 reports the results from our regression on average abnormal returns in stock markets during the cabinet formation period for the sample of proportional representation democracies. The parameter estimate on the dummy variable representing the existence of a strong party is positive and statistically significant. Strong parties increase average abnormal returns. Note that the parameter estimate for strong party is opposite in sign and almost identical in magnitude to the intercept. That is, holding constant the AARs from the campaign period, the absence of a strong party leads to negative abnormal returns during coalition formation periods. Further, we cannot reject the null hypothesis that the combination of the intercept and slope coefficient on strong party are equal to zero. That is, when a strong party exists, abnormal returns are essentially zero. Strong parties negate the political risk surrounding periods of potential political change. Interestingly, the control for the campaign AAR is not statistically significant. Stock market behavior during the campaign period has no systematic influence on abnormal returns in the coalition formation period.

Column 2 of Table 3.4 reports the results of using a continuous measure of strong party status: the number of times that a strong party does not exist based on 1000 Monte Carlo experiments. The parameter estimate is negative and statistically significant, allowing us to reject the null hypothesis that political expectations have no influence on abnormal stock market returns. That is, as the number of times there is no strong party increases – i.e., as the uncertainty over cabinet negotiations increases – stock market returns fall.

Table 3.4. *Average abnormal returns: stock market*

Variable	Model specification I	II	III	IV
Campaign AAR	−0.090	−0.132	−0.067	−0.084
	(0.282)	(0.270)	(0.259)	(0.279)
Strong party	0.014**		0.014**	0.014**
	(0.006)		(0.006)	(0.006)
No strong party		−0.000**		
		(0.000)		
Majoritarian system			0.011**	0.014*
			(0.005)	(0.007)
Year				0.000
				(0.000)
Event duration				0.000
				(0.000)
Partisan change				0.003
				(0.005)
Clock/term				0.002
				(0.005)
Constant	−0.012**	−0.012**	−0.012**	−0.237
	(0.005)	(0.004)	(0.005)	(0.599)
Jarque−Bera (*p*-value)	0.3358	0.4541	0.7557	0.8099
N	73	73	110	108

Cell entries are OLS entries with Huber/White standard errors (adjusted for clustering across countries) in parentheses.
$^{*}p < 0.10$, $^{**}p < 0.05$.

Including the majoritarian cases in the sample does not alter the results on the strong party variable (column 3). Both the dummy for the presence of a strong party and the dummy for majoritarian systems are statistically significant and positive. Indeed, they are almost identical in magnitude and, as before, the opposite sign from the intercept. Holding constant the AARs from the campaign period, stock market returns during the cabinet formation period are unaffected in the presence of a strong party or in a majoritarian system. In proportional representation systems, however, the absence of a strong party contributes to depressed stock returns during the cabinet formation period.

We check the robustness of the results in several ways. First, we add a battery of control variables to the model from column three, including a time trend variable (*Year*), the duration of the cabinet formation period (*Event Duration*), the degree of change in the partisanship of the cabinet (*Partisan Change*),[23] when the event occurred in the electoral term (*Clock/Term*),[24] interest rates for 10 year government bonds, and a battery of country-specific dummy variables. None of these variables is statistically significant, whether we include all of them or add them to the model individually. The variables of interest remain statistically significant and in the predicted direction. Second, we employed stock indices from MSCI rather than Datastream. Results (not reported) were similar. Third, an examination of the residuals, via the Jarque–Bera test, revealed that we could not reject the null hypothesis that they are distributed conditionally normal. Finally, diagnostic tests reveal no significant outlying observations.

We perform a similar exercise using returns on government bonds as the dependent variable (Table 3.5). Diagnostic tests reveal that the residuals from models 3 and 4 depart from normality; these models are estimated using robust regression which does not assume conditional normality.[25] Regardless of the statistical method utilized, measures for the presence of a strong party never achieve statistical significance. Only the variable for abnormal returns during the campaign period attains significance in the first two models. This result is, however, not robust as the parameter estimate flips signs and becomes insignificant in the sample that includes majoritarian systems.

Overall, the results indicate that political predictability helps reduce negative abnormal returns in stock markets during periods of cabinet formation. In the absence of a strong party, stock returns are lower

[23] See Chapter 2 for details on the measurement of partisan change.

[24] The Clock/Term variable is formed by calculating the proportion of time left in the constitutionally-mandated term when the election was called. Chapter 5 discusses the measure in more detail. In systems with endogenous electoral timing, strategic governments will call for early elections only if they expect to benefit (Smith 2004). Hence, these electoral outcomes should often be fairly predictable. Elections called late in the term, on the other hand, may result in closer electoral outcomes.

[25] The robust regression algorithm we use proceeds as follows: (1) use OLS to obtain an initial set of regression parameters and an initial set of residuals; (2) use the residuals to form a set of case weights; (3) apply weighted least squares to obtain a new set of parameter estimates and residuals; (4) go back to step (2) and repeat the process until the difference in weights drops below 0.01.

Table 3.5. *Average abnormal returns: bond market*

	Model Specification			
Variable	I	II	III	IV
Campaign AAR	0.394**	0.422**	0.255**	0.230**
	(0.101)	(0.105)	(0.098)	(0.100)
Strong party	−0.001		−0.000	−0.000
	(0.001)		(0.001)	(0.001)
No strong party		0.000		
		(0.000)		
Majoritarian system			0.001	0.001
			(0.001)	(0.001)
Year				−0.000
				(0.000)
Event duration				0.000
				(0.000)
Partisan change				0.001
				(0.001)
Clock/Term				−0.001
				(0.002)
Constant	0.000	−0.001	−0.000	0.091
	(0.001)	(0.001)	(0.001)	(0.127)
Jarque–Bera Test (*p*-value)	0.6705	0.8267	0.0000	0.0000
N	47	47	66	65

Cell entries in columns I and II are OLS entries with Huber/White standard errors (adjusted for clustering across countries) in parentheses. Cell entries in columns III and IV are estimates from robust regression estimation.
* $p < 0.10$.
** $p < 0.05$.

during these periods than what would have been predicted. When a party enjoys a privileged position in the process of cabinet bargaining, asset owners have clearer expectations about the political outcome and, as a result, stock markets are unaffected. The predictability of cabinet formations, however, does not systematically affect bond markets. Could it be that economic actors are purchasing government bonds with the cash acquired from sales of equities during periods of potential political change?

While it is impossible to answer this question definitively without access to survey data on portfolio allocation decisions, we can test whether the

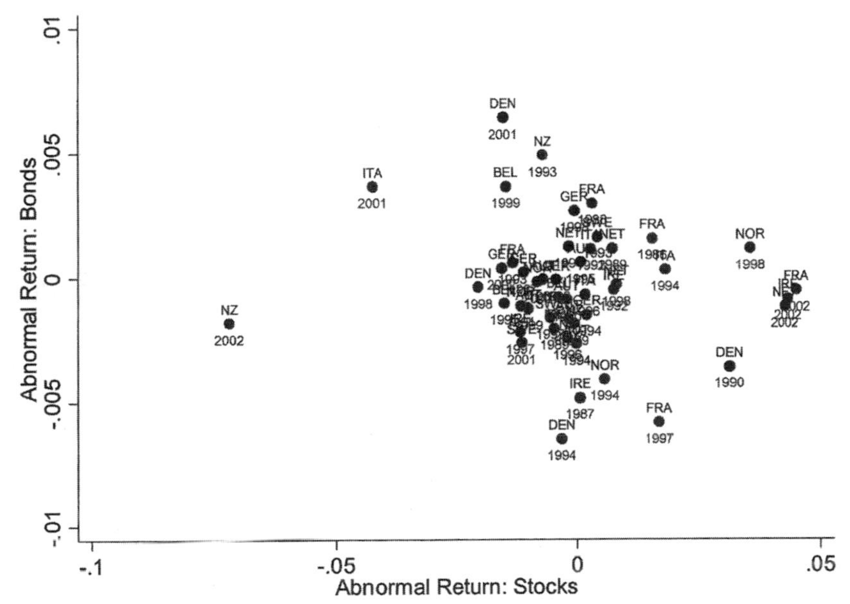

Figure 3.6. Abnormal returns in stock and bond markets during cabinet formation periods.

abnormal returns of stocks and bonds are correlated. Figure 3.6 plots the abnormal returns for both stock and bonds during cabinet formation periods in non-majoritarian countries. The correlation is low ($r = -0.14$) and not statistically significant ($p = 0.32$). Including majoritarian countries in the sample depresses the correlation ($r = -0.06$).

We next estimate the models of abnormal returns of stocks and bonds using Zellner's Seemingly Unrelated Regression (SURE). This procedure estimates two OLS models simultaneously and allows us to test explicitly whether the errors of the two models are correlated.[26] Two findings are noteworthy (Table 3.6). First, the correlation between the error terms of the two models is not statistically significant and does not allow us to reject the null hypothesis that the errors are independent. It follows that, second, the parameter estimates from the SURE model do not differ greatly from the OLS models estimated separately. Consequently, we cannot make a link between the stock and bond markets during periods of political uncertainty. Investors shift their portfolios out of stocks, but the destination of those funds is not clear.

[26] See Wooldridge (2002) for a useful exposition.

Table 3.6. *Seemingly unrelated regression of abnormal stock and bond returns*

	Model Specification	
	I	II
Abnormal return: stocks	All Cases	Only PR
Campaign AAR	0.051	0.000
	(0.173)	(0.168)
Strong party	0.013**	0.013**
	(0.007)	(0.006)
Majoritarian system	0.008	
	0.008	
Year	−0.000	−0.000
	(0.001)	(0.001)
Event duration	−0.000	0.000
	(0.000)	(0.000)
Partisan change	0.001	0.000
	(0.005)	(0.006)
Clock/Term	0.015	0.005
	(0.017)	(0.016)
Constant	−0.005	0.179
	(1.130)	(1.241)
Abnormal return: bonds		
Campaign AAR	−0.105	0.348**
	(0.325)	(0.118)
Strong party (2)	−0.001	−0.001
	(0.002)	(0.001)
Majoritarian system	−0.001	
	(0.003)	
Year	0.000	0.000
	(0.000)	(0.000)
Event duration	0.000	0.000
	(0.000)	(0.000)
Partisan change	0.003	0.001*
	(0.002)	(0.001)
Clock/Term	0.003	−0.000
	(0.006)	(0.002)

	Model Specification	
	I	II
Constant	−0.399	−0.071
	(0.413)	(0.136)
Correlation between errors (*p*-value)	−0.0667	−0.1241
	(0.5906)	(0.4001)
N	65	46

Cell entries are seemingly unrelated regression estimates with standard errors in parentheses.
* $p < 0.10$.
** $p < 0.05$.

Stock and Bond Returns During Cabinet Formation

The results from the two previous tests indicate that returns during periods of potential political change differ from those during periods when the government's position in office is secure. In particular, when the outcomes of democratic political processes are unclear, stock returns tend to be lower than when outcomes are predictable. In this section, we take an alternative and more direct approach to estimating the impact of political events on market returns. Specifically, we estimate a panel regression for the full sample of countries with daily stock and bond returns as the dependent variables. We modify Eq. (3.3) to include dummy variables for the campaign period (*Campaign*), the cabinet formation period (*Negotiation*), whether a strong party exists during the formation period (*Strong Party**Negotiation*), and whether the country has a majoritarian electoral system during the political periods (*Majoritarian**Campaign, Majoritarian**Negotiation*). Again, we are interested in determining how political predictability affects returns during the cabinet formation process. The use of a full daily time series – from January 1, 1980 through December 31, 2002 – also provides a framework that is biased against a finding that political periods influence asset market returns. Given that the panel has over 85,000 observations and periods of cabinet negotiation comprise approximately two percent of the total number of observations (1757 observations) it is unlikely that significant results for the negotiation periods would occur by chance.

We also include a number of additional variables to capture domestic political events as well as global economic shocks, including dummy variables for: the U.S. stock market crash in 1987 (October 14–19), the crisis in the European Monetary System in September of 1992 (Sept 12–30) and the week when the U.S. stock market was closed following the terror attacks in September of 2002 (Sept 11–20). The model is estimated with a full battery of nation dummy variables.

The models for both stock and bond returns are estimated via ordinary least squares. We account for the possibility of unequal variance across countries by reporting Huber/White robust standard errors; country specific intercepts are also included (though not reported) as additional controls for cross-country heterogeneity. The residuals are serially uncorrelated – both single country and panel tests for serial correlation did not lead to a rejection of the null at the 0.05 level.

Using such a long time series to investigate the impact of political events means that we are likely to miss global economic cycles that are not captured by sectoral and economic variables. A very conservative approach to dealing with this potential problem is to measure asset returns as the net (or loss) over a "risk-free" rate. This is standard practice in the equity premia literature (Mehra and Prescott 1985, 2003; Canova and de Nicolo 2003) and we follow it here by measuring the dependent variable as the difference between the local return and the return in the United States. When we examine stock market returns, then, the dependent variable is the difference between the return in country *i* and the United States both at time *t*. This does not change the substance of the results but does substantially decrease the average variance of the residuals.

Results

Column 1 of Table 3.7 contains the results for stock market returns. The parameter estimates for the campaign period and for the majoritarian*campaign period interaction are not significant. Stock returns do not systematically differ during campaign periods. While these results may seem surprising, they should not be. The previous tests indicate that stock returns are, in many cases, lower than returns during non-political periods. We would hypothesize that returns will be lower when the electoral results are in doubt. But we do not have any measure of those campaign expectations that covers the full sample of countries over such a long period of time. As a result, the simple period variables, which aggregate both predictable and unpredictable campaigns, fail to attain significance.

Table 3.7. *Panel data model*

Variable	Stock Returns	Bond Returns
Formation period	−0.057*	0.004
	(0.027)	(0.040)
Strong Party * Formation period	0.114*	−0.002
	(0.043)	(0.054)
Majoritarian * Formation period	0.039	−0.065
	(0.089)	(0.095)
Political campaign	−0.024	−0.003
	(0.028)	(0.034)
Political campaign * Majoritarian	0.037	0.003
	(0.039)	(0.004)
Cabinet dissolution	0.102	0.041
	(0.078)	(0.040)
Δ Gold price	0.038*	−0.016*
	(0.003)	(0.002)
Δ Brent crude price	0.046*	−0.085*
	(0.017)	(0.007)
Δ Sectoral index	0.056*	−0.003
	(0.008)	(0.007)
U.S. Stock Market Crash − 1987	5.21*	0.456*
	(0.306)	(0.241)
EMS Crisis − 1992	−0.001	−0.012
	(0.082)	(0.082)
September 11, 2001	0.164	−0.001
	(0.113)	(0.001)
Constant	−0.010*	−0.016*
	(0.002)	(0.003)
N	80575	62271

Dependent variable is the local rate (stock or bond) minus the comparable rate in the U.S. Both models are estimated with a set of 14 country specific dummy variables. Standard errors are calculated using the Huber/White robust covariance matrix.

The coefficients on the cabinet formation variables square with expectations. During coalition formation periods when a strong party is not present, stock market returns are 0.05 percent lower than during non-political periods. When a strong party does exist during the cabinet formation process, stock market returns are higher; the overall return, however, is not statistically different from zero. This is consistent with earlier results: unpredictable cabinet negotiations decrease returns. The presence of a strong party mitigates this impact. Somewhat surprisingly, the parameter estimate for the majoritarian*cabinet formation period interaction is not significant. This probably reflects the fact that there are so few observations during these periods – only 0.25 percent of the total observations.

There is no evidence that either the EMS crisis or the events associated with September 11th had a statistically significant effect on stock market returns. This is likely due to the fact that the influence of these events is captured by the economic indicators in our factor model. The U.S. stock market crash of 1987, however, was a period when the U.S. stock market performed far differently from markets in other industrial democracies. The statistically significant and positive coefficient shows that local stock markets experienced returns far greater than those in the United States.

Column two reports the same specification for returns on 10-year government bonds. As before, none of the political variables attain statistical significance. Re-estimating the stock and bond equations using robust regression or linking the two models via a SURE model does not change the results. Political events affect returns in equity markets but not in markets for government bonds.

CONCLUSION

Asset owners allocate their portfolios based on information from both economic and political sources. Since political events like elections and cabinet formations affect future policy choices that, in turn, condition the investment environment, investors will want to forecast those outcomes. They employ the information available to them from news sources. They also rely on their own understandings of the political process to arrive at a forecast. That prediction shapes their investment behavior. Where asset owners have a clear sense of the political outcome, they will behave one way. Where they are unsure about what will happen politically, they will shift their assets in other ways.

That the predictability of the outcome shapes the market response to an event is not a new argument. What is new, however, is the measurement of political predictability to test the argument. We argue that political science models can provide information about the ability of investors to forecast political events. These models provide logical analyses of political processes. Further, these models rely on the same information that is available to investors at the beginning of a political event – opinion polls, the distribution of legislative seats, the policy positions of the players, etc. – to make predictions. These models, therefore, represent more systematic, rigorous assessments of the informal intuitions of political observers, including investors. As a result, we contend that the predictions of these models can serve as a proxy for the beliefs of market actors about political outcomes.

In this chapter, we employed a model of coalition government to evaluate how investors respond to the process of cabinet formation after an election. The predictions of the political science models provided a measure of the ability of investors to predict cabinet outcomes. And, indeed, the presence of a strong party in the coalition negotiations did correlate with the behavior of stock markets during the formation process: political predictability affects how asset owners make their decisions. Cabinet negotiations, however, are only a part of the political process. We expect that political science models of other processes will provide useful insight into the ability of market actors to forecast other outcomes as well. Using these models, therefore, should provide further understanding of how markets process political information.

4

The Cross-National Financial Consequences of Political Predictability

With capital accounts more open and technological innovations changing the pace of transactions, financial markets are increasingly integrated. Trading occurs twenty-four hours a day throughout the globe. Fluctuations in one market can affect the behavior of markets across borders. A glance at the worldwide financial news media illustrates this phenomenon: Trading on the New York Stock exchange conditions trading in Tokyo, which, in turn, influences market activity in London, which then affects New York. More spectacularly (and more destructively), the Asian crisis of 1997–98 quickly spread to markets in other developing countries, a process of contagion that has been widely studied in the finance and economic literatures.[1]

As the previous chapter demonstrated, political events do, under certain conditions, affect market performance in domestic equities and bond markets. In a world of integrated financial markets, those political events may touch off reactions in markets in other countries. We investigate this possibility in this chapter. We contend that the configuration of political and economic institutions at both the domestic and international levels can mitigate the effect of cross-border political shocks. To evaluate the argument, we adopt a two-stage research design.[2] Drawing on arbitrage pricing theory, we first measure the size of foreign political shocks. In the second stage, we test alternative explanations for the variation in the size of those shocks. Consistent with the findings in Chapter 3, the results indicate

[1] See Brooks and Del Negro (2002), King and Wadhwani (1994), Cheung and Lai (1998), Braker, Docking, and Koch (1999), Ammer and Mei (1996), Boyer, Gibson, and Loretan (1997), Longin and Solnik (2001), Forbes and Rigobon (2002), and Corsetti, Pericoli, and Sbracia (2002).

[2] As discussed in detail below, our approach emerges from research in the finance literature (Fama and McBeth 1973; Forbes and Chinn 2004).

that political events with a predictable outcome have less impact on markets (both foreign and domestic) than unpredictable events. Further, we find evidence that exchange rate arrangements influence the size of cross-border political shocks.

CROSS-BORDER POLITICAL SHOCKS

With increased levels of financial integration, financial economists are interested in how asset owners take advantage of the opportunities to diversify portfolios across political borders. Do market actors shift their portfolios from country to country? Is there a "home country bias" to the decision to allocate capital? Since individual-level data on portfolio allocation decisions are generally unavailable, however, financial economists must evaluate the behavior of national markets to infer the cross-border allocation decisions of investors, focusing on the transmission of financial shocks across borders, the role of contagion, and so on.

Much of this research examines the comovement of different national markets over time. The comovement of asset returns affects the diversification decisions of investors. Consider the correlation between the returns on assets in two national markets.[3] The correlation coefficient can range between −1 and +1, where −1 means that the two assets move in exactly opposite directions and +1 means that the two assets move perfectly in unison. If the returns are perfectly positively correlated ($r = 1.0$), then investors have no opportunities to reduce risk through diversification. Nothing is gained by investing in both assets. If returns are perfectly negatively correlated (−1), then the risk on the portfolio as a whole decreases – an increase in risk by one asset is offset by a decrease in risk by the other asset. But the expected return of the portfolio is not affected since an increase in the return of one asset is offset by a decrease in the return of the other. If the correlation between the return of two assets is zero, then the portfolio has "minimum risk" since there is no systematic relationship between either the riskiness or the return of the assets.

The comovement literature focuses on how markets move together, rather than how specific political development affects markets. In contrast, we are interested in how political events in one country affect asset returns in another. In our tests, therefore, we control for the comovement between markets, but it is not our main focus. Instead, we want to evaluate what determines the size of specific cross-border political shocks.

[3] See Chapter 5 of Elton et al. (2003) for a detailed discussion of these issues.

How might political events in a foreign country influence asset market behavior in the home country? We identify three possible market reactions to a foreign political event. First, a political event in country *j* may potentially increase returns on domestic assets in country *i*. If market actors respond to the event in *j* by shifting assets out of *j* and putting them into *i*, returns will increase there. That is, asset owners may view markets in country *i* as a safe haven during periods of potential political change in country *j*.

Second, a political event in country *j* may decrease market returns in country *i*. Here, asset owners in country *i* shift out of assets during the political event in country *j*. An uncertain political outcome in country *j* may raise questions about future economic performance and the business environment there. If the economies are integrated, those uncertainties may spill over into concerns about country *i*'s economy and those firms in *i* that do business in country *j*. Asset owners in *i*, therefore, will behave in a way similar to asset owners in *j*, shifting portfolios away from assets that are vulnerable to political shocks.

Third, a political event in country *j* may have no direct effect on an asset market in country *i*. It is possible that investors simply do not take into account information about foreign political events in making their decisions. Alternatively, as we argue, the lack of a direct effect could reflect the configuration of political and economic institutions in the two countries. For instance, a political event in *j* may have a predictable outcome and not cause any major asset reallocation either domestically or internationally. A second possibility is that country *i* or county *j* has adopted financial and monetary institutions that help insulate domestic markets from specific foreign shocks.

What then explains the size and direction of these cross-border political shocks? We contend that the impact of periods of potential political change on asset markets across countries reflects the degree of policy stability in both countries. If political institutions and economic commitments allow asset owners to anticipate and forecast government policy, then periods of potential change in the partisan identity of the government will have less impact on market returns across borders. Where policy is less stable, however, asset owners will be less able to predict future policies. In these systems, periods of potential political change are likely to be associated with the cross-border political shocks to markets.

The Predictability of the Political Event

As demonstrated in Chapter 3, political events with predictable outcomes allow market actors to adjust to a changed policy environment. A lack of political predictability can depress returns as market actors shift out of assets that are vulnerable to different political outcomes. A similar logic applies to cross-border political shocks. If the political event in country *j* is predictable, then we expect no evidence of a cross-border shock due to the event.

We again employ the literature on cabinet government in parliamentary systems to provide our measure of political predictability. We include the *Strong Party* dummy variable for each event in country *j* (see Chapter 3 for a full discussion). We expect this variable to have a positive impact on stock returns and a negative impact on bond returns.

A Change in Partisanship

A change in the partisanship of the government in country *j* may affect the investment decisions of asset owners. The globalization literature implies that a leftward change in government in country *j* might increase returns in country *i*. If left parties provide a less hospitable environment for investment, asset owners might relocate their holdings to a different country. A rightward shift might attract capital to country *j*, depressing returns in country *i*.

We include a variable, *Change in Partisanship*, that measures the shift in the partisan identity of the government in country *j*. To calculate the measure, we multiply the percentage of cabinet seats held by left parties by the percentage of a legislative majority held by left parties (Cameron 1984). We then subtract the value for the outgoing government from the incoming government. Positive values indicate a shift to the left; negative values a shift to the right. If the globalization arguments are correct, the parameter estimate for this variable should be positive for stocks and negative for bonds.

Central Bank Independence

An independent central bank enhances monetary policy stability, insulating policy from short-term political pressures. With a dependent central bank, government ministers have more influence over interest rates. A shift in the partisan identity of the government, therefore, may alter monetary policy. Consequently, in countries with a dependent central bank, asset owners may be less able to predict economic policy during a period of potential partisan change in the government.

We include a measure of *central bank independence* for both country *i* and country *j* from Cukierman, Webb, and Neyapti (1992). We update this measure to reflect central bank reform in Belgium, France, Italy, and New Zealand during the sample period.[4] If central bank independence shields markets from periods of potential political change, the variables should have a positive estimate for stock returns and a negative effect for bond returns.

Exchange Rate Commitments

An exchange rate commitment can also help insulate monetary policy from the potential effects of a change in the partisan identity of the government. With a floating exchange rate, governments have the autonomy to pursue domestically-oriented objectives – objectives that can change easily with the arrival of a new government. Consequently, an exchange rate commitment by country *j* may help reduce the reallocation of portfolios due to a political event in the country. An exchange rate commitment by country *i* will also enhance the predictability of the external policy environment, reducing the need for asset owners to shift their portfolios in response to foreign events. Multilateral commitments will reinforce these incentives.

We include six variables to account for exchange rate commitments. The first dummy variable, *Fixed Exchange Rate*, is coded one when a country had a pegged exchange rate outside the European Monetary System. The second dummy variable, *European Monetary System*, is coded one when country *i* participated in the EMS between 1985 and 1999.[5] The third dummy variable, *Euro*, is coded one when country *i* participated in the single currency after 1999. We include three other variables to capture the exchange rate arrangements in each country pair: *Both Fix, Both EMS, Both Euro.*

Data are from Cobham (1994), Gros and Thygesen (1998), and the IMF's "Exchange Arrangements and Exchange Restrictions Annual Report"

[4] The rankings of central bank independence for reformed central banks are based on Tavelli, Tullio, and Spinelli (1998), who used the Grilli, Masciandaro, and Tabellini (1991) criteria. We used the same criteria to compute the value for the reformed New Zealand central bank. We then used these updated rankings to impute the new values in the Cukierman, Webb, and Neyapti (1992) index.

[5] This includes Denmark and, after 1995, Sweden – countries that participated in the EMS until 1999, but then opted out of the single currency. For Austria and Sweden, countries that joined the EU in 1995–96, we code them as participating in the EMS beginning in 1996.

(various years). We expect all three variables to have a negative parameter estimate.

Capital Controls

The impact of capital controls on how markets respond to periods of potential political change is less clear. Without capital controls, asset owners can easily shift their assets out of the country, potentially contributing to market shifts across countries during these periods. If controls are in place, however, asset owners have fewer exit options in the face of a political event, preventing them from moving assets across borders.

On the other hand, capital mobility may act as a disciplining device on economic policy. With controls, governments have more domestic policy autonomy – autonomy they could use to pursue alternative partisan objectives.

We include a variable, *Capital Account Openness*, from Quinn (1997) for country *i*. Low values indicate more restrictions on the capital account. We expect the presence of capital controls to limit the size of the cross-border shock.

Control Variables

The literature identifies a variety of factors that may condition the effect of events in country *j* on markets in country *i* (e.g., Forbes and Chinn 2004). For each country pair, we included variables for distance between the two capitals, common language, trade competition, total GDP, and the difference in GDP between the two countries. In no specification were any of these variables statistically significant.

RESEARCH DESIGN AND METHODOLOGY

Following Fama and MacBeth (1973), we adopt a two-stage estimation strategy to evaluate our argument about the impact of foreign political events on the behavior of stock and bond markets in a domestic economy. In the first stage, we draw on the Arbitrage Pricing Theory (APT) framework to measure the impact of foreign political events on domestic asset markets. In the second stage we use the estimated foreign political shocks from stage one as the dependent variable to test whether the configuration of political and economic institutions influences the size of these shocks.

THE FIRST STAGE: ESTIMATING THE IMPACT OF FOREIGN POLITICAL EVENTS ON DOMESTIC MARKETS

As in Chapter 3, we employ Arbitrage Pricing Theory (APT) to provide a framework for the analysis. Recall that APT models explain a country's stock and bond market performance with reference to a host of risk factors. The basic APT model is:

$$R_t = \alpha + \beta X_t + \varepsilon_t \tag{4.1}$$

where R_t is the return on an asset (stock or bond); X_t is a set of "risk" factors (domestic, sectoral and/or global factors hypothesized to have an impact on the return R_t); and the error term, ε_t, represents asset specific returns (the returns that are not accounted for by the domestic, sectoral or global factors included in X_t). The parameter β on the X_t's represents the factor or "risk" sensitivities of R_t to the X_t in question. That is, the β measures how much the return, R_t, responds to a change in one of the factors.

We want to determine how an asset in country *i* is affected by a political event in country *j*. We, therefore, include a political event in country *j* as a factor, one of the "X's," in a model of asset returns for country *i*. More specifically, denote the local country with the subscript *i* and the foreign country with the subscript *j*. For each country *i*, we estimate the following model for both stock and bond returns:

$$R_{it} = \alpha + X_t\beta + \lambda R_{jt-1} + \theta \sum_{i=1}^{I} P_i + \phi \sum_{j=1}^{J} P_j + \varepsilon_t. \tag{4.2}$$

In this specification, the return on an asset in country at time t is a function of four sets of factors: (1) global and sectoral factors, X_t, that are constant across countries but vary over time; (2) market (stock or bond) returns, R_{jt-1}, in the other countries in the sample at time $t-1$;[6] (3) political events in country i, P_i, measured by dummy variables corresponding to individual political campaign and election periods; and (4) individual political events in the other countries in the sample, P_j. The parameter β represents the risk sensitivity of returns in the local market to global factors; λ captures the co-movement between assets in country i and country j; θ captures the impact of local political events; and

[6] We lag the return in country *j* to avoid problems of simultaneity.

ϕ measures the impact of political events in country j on returns in country i.

Data, Sample, and Methodology

We use the change in daily stock market indices and the change in annualized daily returns on ten-year government bonds as the dependent variables. The data are from Datastream.

Global factors include changes in gold prices, oil prices, and a global market index. We include a summary indicator of sectoral performance generated by performing a factor analysis of 36 MSCI sectoral indices. We also include the behavior of U.S. asset returns (stocks or bonds) as an additional global factor.

We identify two political periods: the campaign period and the cabinet formation period. The campaign period extends from the day that the election was called through the election day (see Chapter 2). The cabinet formation period begins the day after the election and lasts until the day a new cabinet is installed.

We estimate Eq. (4.2) for eleven parliamentary systems: Austria, Belgium, Denmark, France, Germany, Ireland, Italy, the Netherlands, New Zealand, Norway, and Sweden. This gives us a set of 55 country pairs. The sample period extends from January 1, 1985 to December 31, 2001.

We pool the daily observations for each country. The use of such a long panel leads us to employ Prais–Winsten regression and adjust the residual for first-order serial correlation. We also estimate panel corrected standard errors to account for unequal error variances across countries. This approach produces unbiased parameter estimates and efficient standard errors even if the error terms deviate from traditional assumptions.

Table 4.1 includes descriptive statistics.

Results

Since each equation includes dummy variables for political events in ten other countries over the sixteen year time period, each model contains over forty parameters. Hence, reporting the full results is not feasible. Our interest in estimating Eq. (4.2) is to measure the extent to which a political event in country j affects the stock (bond) market in country i. The parameter estimates, $\hat{\phi}_{ijt}$, capture the independent effect – or shock – of a political event in country j at time t on asset markets in country i.

Table 4.1. *Descriptive Statistics*

Variable	Mean	Std. Dev.	Minimum	Maximum
Equity Models				
$\hat{\phi}_{ijt}$	−0.369	11.617	−65.335	67.362
Strong party$_j$	0.82	0.384	0	1
Capital openness$_i$	89.376	11.607	62.5	100
Change partisanship$_j$	0.0006	0.004	0	0.029
EMS$_i$	0.51	0.500	0	1
Euro$_i$	0.13	0.337	0	1
Fix$_i$	0.164	0.371	0	1
Both EMS	0.294	0.456	0	1
Both euro	0.06	0.238	0	1
Both fix	0.028	0.165	0	1
Central bank independence$_i$	0.415	0.164	0.17	0.69
Central bank independence$_j$	0.403	0.165	0.17	0.69
N = 500				
Bond Models				
$\hat{\phi}_{ijt}$	−0.002	0.045	−0.327	0.239
Strong party$_j$	0.794	0.405	0	1
Capital openness$_i$	91.641	10.304	62.5	100
Change partisanship$_j$	0.0003	0.003	0	0.029
EMS$_i$	0.504	0.501	0	1
Euro$_i$	0.159	0.367	0	1
Fix$_i$	0.120	0.326	0	1
Both EMS	0.275	0.447	0	1
Both euro	0.074	0.262	0	1
Both fix	0.017	0.130	0	1
Central bank independence$_i$	0.449	0.157	0.17	0.69
Central bank independence$_j$	0.408	0.163	0.17	0.69
N=348				

To get a sense of the relationship between political periods in country *j* on asset markets in country *i*, we use Germany as an example. In Fig. 4.1 we graph the impact of German political events on the other countries in the sample. German elections occurred in 1987, 1990, 1994, and 1998.

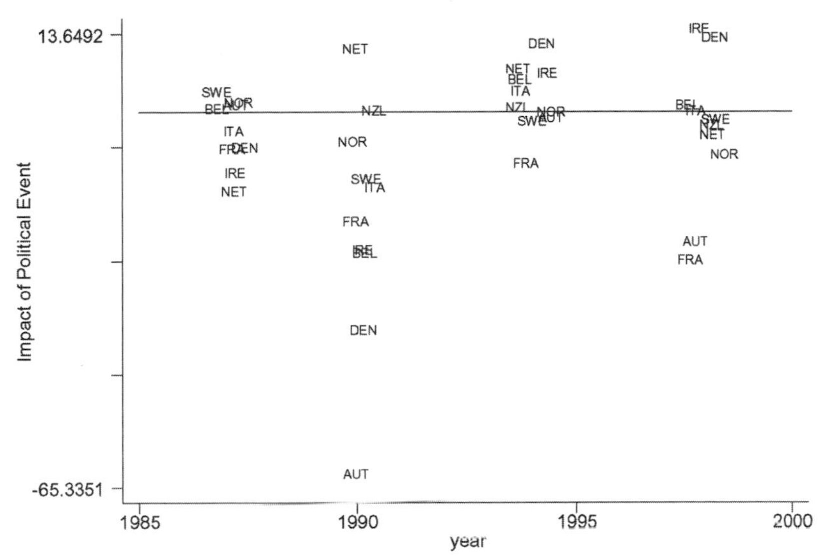

Figure 4.1. Impact of German political events on foreign markets.

For each of these elections, Fig. 4.1 shows the impact of the German political periods, $\hat{\phi}_{ijt}$, on stock market returns for the other ten countries in the sample. Consider the impact of the 1990 German election – the first after reunification – on the Austrian stock market. Holding constant the co-movement between German and Austrian stock markets, this election is associated with a decline in the Austrian market of 65 points. Market actors who may ordinarily invest in Austrian equities may have viewed this election as an opportunity to shift their assets out of Austria. On the other hand, the 1990 election is also associated with increased equity returns in the Netherlands, New Zealand, and Norway, suggesting that asset owners may have shifted portfolios out of German equities toward these markets.

Figure 4.2 graphs the impact of political events in all countries j on German (country i) stock market returns. In most situations, German equities are relatively unaffected by political events in other countries (holding constant the co-movement between markets). But Germany is attractive investment option during periods of potential political change in other countries. Again Austria presents an excellent example. The Austrian election of 1999 had favorable consequences for German equities as they rose by 37 points.

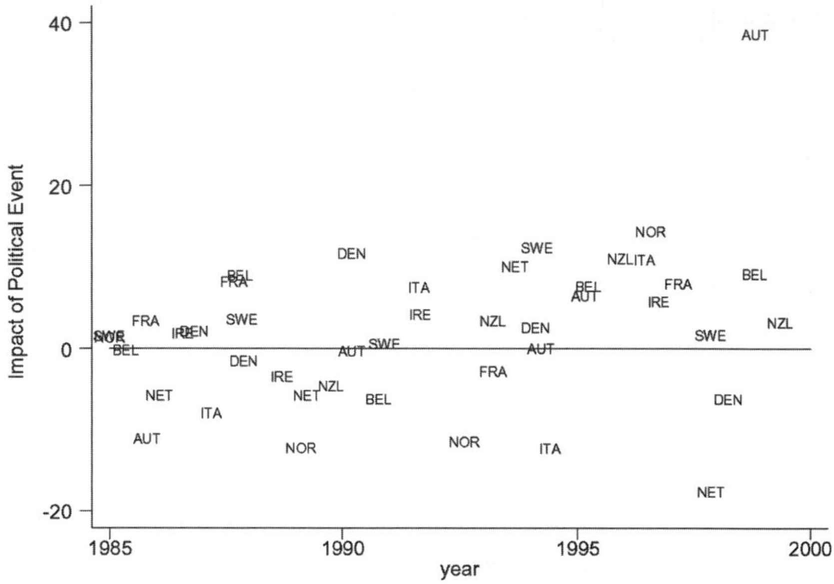

Figure 4.2. Impact of foreign political events on German markets.

THE SECOND STAGE: EXPLAINING THE IMPACT OF FOREIGN POLITICAL EVENTS ON DOMESTIC MARKETS

The parameter estimates, $\hat{\phi}_{ijt}$, can be interpreted as the degree to which political events in country *j* affect market returns in country *i*. We want to explain the variation in $\hat{\phi}_{ijt}$ across political events. Why is it large for some events and small for others? Why is it positive or negative? What determines how a foreign political event will affect the domestic market?

We hypothesize that the estimated impact of a foreign political event, $\hat{\phi}_{ijt}$, is a function of the configuration of political and economic institutions. One way to test these hypotheses directly would be to create a set of interactions between political events in country *j* and the conditioning variables. While this approach would not be problematic statistically, it would require a model with over seven hundred additional parameters.[7] Interpretation and presentation of the results for such a model would be cumbersome.

Fama and MacBeth (1973) propose a strategy to deal with the proliferation of parameters inherent in estimating CAPM models for large numbers of securities.[8] Their methodology proceeds in two stages.

[7] The models include over seventy political periods and eleven conditioning variables.

In stage one, Eq. (4.1) is estimated for each security and the betas are collected. Fama and MacBeth interpret the estimated betas as a shock to the return on security i. The second stage treats the estimated betas as the dependent variable to be explained by exogenous variables.

Our approach follows this two-stage method. After estimating Eq. (4.2) for each country i, we collect the parameter estimate, $\hat{\phi}$, and the standard error, $SE_{\hat{\phi}}$, for each political event in country j at time t. We denote the political shock caused by a political event in country i on an asset in country j at time t by $\hat{\phi}_{ijt}$. We then stack the $\hat{\phi}_{ijt}$s to create a panel dataset ordered by country i, country j, and time t.

We then estimate

$$\begin{aligned}\hat{\phi}_{ijt} = {} & \delta_0 + \delta_1 * Strong\ Party_j + \delta_2 * Capital\ Openness_i \\ & + \delta_3 * \Delta Government\ Partisanship_j + \delta_4 * Euro_i + \delta_5 * EMS_i \\ & + \delta_6\ Fix_i + \delta_7 * Both\ Euro + \delta_8 * Both\ EMS + \delta_9\ Both\ Fix \\ & + \delta_{10} * \mathrm{CBI}_i + \delta_{11}\mathrm{CBI}_j + \nu_{it}.\end{aligned} \tag{4.3}$$

Methodology

Estimating Eq. (4.3) via OLS with adjustments appropriate to panel data is an obvious place to start. For instance, to control for potential heterogeneity over time, we include a time trend variable. (The parameter estimate and standard error are not reported to conserve space.) In initial specifications, we also included a set of dummy variables corresponding to country pairs *ij*, individual countries i, and individuals countries j. *F*-tests for the joint significance of these dummy variables failed to reject the null hypothesis of no effect. Due to the uneven spacing of political events in country j, we also failed to find statistically significant serial correlation in the residuals using any estimation methods.

Nevertheless, the nature of the dependent variable complicates the estimation strategy. The dependent variable, $\hat{\phi}_{ijt}$, is measured with error: it is an estimated regression coefficient and has an associated standard error.

[8] Elton et al. (2003) contains a lucid exposition of the Fama–MacBeth (1973) methodology. We are grateful to Campbell Harvey for helpful discussions regarding this approach.

The use of a generated variable on the left hand side of a regression leads to residuals that are not homoscedastic (Hanushek 1974). In the situation of measurement error in the dependent variable, therefore, the estimated δs and their variances remain unbiased; the variances, however, are inefficient (they are larger) when compared to a model where the dependent variable has no measurement error.[9] If left unchecked this would result in more conservative standard errors; standard errors that would lead us to fail to reject the null when the null was not true.

We deal with the problem of measurement error in the dependent variable in two ways. First, efficient second stage estimates of parameters and standard errors can be obtained by weighting each observation by the inverse of the standard error of $\hat{\phi}_{ijt}$ (Hanushek 1974). The second strategy is to employ non-parametric regression techniques that do not assume that the residuals (v_{it}) are normally distributed. We estimate the model using both robust regression and quartile regression. Robust regression produces estimates of parameters and standard errors that are not unduly influenced by outlying or aberrant observations.[10] Quartile regression estimates the conditional median rather than the conditional mean of the dependent variable. The median regression estimator also uses bootstrap resampling techniques to estimate the variance-covariance matrix of the regressors; standard errors are thus based on simulation and not on reference to an asymptotic distribution.

Results

Table 4.2 reports the results for estimating Eq. (4.3). Columns one through three contain the results for stock market returns while columns four through six are for bond market returns.

Column one reports the weighted least squares estimates with robust standard errors (adjusted for unequal variances across country-pairs) in parentheses. (Each observation is weighted by the inverse of the standard error of $\hat{\phi}_{ijt}$.) The negative parameter estimate on the constant indicates

[9] Gujarati (2003) provides a simple proof of this conclusion.

[10] The procedure we employ does an initial screening of residuals from an OLS model and excludes observations that have values of Cook's Distance (a standard measure of statistical influence) greater than one. In our stock and bond samples no observation satisfied this condition. The robust procedure then proceeds to use residuals from the OLS regression as case weights and applies weighted least squares to the weighted sample. This procedure – estimating a WLS model, obtaining residuals, re-estimating a WLS model based on new weights – continues until the maximum difference in weights drops below 0.01. See Berk (1990) for a discussion of robust regression in both theory and practice.

Table 4.2. *Second stage regression*

	Stocks			Bonds		
	WLS	R. Reg.	Q. Reg.	WLS	R. Reg.	Q. Reg.
Strong party$_j$	5.117**	2.306**	0.943	−0.020**	−0.019**	−0.019**
	(1.754)	(1.030)	(0.843)	(0.006)	(0.005)	(0.007)
Capital openness$_i$	0.019	0.004	0.036	−0.013	−0.011	−0.014
	(0.062)	(0.039)	(0.051)	(0.018)	(0.014)	(0.014)
Change partisanship$_j$	232.068	160.462*	174.032**	0.069**	0.066**	0.077**
	(161.922)	(91.132)	(47.824)	(0.017)	(0.013)	(0.022)
EMS$_i$	1.074	−2.286*	0.079	−0.000	−0.000	−0.001**
	(2.665)	(1.262)	(1.426)	(0.000)	(0.000)	(0.000)
Euro$_i$	−1.824	−4.040**	−0.774	−0.185	−0.054	0.141
	(3.302)	(1.780)	(3.784)	(0.838)	(0.610)	(0.442)
Fixed exchange rate$_i$	−3.032	−1.753	−1.070	0.002	0.001	0.002
	(3.103)	(1.433)	(0.993)	(0.008)	(0.006)	(0.008)
Both EMS	−3.836**	−0.663	−3.184**	−0.001	−0.004	−0.001
	(1.608)	(1.061)	(1.370)	(0.010)	(0.008)	(0.010)
Both euro	5.826*	5.013**	2.327	0.013	−0.001	−0.003
	(3.365)	(2.126)	(5.120)	(0.010)	(0.008)	(0.009)
Both fix	5.201	1.802	1.886	0.005	0.005	0.005
	(5.227)	(2.429)	(2.670)	(0.008)	(0.006)	(0.007)
Central bank independence$_i$	4.315	5.082**	3.097	0.022*	0.024**	0.024**
	(4.951)	(2.569)	(2.485)	(0.012)	(0.009)	(0.012)
Central bank independence$_j$	−6.708	0.312	−0.708	0.022	0.035	0.033**
	(4.144)	(2.445)	(2.540)	(0.031)	(0.025)	(0.013)
Intercept	−17.454**	−7.505**	−6.195	−0.002	−0.001	−0.002
	(6.317)	(3.744)	(4.295)	(0.002)	(0.001)	(0.002)
N	500	500	500	348	348	348

* $p < 0.10$.
** $p < 0.05$.
WLS = weighted least squares (observations weighted by inverse of the standard error from stage one regression).
R. Reg. = robust regression.
Q. Reg. = median regression.

that, with all independent variables held at zero, periods of potential political change in country *j* are associated with lower stock market returns in country *i*. That is, in countries with a floating exchange rate, low levels of central bank independence, and unpredictable political outcomes in the foreign country (i.e., no strong party), a political event in the foreign country will depress stock returns in the home country. An unpredictable political environment in the foreign country will cause domestic asset owners to shift out of stocks. This result is consistent with findings in Chapter 3 that political periods in country *i* depress stock markets in country *i*.

We argue that the configuration of political and economic institutions may mitigate these cross-border consequences, especially if those factors enhance the predictability of policy outcomes. The existence of a strong party provides market actors with a common focal point to predict the outcome of elections in parliamentary systems. The parameter estimate for strong party is positive and significant: the presence of a strong party in the foreign country mitigates the impact of the foreign political event on the domestic market. Interestingly, a change in the partisanship of the foreign government does not appear to affect foreign markets. The variable fails to attain conventional levels of statistical significance.

Economic and monetary institutions have a mixed impact on cross-border political shocks. First, consider exchange rate commitments. Country *i*'s membership in the EMS, participation in the Euro, and a fixed exchange rate do not have a statistically significant independent effect on cross-border political shocks. The coefficients for all three variables are individually insignificant. Note, however, that these variables correlate with the variables measuring whether a country pair shares the same exchange arrangement. A joint test of EMS_i and Both EMS shows that the combination is statistically significant ($p = 0.008$). When compared to a pair of countries that have floating exchange rate regimes, a political period in country *j* decreases equities in country *i* by 1.6 more points when both countries are members of the EMS.

A joint test of $Euro_i$ and Both Euro also reveals statistical significance ($p = 0.003$). Joint membership in the Euro mitigates cross-border political shocks. When both countries are members of the Eurozone, a political period in country *j* increases the impact on country *i*'s market by about six points.

The other monetary variables fail to attain statistical significance. A joint test for the fixed exchange rate variables is insignificant ($p = 0.4533$). Surprisingly, central bank independence in either country does not condition the impact of political periods in country *j* on equity markets in country *i*. Finally, capital openness in the home country has no significant effect on cross-border shocks.

Column two reports the parameter estimates from using the robust regression technique. The results are broadly similar. In the absence of a strong party and a joint exchange rate commitment, a foreign political event decreases stock returns in the domestic market. The presence of a strong party in country *j* and joint membership in the Euro, however, mitigate this effect. Because robust regression down-weights outlier observations, each of these variables has a smaller substantive impact than with the weighted-least squares estimate, but each remains statistically significant. With the robust regression, the institutional status of the central bank in the home country has a positive and statistically significant effect, suggestions that an independent central bank can help insulate home equity markets from cross-border political shocks.

Column three reports the results from the median regression technique, where the regression line is fit through the conditional median rather than the conditional mean of the estimated cross-border political shock. Given how conservative the technique is, it is unsurprising that this approach provides us with the weakest results. The constant is no longer statistically significant, nor is participation in the Euro. The parameter estimate for the presence of a strong party in country *j* remains positive, but is no longer statistically significant. Interestingly, the change in partisanship variable is statistically significant in this specification. A rightward shift in country *j* decreases market returns in country *i*. A move to the left increases domestic returns. This result suggests that asset owners shift portfolios across borders based on the policy priorities of the incoming government.

Overall, the results across the three estimation techniques suggest that asset owners will reallocate their portfolios away from equities if they cannot predict the political outcome in a foreign country. Participation in the euro also appears to help mitigate the size of cross-border political shocks.

Columns four, five, and six report the parameter estimates from similar models and estimation techniques using interest rates on ten year government bonds as the dependent variable. Note first the constant which reports the effect of a foreign political event holding all other variables at zero (i.e., for a country with a floating exchange rate, low central bank independence, and no strong party in the foreign country). For all of the estimation techniques, the parameter estimate is not statistically significant: political events in country *j* have no impact on interest rates in country *i*.[11] The presence of a strong party in the foreign

[11] The WLS results differ due, in part, to the presence of a major outlier. The 1994 election in the Netherlands is associated with a large decrease in Swedish interest rates (0.327). If that observation is deleted, the WLS results show a statistically significant intercept of 0.041.

country *j*, however, decreases bond returns. For all three estimation techniques, the strong party variable is negative and statistically significant. Political predictability in country *j* helps keep interest rates in country *i* lower.

The direction of partisan change in country *j* influences interest rates in country *i*. A leftward shift in the foreign country causes interest rates in country *i* to increase. If interest rates tend to be higher under left governments, other countries might have to increase their own interest rates to keep capital from leaving the country.

The independence of the central bank in the home country is also associated with higher interest rates during foreign political events. This may be a policy response to insulate the home economy from the influence of outside political events.

Neither participation in the Euro or capital openness affects the size of foreign political shocks on bond markets.

CONCLUSION

Democratic political events do not just affect domestic markets. With high levels of financial integration, elections and cabinet formations have consequences for markets across borders as asset owners shift their portfolios in response to political developments. We demonstrate that variations in the size of these cross-border political shocks reflect not only the predictability of the outcome in the political event, but also the configuration of political and economic institutions within and between countries. Adopting a single currency, for instance, has reduced the cross-border impact of political events on markets within Europe.

The potential for cross-border political shocks does not have implications for market performance only. Instead, the possibility of these shocks affects the ability of politicians to remain in office. If foreign political events affect the performance of domestic markets, and if the performance of domestic markets has consequences for politicians, then politicians may be vulnerable to the unpredictability of foreign political events, making their own positions in office more tenuous. These potentially negative political consequences may provide incentives for politicians across highly-integrated countries to pursue common packages of institutional reform to protect their own positions.

5

Cabinet Dissolutions and Interest Rate Behavior

In this chapter, we investigate the political impact of financial market behavior by focusing on the costs of borrowing. We show that expectations of political outcomes can affect interest rates in both the public and private sectors. As market actors are less confident of the government's economic policy commitments, interest rates increase – with potentially harmful consequences for public finances and economic outcomes.

Higher interest rates complicate the task of balancing the state's finances. Citizen demands for expansive social programs and the increasing pool of citizens eligible for state-sponsored retirement plans have dramatically ratcheted up the debit side of the state's ledger. This would not be problematic if the revenue side were expanding as well. Open financial markets, however, have exacerbated the global competition for tax revenues, leading some political economists to suggest that advanced democracies can no longer sustain generous governmental programs and, instead, must engage in a "race to the bottom." Given these constraints, governments must issue public debt. High interest rates on government debt can add millions of dollars to government balance sheets in terms of debt servicing, limiting their ability to use fiscal policy to satisfy constituents. The cost of borrowing, therefore, significantly constrains the ability of politicians to expand programs or pursue new initiatives – policies that might help them retain office.

Private economic activity is also affected by interest rate behavior. In the neoclassical model, investment decisions are driven not only by the expected return from investment, which is a function of the price and volume of output, but also by the cost of capital, which is a function of tax rates and interest rates.[1] Indeed, a recent OECD study (2002) finds that interest rates significantly affect economic performance. The costs associated with borrowing capital, therefore, have economy-wide implications.[2]

Our task in this chapter is not to repeat arguments about the impact of asset market behavior on fiscal policy or economic outcomes. A large literature already documents these issues. Instead, we argue that political processes can affect the costs of borrowing: when political outcomes are less predictable, investors will demand higher rates of return. More predictable outcomes will help keep interest rates low.

To evaluate this argument, we again turn to parliamentary politics. In these systems, the government "emerges from" and "is responsible to" the legislature. That is, a prime minister and her cabinet must garner and maintain the support of a legislative majority to serve in office. Cabinets, therefore, can lose support at any time during the constitutionally-mandated electoral term. In the event that a cabinet loses a no-confidence vote in the legislature, party leaders must re-negotiate to form a new cabinet or, in some systems, they may call for new elections. Political science models have established that cabinets are more likely to end prematurely as the number of parties in the cabinet increases and as the percentage of legislative seats controlled by the parties in the cabinet decreases. We draw on these models to estimate the probability that a cabinet will come to an end. This probability represents our proxy measure of market expectations.

We argue that the expectations of market actors about the duration of a cabinet government will affect the costs of borrowing. As market actors expect a cabinet to come to an end, interest rates will increase. We are therefore able to quantify the interest rate costs of cabinet dissolutions.[3]

[1] Although neoclassical models of investment have been criticized for not incorporating dynamic expectations of future profits, models that address this shortcoming (e.g., models that incorporate Tobin's Q (Tobin 1969)) still find an important relationship between the cost of capital and investment.

[2] A study conducted by HM Treasury (2003) that examines the interest rate implications associated with British accession to the EMU contains a survey of this literature.

[3] We recognize that our argument is potentially subject to the concerns about endogeneity between political outcomes and market behavior. While the argument in this chapter holds political processes (cabinet dissolutions) as exogenous to market behavior, it is possible that changes in the government's fiscal position or slow economic growth due to high interest rates may actually precipitate the end of cabinet.

PARLIAMENTARY PROCESSES AND INTEREST RATES

If economic agents doubt the government's policy commitments, they may demand a premium to hold debt or maintain investments in that country, driving interest rates upward. In parliamentary systems, one of the key pieces of political information about the government's commitment centers on the expected duration of the cabinet government.

In parliamentary democracies, cabinets end for two reasons: a loss of confidence or an election.[4] First, in parliamentary democracies, the government must maintain the support of a legislative majority to remain in office. Cabinets may end due to losing legislative support or, in a multiparty government, parties may withdraw from the coalition. If the cabinet dissolves, parties must negotiate to form a new cabinet. In some instances, politicians may call for new elections in response to the crisis.

Cabinets may also end due to constitutionally mandated elections. In systems with exogenous electoral timing, elections occur at regular intervals. In many parliamentary systems, however, electoral timing is endogenous. That is, government leaders can call for an election at any time within a constitutionally mandated electoral term. As the end of a term approaches, government leaders will attempt to time the election to coincide with opportune conditions.

Anticipated cabinet durability can influence market actors' policy expectations in several ways. First, weak cabinet governments – those cabinets with tenuous support in the legislature or composed of many different parties – may not have the capacity to manage economic policy decisively. Because these governments must rely on a variety of veto players in the policy process, it is hard for ministers to make difficult economic choices (Tsebelis 2002; Haggard and McCubbins 2001). Often, policies are made to ensure that all cabinet supporters are satisfied, even if that means broadly extending benefits while ignoring costs. Indeed, Tabellini and Alesina (1990) show that a higher number of parties in a cabinet exacerbates fiscal policy profligacy (see also Roubini and Sachs 1989a). Hallerberg (2004), and Hallerberg and von Hagen (1998) also demonstrate a link between the number of parties and the size of the budget deficit.

[4] Defining the "end" of a cabinet remains a point of controversy in the literature (Laver and Schofield 1990). Lijphart (1984a), for instance, argues that a cabinet ends only with a change in the party membership of the cabinet. Other political scientists count a change in the prime minister, a formal government resignation, and elections as an end to the cabinet.

Second, as cabinets are likely to come to an end, market actors recognize that policymakers have shorter time horizons. As ministers understand that they may be out of office in the near-term, they may be tempted to pursue policies that will bring short-term benefits, even if it means sacrificing long-term goals (Kydland and Prescott 1977; Barro and Gordon 1983). At the very least, these politicians will be unlikely to implement any policies with significant short-term costs even if those policies promise long-term benefits. In the area of fiscal policy, cabinet ministers with short time-horizons may be tempted to forego the political costs of raising taxes or cutting spending and instead borrow money to cover revenue short-falls (Roubini and Sachs 1989b).

Finally, the prospect of a cabinet dissolution can create tremendous uncertainty about the identity of the next cabinet and, as a result, the future course of economic policy. In some cases, a cabinet dissolution will result in new elections. These elections may change the distribution of legislative seats, and new parties may be tapped to form the next government. Even without a new election, however, a cabinet dissolution may produce a new government, composed of parties whose policy priorities differ from those of the previous government.

In a multiparty system, the bargaining between political parties in the government formation process may create even greater questions, not only about the identity of the new government, but also about its policy priorities. First, the bargaining process can extend for months, leading to policy inactivity. Second, bargaining typically occurs behind closed doors, out of the public's view. This can make it difficult for economic agents to project the partisan identity of the government. Finally, it may be unclear what type of coalition bargain is struck. During negotiations, parties may make policy compromises or trade-off responsibility for different issue dimensions (Laver and Schofield 1998; Laver and Shepsle 1996; Strom and Leipart 1993). The vague language of public coalition agreements often does not clarify responsibility for policy.

Although the policy consequences of a cabinet end are not often clear, we argue that economic agents can have fairly accurate expectations about when a dissolution will occur. Newspaper and media accounts often report when backbench legislators or, in a multiparty government, coalition parties are dissatisfied with the current cabinet, creating the conditions for a vote of no confidence. Economic agents can also recognize when coalition parties have incompatible policy preferences and, thus, be less likely to maintain the coalition. Finally, economic agents are also aware of when constitutionally mandated elections are due. In systems with endogenous timing, there is often extensive discussion about how long the government will wait to call elections. On the basis of this information, economic agents will form expectations of when the cabinet is likely to end.

These expectations about political events, in turn, affect economic behavior. If economic agents are fairly confident that the cabinet will survive, they can make projections about the government's economic objectives. As economic agents come to believe that a cabinet is likely to dissolve, however, they recognize that there is a non-zero probability of change in the composition of the government. This potential change in the government's identity raises the possibility that economic policy will change as well. Consequently, market actors will demand higher returns to hold government debt or to keep money in the country. Therefore, as markets become more confident that the government is going to end – either through an election or a cabinet collapse – then interest rates will increase.

Further, we expect that the effect of an actual cabinet dissolution on interest rates will vary according to whether the event was anticipated. Predicting a cabinet collapse or the date of elections is an imperfect science. A variety of political shocks may cause the sudden collapse of a cabinet: scandal, a foreign policy crisis, a change in party leadership, death of a minister, snap elections, etc. A cabinet dissolution, therefore, may surprise economic agents. If economic agents have not anticipated the cabinet dissolution, their evaluation of the government's policy commitments may suddenly change. Prior to a surprise dissolution, market actors expect the current government's policies to be in place for the medium-term. An unanticipated dissolution, however, suddenly raises the possibility of a new government with different policy priorities. Therefore, if a cabinet ends when markets did not anticipate a dissolution, we expect that event to increase interest rates sharply.

Expectations of a cabinet dissolution and the policy consequences of that dissolution affect how markets evaluate the government's policy commitments. These expectations, in turn, can influence interest rates. Our next step is to provide an operationalization of those expectations. To do this, we first employ a simple model of cabinet dissolution. This model provides a predicted probability of cabinet dissolution for each day in our sample series. These probabilities serve as a proxy of market expectations of a cabinet dissolution.

ESTIMATING THE PROBABILITY OF A CABINET END IN PARLIAMENTARY DEMOCRACIES

We draw on the extensive literature on cabinet durability to model the probability that the cabinet will end.[5] Typically, political scientists have compared the durability of governing coalitions based on coalition attributes (the majority status of the government, the number of parties in the government), regime attributes (fragmentation of the political system, political polarization, etc.), and bargaining situation (number of formation attempts). Lijphart (1984a and 1984b), for instance, compares the durability of governments based on their coalition attributes. He finds that single party majority cabinets are the most durable and minimum winning coalitions are slightly less durable. Minority and oversized cabinets tend to have the shortest life-spans.

We argue that the probability that the cabinet will end is a function of five sets of variables: the duration of the cabinet to that point, the time remaining before constitutionally mandated elections, whether the system has exogenous electoral timing, government type, and party system attributes.

First, consider the duration of the cabinet to that point. Coalition bargains tend to be fragile in the months just after cabinet formation. As cabinets survive over time, however, they are less likely to fall over a policy disagreement (King et al. 1990; Alt and King 1994; Warwick 1994). That is, cabinets that have survived 24 months are very likely to survive another month, while cabinets that have survived only a month are not as likely to make it to a second month. Therefore, we include a variable for *Cabinet Duration*, which counts the number of days the cabinet has existed to that point. We also include a square of that term. We expect the overall effect of these variables to have negative probability on cabinet dissolution.

Second, we also count elections as instances of cabinet dissolution. Most parliamentary systems have endogenous electoral timing. As constitutionally mandated elections approach, government leaders will attempt to dissolve the government at the most optimal time. We include a variable, *Electoral Clock*, counting down the time to when an election must, by law, be called.[6] We also include a square of this term. The time until mandated elections will have a higher probability of a cabinet

[5] Laver and Schofield (1998) and Warwick (1994) provide reviews.

[6] Countries have different constitutionally mandated election periods: 36, 48, or 60 months. We normalized the electoral clock variable to reflect these different periods. The formula for the electoral clock variable is: (Number of Months Until

dissolution as it approaches zero. Consequently, we expect the square term to have a positive estimate.

Third, we include a dummy variable for systems with *Exogenous Electoral Timing.* In these systems, electoral timing is constitutionally mandated. Governing politicians cannot call elections at opportune times. Since politicians know that they must work within the distribution of legislative seats, they will be less likely to dissolve the cabinet. Exogenous electoral timing, therefore, is likely to prolong cabinet durability.

Fourth, we include dummy variables for *Government Type*: single party majority, minimum winning coalition, oversize coalition, single party minority, and coalition minority. Following the literature, we expect that single party majority governments will be most durable, minimum winning coalition slightly less durable, and oversize and minority governments least durable. We also expect that the government type will have an interactive effect with the time-dependent variables (duration, electoral clock). For instance, the probability of a cabinet dissolution with single party majority governments will be very low and relatively constant throughout most of the term. This probability will increase sharply as mandated elections approach. We expect a similar pattern with minimum winning coalitions, except that the probability of cabinet dissolution will be slightly higher just after the coalition forms. With the minority and oversize coalitions, the probability of a cabinet dissolution will be high early in the terms. We include interactive terms to capture these relationships.

Fifth, we include two attributes of the party system: fractionalization and polarization. Political scientists argue that the more fragmented and polarized the political system, the shorter the expected cabinet duration. We include a variable for party system *Fractionalization*, which measures the number of effective political parties in the system (Rae 1971). This variable should have a negative effect on cabinet durability. *Polarization* is measured by the electoral support for extremist parties.[7] More support for extremist parties also implies shortened duration.

Election Must Be Called)/(Constitutional Electoral Period). The electoral clock variable runs from 1 (Full electoral period remaining) to 0 (No time remaining). A value of 0.5 indicates that half the electoral period remains before elections must be called.

[7] Following Powell (1982), we measure polarization as the percentage of electoral support for extremist parties. According to Powell, extremist parties exhibit one of the following characteristics: (1) A well-developed nondemocratic ideology; (2) A proposal to break-up or fundamentally alter the boundaries of the nation; or (3) Diffuse protest, alienation, and distrust of the existing political system. We follow Powell's (1982) classifications with the exception of including France's National Front.

Finally, following King et al. (1990), we include a set of nation dummy variables. The number of cabinet collapses varies substantially across the countries in our sample. Britain, Canada and the Netherlands had the fewest governments (10 each) while Italy and Japan had the most governments (26 and 24, respectively). The dummy variables account for country specific factors that influence the probability of cabinet dissolution.[8]

Sample and Dependent Variable

We examine the duration of cabinets in a set of 15 parliamentary democracies over the period January 1970–December 2002. The countries include Australia, Austria, Belgium, Britain, Canada, Denmark, France, Germany, Ireland, Italy, Japan, Netherlands, New Zealand, Norway, and Sweden. We include only cabinets that began on or after January 1970. Cabinets that did not end before December 31, 2002 are right censored. Overall, the sample includes 210 cabinets.

The dependent variable, *End*, is a dummy variable, coded one for each instance of cabinet dissolution, due either to election or to a change in the composition of the parties in government, and coded zero, otherwise. Of the 210 cabinets, 131 end with an election, while 79 end without an election. The data are from Woldendrop, Keman, and Budge and supplemented by *Keesings Contemporary Archive* and by annual issues of the *European Journal of Political Research.*

Table 5.1 provides descriptive statistics for those variables.

Methodology

Recent work on cabinet duration uses event history analysis. Event history models estimate the underlying hazard of an event (i.e., a cabinet ending), and also analyze the influence of covariates on the length of time a cabinet remains in power. Typically, these models have estimated continuous time survival models of cabinet duration with time-constant covariates (King et al. 1990; Alt and King 1994; Beck 1997; Warwick 1994). That is, they assume that cabinet duration is a function of variables that

[8] We have not incorporated other time-constant covariates suggested by the literature (e.g., number of formation attempts). We did include the variables suggested by King et al. (1990) for those cases which overlapped with ours. In this limited sample, the nation dummy variables absorbed much of the variation attributable to these time-constant covariates.

Table 5.1. *Summary statistics for model of cabinet duration*

Variable	Mean	Std. Dev.	Minimum	Maximum
Government end	0.002	0.043	0	1
Single party majority	0.280	0.449	0	1
Minimum winning coalition	0.256	0.436	0	1
Oversize majority	0.126	0.332	0	1
Single party minority	0.219	0.414	0	1
Coalition minority	0.117	0.322	0	1
Electoral clock	0.498	0.351	0	0.999
Cabinet duration	444.585	332.856	1	1929
Exogenous electoral timing	0.132	0.338	0	1
Government polarization	0.080	0.095	0	0.416
Government fractionalization	0.676	0.108	0.4091	0.891

N = 111,453.

are measured at the time of cabinet formation. This approach is similar to a cross-sectional data set where the dependent variable is the number of days that the cabinet has been in power.

Instead, we want to employ a statistical model that allows us to estimate the probability that a cabinet will end (or survive) on any given day. This probability is a function of both time-constant covariates (e.g., government type, country dummy variables) and time-varying covariates (e.g., cabinet duration, electoral clock). Consequently, we use a discrete-time hazard model with a probit specification (Allison 1984; Beck, Katz, and Tucker 1998). Here, the hazard rate represents the probability that a cabinet will end at a particular time, given that the cabinet has survived to that point. We observe only whether a cabinet survives or ends; the actual probability of a cabinet ending on any particular day is latent. Inclusion of the electoral clock and cabinet duration variables helps control for duration dependence in the analysis. This model provides predicted probabilities of cabinet dissolution for each day included in the sample.[9]

[9] In Leblang and Bernhard (2000) we estimated a similar discrete time model and found that the predicted hazards from Cox and Weibull specifications were highly correlated (above 0.85) with the predicted probabilities generated by this type of probit specification.

Results

Table 5.2 contains the results of the discrete-time probit model. This model was estimated with a set of 15 country specific dummy variables, the results of which are not included in the table. A log-likelihood ratio test rejects the null hypothesis that, as a whole, the model is not

Table 5.2. *Discrete time hazard model of cabinet duration*

Independent variables	Probit coefficient	Robust st. error	Marginal effects (X 100)
Single party majority	−0.364	0.197	−0.13
Minimum winning coalition	−0.608	0.374	−0.14
Oversize majority	−0.415	0.363	−0.10
Single party minority	−0.274	0.255	−0.05
Electoral clock	−1.871	1.258	−0.70
Electoral clock^2	0.826	1.446	0.30
Government duration	0.0006	0.002	0.0004
Government duration^2	−1.01e−06	1.32e−06	−3.35e−07
Electoral clock*single party majority	1.269	1.123	0.47
Electoral clock*minimum winning coalition	1.272	1.273	0.40
Electoral clock*oversize majority	1.603	1.343	0.48
Electoral clock*single party minority	1.498	1.292	0.50
Electoral clock^{2}*single party majority	−1.964	1.433	−0.70
Electoral clock^{2}*minimum winning coalition	−0.746	1.515	−0.16
Electoral clock^{2}*oversize majority	−0.919	1.547	−0.19
Electoral clock^{2}*single party minority	−1.279	1.446	−0.47
Duration*single party majority	−0.0004	0.001	−1.29e−04
Duration*minimum winning coalition	−0.0008	0.002	−2.64e−04
Duration*oversize majority	−0.001	0.002	−4.33e−04
Duration*single party minority	−0.0006	0.002	−2.47e−04
Duration^{2}*single party majority	8.51e−07	1.22e−06	2.75e−07

Independent variables	Probit coefficient	Robust st. error	Marginal effects (X 100)
Duration^{2}*minimum winning coalition	1.57e−06	1.49e−06	5.65e−07
Duration^{2}*oversize majority	1.78e−06	2.01e−06	7.24e−07
Duration^{2}*single party minority	1.05e−06	1.41e−06	3.31e−09
Exogenous electoral timing	−0.173	0.069	−0.11
Government polarization	0.888	0.206	0.07
Government fractionalization	−0.246	0.327	−0.10
Constant	−2.105	0.306	

Joint Hypothesis Tests

Variables	$\chi 2$	**p-value**
Country dummies	22.07	0.054
Single party majority	10.85	0.055
Minimum winning coalition	13.57	0.019
Oversized majority	7.56	0.182
Single party minority	2.26	0.813
Electoral clock	66.61	0.000
Cabinet duration	17.96	0.056

Cell entries are probit coefficients, robust standard errors and marginal effects. The model was estimated with a set of country dummy variables; parameter estimates not reported to conserve space. The marginal effects are for a change from 0 to 1 for discrete variables and for an infinitesimal change from the mean.

statistically different from zero. The model does a good job predicting when a government is going to survive (99 percent of the cases correctly specified) and when a government is going to end (75 percent of the cases correctly specified). This is evidence that the model is fairly well specified.[10]

Maximum likelihood parameter estimates are in column one and robust standard errors (adjusted for unequal error variances across countries) are in column two. There is extensive collinearity among

[10] Given that we observe only 210 observations where a government ends, it would not be surprising if the model produced skewed results. Therefore, we take a case to be correctly predicted if the estimated probability is greater than or equal to the mean of the dependent variable in the sample.

many of the independent variables, resulting from the construction of the duration and electoral clock variables and their interactions with government type variables. Consequently, it is not surprising that most of the independent variables are individually statistically indistinguishable from zero.[11] As a result, we report a set of log-likelihood ratio tests that test for the joint significance of each government type and its interaction with the duration and electoral clock variables. These results are presented at the bottom of Table 5.2 and indicate that we can reject the null hypothesis that none of the sets of variables – with the exception of oversize and single party minority – have any statistically significant influence on the dependent variable at the 0.10 level.

The exogenous electoral timing variable is statistically significant and, consistent with our expectations, negative. The parameter estimate for polarization is positive and statistically significant. As polarization increases, the probability of a dissolution also increases – a finding that is again consistent with the literature. Finally, fractionalization is not statistically significant.

Finally, three of the country dummies are statistically significant. In comparison to Britain (our omitted category), German governments last longer and Italian and Japanese governments last shorter lengths of time. The other country dummy variables were not significant.

Given that few of the independent variables are individually significant, how can we be confident that the results meet with our expectations? The discrete-time hazard model using the probit specification provides predicted probabilities of a cabinet dissolution for each day. We first compare the average predicted probabilities of a cabinet dissolution by government type (Table 5.3). As expected, the average probability of a single party majority cabinet falling and the average probability of a minimum winning coalition falling are lowest. Oversize coalition governments have the highest average probabilities of collapsing followed closely by single party minority governments. Surprisingly, our results find that coalition minority governments have a probability of collapse that lies between single party majority and single party minority governments.

Finally, Table 5.4 reports these probabilities for periods when a cabinet survives (End = 0) and when a cabinet ends (End = 1). As expected, the

[11] This would be a problem if we argued only that different government types had different intercepts. Instead, we contend that there is an interaction between government type and the length of time that a cabinet has been in power.

Table 5.3. *Average predicted probability of a cabinet dissolution*

Government type	N	Average probability of dissolution	95% Confidence interval	
Single party majority	31,249	0.0016	0.001613	0.001657
Minimum winning coalition	28,561	0.0016	0.001583	0.001628
Oversized majority	14,081	0.0027	0.002633	0.002695
Single party minority	24,502	0.0021	0.002092	0.002131
Coalition minority	13,060	0.0018	0.001790	0.001842

Table 5.4. *Predicted probability of a cabinet dissolution*

Periods	N	Mean	95% Confidence interval	
All periods	111,453	0.001883	0.001872	0.001894
End = 0	111,243	0.001880	0.001869	0.001890
End = 1	210	0.003837	0.003437	0.004239

mean probability of a cabinet dissolution is substantially higher in periods when the cabinet ends than when it survives. In fact, when a cabinet survives, the predicted probability of cabinet dissolution never exceeds 0.22. The predicted probabilities for when a cabinet dissolves, however, range from (essentially) zero to (essentially) one. Where the predicted probability of cabinet dissolution is low, the cabinet dissolution is unanticipated.

Discussion

These predicted probabilities are a proxy for market uncertainty in parliamentary democracies. We use the predicted probabilities from our model of cabinet duration as an independent variable, *Expectations*, in our interest rate spreads models. Cabinet dissolutions create uncertainty about the future of economic policy. Consequently, as economic agents anticipate a cabinet dissolution, they are more likely to be uncertain about economic policy. The expectations variable, therefore, will have a positive effect on interest rates.

Further, we argue that the effect of an actual cabinet dissolution on interest rate spreads will be contingent on expectations of a cabinet collapse. We include an interaction between the dummy variable for a cabinet dissolution (*End*) and the predicted probability of cabinet dissolution (*End*Expectations*). Higher values indicate that the cabinet dissolution was anticipated. Lower values suggest the cabinet dissolution was a surprise. Since we hypothesize that unanticipated cabinet events have a greater effect on interest rates, this interactive term should have a negative estimate.

CABINET EXPECTATIONS AND INTEREST RATES

To evaluate the effect of the expectations of a cabinet end on interest rates, we perform two tests. The first test examines bond issues. We employ a selection model to determine how the fragility of a cabinet affects the government's decision to issue debt and, in turn, the interest rate spread of those bonds in the primary market. The second test focuses on the behavior of interest rates in the private sector. Specifically, we test how cabinet dissolutions affect the onshore–offshore interest rate spread.

Cabinet Ends and the Market for Government Bonds

In this section we examine interest rate spreads on sovereign government bonds offered in primary markets.[12] Most securities – stocks, bonds, etc. – trade in two different markets during their lifetime. Issuing entities – governments or corporations – initially sell securities directly to investors; this is the primary market offering.[13] Once purchased these securities are then traded (bought and sold) between investors on secondary markets.

Studying the launch of new government bonds, however, presents issues of potential selection bias. Poor economic conditions or unclear political outcomes may increase the premium that governments would have to pay for new issues. The anticipated premium on a new issue may,

[12] Most studies of interest rate spreads employ U.S. or German bonds (of comparable maturity) as the "benchmark" – the bond against which the local interest rate will be measured. In this study, U.S. bonds serve as the benchmark for bonds issued in U.S. dollars (and for German bonds) and German bonds as the benchmark for bonds issued in the DM. For bonds issued in either the Euro or the local currency, we use the bond of the country that is its larger trading partner (e.g., for Japanese bonds issued in Yen, U.S. serve as the benchmark).

[13] It is also known as an initial public offering (IPO).

in turn, affect the government's decision to issue debt in the first place. To deal directly with these issues, we must jointly estimate models for the issuance and spread on government bonds.[14] Following Eichengreen and Mody (2004), we model both the decision by governments to issue debt and, if a bond is issued, the interest rate spread. The spread is measured as the difference between the interest rate on the issued bond and a benchmark bond of similar maturity issued in the same currency.

The decision to issue a bond

Consider first the government's decision to issue a new bond. We argue that higher expectations of a cabinet end are likely to increase the probability of issuing debt. First, the expectations measure reflects a government's decision-making capacity. Strong governments – single party majority governments or minimum winning coalitions – have a relatively low probability of coming to an end. These governments have the capacity to act decisively, either finding new sources of revenue or making budget cuts to manage fiscal pressures. For other government types, however, the probability of a cabinet end is higher, reflecting their weakness and fragility. These governments may lack the ability to push through tax hikes or cut spending, instead of relying on debt to finance spending initiatives.

For all government types, the probability of a cabinet end increases as constitutionally-mandated elections come due. In the run-up to an election, an incumbent government will be less willing to cut spending or increase taxes to finance new government programs. (Indeed, they may be likely to increase spending and reduce taxes just prior to an election!) As a result, they will seek to finance spending through borrowing. In both situations, the expectations variable should have a positive impact on the probability of issuing new debt.

CONTROL VARIABLES. We control for the following characteristics in modeling the government decision to issue debt.

Prior borrowing: Borrowing can often feed on itself, as governments borrow more to help cover for past obligations. Governments with higher levels of debt and budget deficits, therefore, are likely to issue debt more frequently.

[14] Eichengreen and Mody (2004) study launch spreads in emerging markets. The only study of launch spreads on bonds issued in OECD markets that we know of is Bernoth, von Hagen, and Schuknecht (2004).

We include two measures to capture these pressures: *Debt* and *Deficit*, both measured as a percentage of GDP. Data were collected from Source OECD and various national sources on January 1 of each year. Unfortunately, these measures are available only an annual basis, precluding us from making anything other than cross-national comparisons.

Capital account liberalization: Governments that have relatively closed capital markets have less access to international sources of capital and are thus more likely to issue debt as compared to governments that have liberalized their capital markets. We include an annual measure of capital account liberalization, *Liberalization*, from Quinn (1997) and lag it one year.

National economic performance: The more productive and robust the national economy the greater the proportion of government revenue that will be generated by tax revenue.

We measure national economic performance using daily returns on national stock market indices (*Returns*). We expect larger national returns will be associated with a lower probability that the government will issue public debt.[15]

Government partisanship: The partisan composition of the government affects budgetary priorities. But the implications for government borrowing are not clear. Left governments are often assumed to favor expanded public spending without necessarily raising taxes to meet these new expenditures. Right governments, on the other hand, may be more likely to reduce taxes, but often fail to make commensurate cuts in spending. In both cases, governments may be forced to rely on borrowing to cover revenue short-falls.

We include a measure of partisanship, *Partisanship*, that multiplies the percentage of Left party members in the cabinet with the percentage of Left party members in the legislature (Cameron 1984). We do not anticipate that partisanship will have any significant effect on the decision to borrow.

Time since previous issue: Governments may issue debt on a regular schedule. To account for this, we include a variable, *Time Since Last Issue*, counting the number of elapsed days since the government last issued debt. If governments do issue bonds on a regular schedule, this variable will have a positive sign since the longer the elapsed

[15] We employ MSCI indices. Results do not differ if alternative indices are used (e.g., Datastream).

time since the last issue increases the probability of a bond being floated. Alternatively, this variable could capture the cross-national difference in the propensity of different governments to issue bonds. In alternative specifications, we also included the square of this term.

Unmeasured national and temporal characteristics: The frequency of debt issue varies tremendously across countries. Italy, for instance, issues debt much more often than other countries in the sample. Further, the frequency of new issues increases over time. To minimize the risk of biased parameter estimates due to omitted variables, we include a set of 13 country specific dummy variables and a time trend variable in the model of new issues.

The interest rate spread

Once a government has decided to issue new debt, markets decide how much to pay for it. We model the spread between the new issue and the benchmark bond in a second equation. The spread also reflects expectations that the cabinet is likely to end. If market actors anticipate that a government's coalitional status makes it weak or indecisive, they are likely to demand a higher premium since it is reasonable to believe that such a government will continue to borrow. Further, as governments borrow toward the end of their constitutionally-mandated terms, markets actors may not be able to forsee the policy priorities (and capacity) of the incoming government. This may lead them to demand a higher premium as well. For both reasons, therefore, the expectations variable should have a positive coefficient in the spread equation.

CONTROL VARIABLES. Eichengreen and Mody (2004) suggest a number of variables that affect the spread on government bonds.[16] In addition to the measures of debt,[17] deficit, capital account liberalization, and government partisanship, we control for the following:

Exchange Rate Regime: A country's exchange rate commitment may affect how market actors evaluate default risk. In the European

[16] Persson and Tabellini (2002) and Drazen (2000) provide a review of theoretical models linking political institutions to public debt.

[17] Alesina et al. (1992), Lemmen and Goodhart (1999), and Flandreau, Cacheux, and Zumer (1998) find a relationship between public debt and spreads between public and private borrowing costs for European governments. Lonning (2000), Copeland and Jones (2001), Codogno, Favero, and Missale (2003), and Bernoth, von Hagen, and Schuknecht (2004) show that higher levels of debt help explain cross-national differences in interest rates on government bond issues.

context, much of this policy debate centers on the consequences of participation in the EMU. Some economists contend that EMU increases default risk since domestic policymakers have surrendered their monetary policy autonomy and cannot monetize their debt. Further, there is no guarantee that the European Central Bank (or other governments) will offer assistance if a member state experiences a financial crisis.[18] Bernoth, von Hagen, and Schuknecht (2004) point out, however, that membership in a monetary union may decrease default risk (and subsequently risk premia) if market actors believe that a central authority will bail out countries in fiscal crisis.

We include dummy variables for participation in alternative exchange rate regimes: *Unilateral Peg, Member of the EMS* (European Monetary System), and *Euro.* A floating exchange rate regime is the comparison category.

Country risk: Investors will likely rely on ratings from major credit ratings agencies to help them evaluate bond issue. Poor credit ratings mean a higher premium. We include the S&P sovereign credit rating, *S&P Rating*, at the time of issue.

Investors' appetite for risk: The decision by investors to hold newly issued assets is based on an evaluation of the risk versus the return. Direct measure of investors' risk aversion, however, are not available. According to the literature on sovereign bonds, bond spreads are sensitive to U.S. based risk factors (e.g., Eichengreen and Mody 2004; Bernoth, Von Hagen, and Schuknecht 2004). As a proxy for investor's risk aversion, therefore, we use the spread between U.S. corporate and government bond yields – specifically, the spread between low grade U.S. corporate bonds (BBB) and the benchmark U.S. government bond. Both bond series are available from the U.S. Federal Reserve bank on a daily basis. We expect a positive relationship between investors' appetite for risk and spreads on newly issued government bonds.

Maturity: Default risk usually varies with the length of the contract. Longer-term bonds naturally entail more risk and, therefore, should have higher premia. We include a measure of the time to maturity of the bond at the time of issue (*Time to Maturity*).

Issue size: A government that issues a larger amount of bonds should expect, all things being equal, a smaller return on those bonds. Additionally, larger issues provide greater liquidity on secondary

[18] This is implicit in the "no bail-out clause" of the Maastricht Treaty.

markets, decreasing marginal demand for government bonds (McBrady 2003). Therefore, we expect a negative relationship between issue size and the spread. Issue size is measured in U.S. dollars.

Currency of issue: We include two dummy variables reflecting whether the bonds were issued in the Euro or in the U.S. Dollar. The default category is the local currency.

Data

We examine initial offer or "launch" spreads on specific bonds offered between January 1, 1990 and December 30, 1999.[19] Euromoney's Bondware reports all bonds issued by sovereign entities in 13 parliamentary democracies: Austria, Belgium, Britain, Canada, Denmark, France, Germany, Ireland, Italy, the Netherlands, New Zealand, Norway and Sweden.[20] Table 5.5 reports the number of bonds issued by country and by year, the total amount of the annual issue (in U.S. dollars), and the average spread between the primary market price and the risk free rate charged for bonds of comparable maturity and issued in the same currency. A cursory inspection of the table reveals that Italy and Sweden are the countries that most often issue debt. Further, countries issue more bonds toward the end of the sample period than at the beginning. Finally, the spread for members of the Euro-zone appears to be smaller than for countries outside it.

Table 5.6 reports descriptive statistics. The sample includes over 31,000 daily observations and 1272 bond issues.

Method

The decision to issue government debt and the actual price of the debt represent potentially interdependent outcomes. We can observe spreads only for bonds that have been launched. Failing to model the issuing decision may lead to biased parameter estimates of variables in the spread model. To deal with this possibility we employ a standard sample selection model (e.g., Heckman 1979). A selection model follows a two equation set-up, one equation to model the initial decision (in this case, whether or not to launch a bond) and a second one to model the observed outcome (the spread on the bond).

[19] All but two of the bonds in our sample are fixed income securities. Italy issued two convertible rate bonds in 1996.

[20] We exclude Australia and Japan due to lack of comparable data.

Table 5.5. *Bond issues:*
Cell entries are spread, total amount issued in millions of U.S. Dollars, and number of bonds issued

	1990	1991	1992	1993	1994	1995	1996	1997	1998	1999	2000
Britain		0	0.201556	0.389	0.367695	0.485664	0.416504	0.498342	0.417328	0.516767	0.639883
	0	3868.336	6878.729	1391.422	3092.23	3335.938	8688.86	19180.18	18052.1	18995.33	9371.233
	0	**1**	**4**	**5**	**16**	**16**	**20**	**23**	**11**	**9**	**6**
Austria	0.002917	0.005406	0.003563	0.00518	−0.01905	−0.01758	0.012113	−0.04172	0.013394	0.00337	0.001042
	2718.528	1151.963	3059.926	4618.035	4687.508	3072.636	4750.048	3458.56	20244.31	20861.37	15799.9
	12	**8**	**8**	**10**	**13**	**8**	**6**	**15**	**21**	**20**	**12**
Belgium	0.00255	−0.00733	0.004327	0.019292	−0.02394	−0.03225	0.017818	0.083956	0.102333	0.039864	−0.01786
	1586.114	12984.97	17767.81	13598.2	11903.63	11669.41	12202.92	11066.02	14117	22370.41	18796.48
	5	**16**	**28**	**30**	**29**	**25**	**28**	**27**	**34**	**25**	**15**
Denmark	0.004483		0.005446	0.007428	−0.0191	−0.08112	0.00426	−0.01326	0.007416	0.00135	−0.06342
	2376.98	0	2574.366	9840.201	500.05	2189.713	2706.248	4707.262	1788.627	2212.014	1496
	8	**0**	**6**	**23**	**2**	**9**	**15**	**16**	**11**	**10**	**22**
France				−0.70366	−0.17053	−0.16342	0.010743	0.021747	0.019835	−0.00232	−0.01659
	0	0	0	46.453	4989.574	14385.26	33561.31	10887.97	86069.46	87263.56	79759.75
	0	**0**	**0**	**1**	**7**	**9**	**21**	**15**	**56**	**55**	**63**
Germany									0.010279	0.000443	−0.00452
	0	0	0	0	0	0	0	0	67232.79	77110.44	62531.34
	0	**0**	**0**	**0**	**0**	**0**	**0**	**0**	**14**	**14**	**12**
Italy	−0.00123	−0.014	−0.30988	−0.00377	−0.00171	−0.04069	−0.00334	0.015358	0.037324	−0.01278	−0.007
	6239.177	6941.078	1211.837	12753.44	11633.35	10322.18	17300.34	24396.37	119872.6	143447.5	119686.3
	5	**2**	**18**	**8**	**7**	**7**	**14**	**17**	**62**	**70**	**80**

	1990	1991	1992	1993	1994	1995	1996	1997	1998	1999	2000
Netherlands				−0.0007	−0.0049	−0.031	0.0013	0.0279	0.036233	−0.03494	−0.00135
	0	0	0	4283.112	5674.187	2083.722	4476.81	2488.802	20457.86	25194.4	14083.44
	0	**0**	**0**	**1**	**1**	**3**	**1**	**1**	**9**	**10**	**8**
Norway		−0.003	0.004788	0.047348	−0.106	−0.1505	−0.01733	0.0315	0.0066	0.0112	0.02314
	0	2161.98	4685.97	5621.836	842.158	931.273	2181.954	1749.96	1869.506	1752.055	1724.845
	0	**2**	**8**	**8**	**2**	**2**	**3**	**4**	**5**	**5**	**5**
Sweden			−0.02594	−0.01613	−0.00307	−0.04765	−0.00226	0.005089	0.036082	0.020338	0.000995
	0	0	5884.227	14264.68	13315.31	15394.75	14662.07	11355.24	14298.11	12758.84	4255.32
	0	**0**	**5**	**25**	**33**	**38**	**65**	**54**	**30**	**28**	**12**
Canada					0.004518	−0.00755	−0.00528	−0.00111	0.005154	0.00115	
	0	0	0	0	4000	3000	2000	1843.302	8375.102	2815.435	0
	0	**0**	**0**	**0**	**2**	**2**	**2**	**4**	**7**	**4**	**0**
Ireland	−0.00535	−0.00816	0.009705	0.01274	0.011071	0.0165		−0.01143	0.072954	−0.04303	−0.10203
	857.055	914.81	1694.389	1655.799	953.814	467.96	0	772.417	1103.024	1178.389	1206.658
	5	**8**	**11**	**5**	**6**	**5**	**0**	**3**	**7**	**7**	**8**
New Zealand	0			0.00416	0.02835		0	0.006358	−0.05283	−0.003	0
	845.063	0	0	387.515	1172.375	0	100	926.795	100	300	257.073
	3	**0**	**0**	**2**	**3**	**0**	**1**	**5**	**1**	**1**	**4**

Table 5.6. *Summary statistics for selection model*

Variable	Obs	Mean	Std. Dev.	Minimum	Maximum
Bond spread	1272	0.035	0.159	−0.781	1.255
Political expectations	31743	0.002	0.002	6.67e−06	0.013
Government partisanship	31743	0.369	0.401	0	1.27
Bond issued in euro	1272	0.006	0.078	0	1
Bond issued in U.S. dollar	1272	0.004	0.061	0	1
Fixed exchange rate	31743	0.083	0.275	0	1
EMS	31743	0.418	0.493	0	1
Euro	31743	0.110	0.313	0	1
Debt/GDP	31743	61.491	26.889	19.8	121.6
Deficit/GDP	31743	−2.969	3.754	−11.765	7.765
Investor appetite for risk	30725	1.823	0.308	1.228	2.786
Log(issue amount)	1312	6.024	1.326	1.125	9.476
Time to maturity	1312	3685.149	2630.275	107	13353
Capital Account Liberalization(t−1)	31743	93.159	10.240	62.5	100
S&P rating	1312	4.279	0.743	3	5
Bond issued	31743	0.040	0.196	0	1
Return on DS stock index	31743	0.0003	0.012	−0.145	0.130
Time since last issue	31743	341.787	688.381	0	3651

A continuous outcome model with a probit selection equation can be written as:

$$y = \beta' x + \varepsilon_1$$
$$z^* = \alpha' w + \varepsilon_2$$
$$z = \begin{Bmatrix} 1 & \text{if } z^* > 0 \\ 0 & \text{if } z^* \leq 0 \end{Bmatrix}$$
$$\varepsilon_1, \varepsilon_2 \sim N(0, 0, \sigma^2_{\varepsilon_1}, \sigma^2_{\varepsilon_2}, \rho)$$

where y is the launch spread on government bonds, which is a function of a set of exogenous variables, x, and a normally distributed error term with mean zero and constant variance ε. z^* is the latent (unobserved) probability that the government will issue a bond, normalized to have mean zero and variance equal to one. Zero is the cut point between categories in the observed z. That is, $z = 1$ only when the latent probability (z^*) is greater than zero. We estimate these two equations jointly using maximum likelihood. This allows us to obtain estimates of the parameters α and β and the correlation between the errors in the two models, ρ.[21]

Results

Table 5.7 reports the results from estimating the sample selection model. Our estimated value of ρ, which indicates the correlation between the errors in the selection and outcome equations, is not statistically significant. This indicates, surprisingly, that launch spreads are not systematically related to the government's decision to issue bonds.[22]

The first column of table 5.7 reports the results from the selection equation – a probit model that estimates the probability that governments will issue a bond. Cell entries are marginal effects followed by probit parameter estimates and robust standard errors in parentheses.[23] The expectations variable – the estimated probability that the cabinet will end at any particular point in time —is positively associated with the likelihood that a government will issue new bonds and is statistically significant.[24] The marginal effect indicates that a small change in the probability of a cabinet end from the mean increases the likelihood of issuing a bond by 0.4 percent, holding everything else constant. While this impact is small, it is important to remember that our sample contains only 1396 instances of bonds being issued, just about 4 percent of the entire sample.[25] We graph this relationship in Fig. 5.1. As the probability

[21] Details on maximum likelihood estimation of this type of selection model can be found in Greene 2003 and Wooldridge 2002.

[22] The inverse of the Mills-ratio (lambda) is negatively signed (−0.018) with a standard error over twice its value (0.039).

[23] The marginal effects for dichotomous variables are calculated as the change from zero to one.

[24] This model is similar to two-stage least squares in that the variable of interest – political expectations – is a generated variable (from a model of cabinet duration). Generated variables contain two sources of error: (1) it is a predicted probability that has an associated standard error and (2) it likely contains a degree of measurement error. To deal with the first issue, we re-estimate the models substituting the estimated probability divided by its standard error (akin to a t-statistic) as the measure of political expectations. For the second potential problem, we re-estimate the model using a parametric bootstrap. Neither alteration results in substantially different findings from those reported.

[25] The infrequency of bond issues raises a concern that probit may be inappropriate for modeling such rare events. We re-estimated the selection equation using the rare-events logit estimator of King and Zeng (2001) and did not obtain substantively different results with one exception. The rare events estimator provided an estimate of left government that is positive and statistically significant, although the size of the parameter (once an adjustment was made to compare logit and probit coefficients) was not different from the reported result.

Table 5.7. *Heckman selection model*

Independent variables	Issue equation	Spread equation
Expectations	0.004	
	0.198**	0.128**
	(0.085)	(0.026)
Government partisanship	0.00083	
	0.041	−0.039*
	(0.047)	(0.021)
Unilateral peg		−0.138**
		(0.017)
European monetary system		−0.153**
		(0.017)
EURO		−0.090**
		(0.014)
Government debt/GDP	0.0004	
	0.019**	0.001**
	(0.003)	(0.000)
Government deficit/GDP	−0.0001	
	−0.006	0.004**
	(0.008)	(0.001)
World appetite for risk		0.008
		(0.016)
Log(Issue amount million US$)		0.001
		(0.004)
Length to maturity (Days)		0.000**
		(0.000)
Capital Account Liberalization(t−1)		0.005**
		(0.001)
S&P rating		0.104**
		(0.014)
Bond issued in Euro		−0.072**
		(0.012)
Bond issued in USD		−0.048**
		(0.010)
Capital market openness	0.0002	
	0.005	
	(0.003)	

Independent variables	Issue equation	Spread equation
MSCI stock market return	−0.030	
	−1.170	
	(1.308)	
Time (days) since last issue	−0.0001	
	−0.001**	
	(0.000)	
Issue date	0.0002	
	0.000**	
	(0.000)	
United Kingdom	−0.001	
	−0.034	
	(0.164)	
Austria	−0.004	
	−0.212*	
	(0.129)	
Belgium	−0.009	
	−0.978**	
	(0.240)	
Denmark	−0.007	
	−0.581**	
	(0.152)	
France	−0.007	
	0.243**	
	(0.108)	
Italy	0.007	
	−1.013**	
	(0.231)	
Netherlands	−0.009	
	−0.824**	
	(0.147)	
Norway	−0.008	
	−0.161	
	(0.129)	
Sweden	0.003	
	−0.008	
	(0.161)	

(*continued*)

Table 5.7. *(continued)*

Independent variables	Issue equation	Spread equation
Canada	−0.003	
	−0.807**	
	(0.133)	
Ireland	−0.008	
	−0.681**	
	(0.166)	
New Zealand	−0.007	
	−0.626**	
	(0.179)	
Constant	−5.662**	−0.880**
	(0.455)	(0.122)
Prob > $\chi 2$	0.0000	
Total observations	31743	
Censored observations	30471	
Uncensored observations (in issue equation)	1272	
Rho	−0.1317392	
(p−value)	(0.6346)	

Cell entries in the issue equation are marginal effects, parameter estimates, and robust standard errors. (Cell entries in the spread equation are parameter estimates and robust standard errors.)

of a cabinet end increases, the probability of a new bond issue also increases.

The parameter estimates for the control variables are generally in line with expectations. Partisanship, as predicted, has no clear relationship with the probability of issuing new bonds. Both left and right governments are equally likely to borrow. Countries with higher debt ratios are more likely to issue bonds. The time since last issue negatively affects the probability of an issue. In contrast, the size of the deficit, stock market returns, and capital account openness appear to have no systematic relation to a government's decision to issue bonds. These results could reflect the fact that we included a battery of specific country dummy variables. Almost all of these variables have a significant parameter estimate. Additionally, the time trend variable, Issue Date, is also significant and positive: the probability of issuing new debt increases over time.

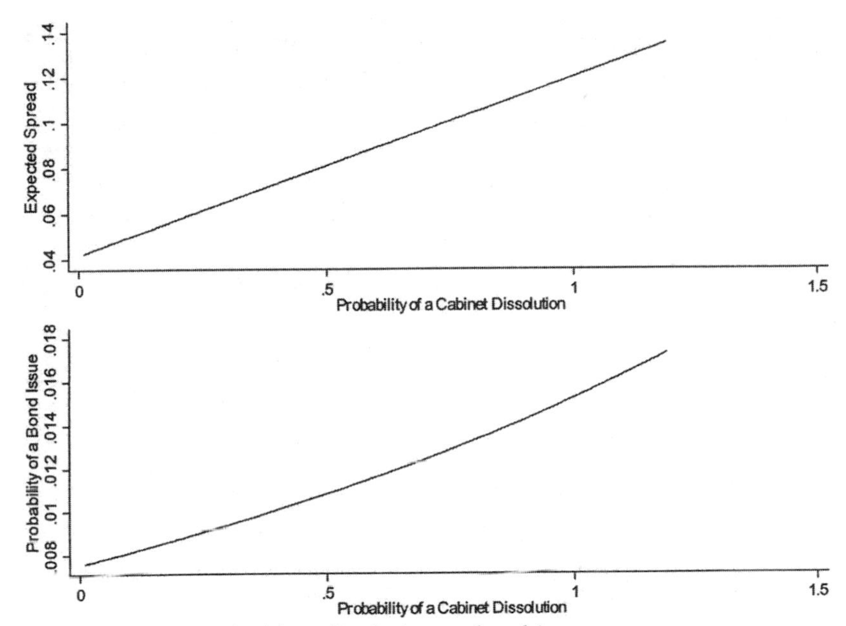

Figure 5.1. Impact of cabinet dissolution on bond issues.

Column two of Table 5.7 reports the results for the model of launch spreads. Cell entries are maximum likelihood estimates with robust standard errors in parentheses. These parameter estimates are equivalent to OLS estimates. The slope coefficient, therefore, is identical to the marginal effect. As predicted, the probability of a cabinet coming to an end increases the spread on new government bonds. Market actors demand higher premia when the government appears likely to change in the near future. Increasing the probability of a cabinet end by one percent increases launch spreads by 12 basis points (Fig. 5.1).

With a few exceptions, the remaining variables in the spread equation are statistically significant and correctly signed. Consistent with previous literature, governments with higher deficits and debts relative to GDP pay higher spreads. Longer time to maturity and poor S&P ratings are also associated with larger spreads. The exchange rate regime affects the price paid by governments for debt. Governments with a floating exchange rate (the omitted category) pay a higher premium compared to countries with either a unilateral or a multilateral commitment. Capital market openness is associated with increased spreads, although the effect is small. The variables for the currency of issue are also significant: Bonds denominated in local currency cost more.

The variables for government partisanship, the world appetite for risk, and (surprisingly) the amount of the bond issue failed to attain statistical significance.

Overall, the results indicate that political uncertainty in parliamentary democracies – measured by the probability that a cabinet will come to an end – does affect the primary market for government debt. Cabinets are more likely to issue new debt if they are unlikely to survive for a long period of time. In turn, as market actors expect the cabinet to end, they will demand a higher premium for purchasing government debt.

Cabinet Ends and Onshore/Offshore Interest Rate Spreads

To examine how the prospect of a cabinet end affects interest rates in the private sector, we compare the difference between interest rates on assets denominated in the same currency but deposited in different financial centers, a measure commonly called the onshore/offshore spread. "Onshore" assets are deposited in the home country. "Offshore" assets are denominated in the same currency but deposited in a foreign country. Holders of U.S. dollars, for instance, can deposit their funds "offshore" in banks in, say, the Cayman Islands.

Economists argue that the spread between the onshore and offshore rate is a useful measure of political risk (e.g., Marston 1995; Aliber 1973; Dooley and Isard 1980; Ito 1986).[26] Because onshore and offshore deposits are denominated in the same currency, exchange rate risk does not exist. Instead, the spread reflects a probability assessment by investors that they will be unable to withdraw their money from the domestic market due to the potential imposition of capital controls or other financial market restrictions. Since we measure the onshore/offshore spread by subtracting the offshore (London) deposit rate from the onshore (interbank) rate for short-term deposits, a positive differential means that investors are demanding a higher rate of return from domestic financial institutions. A negative spread suggests that domestic banking institutions provide investors with (relatively) risk-free investment opportunities.[27]

We argue that expectations of a cabinet end will affect the onshore–offshore spread. As the probability of a cabinet end increases, the spread should also increase, reflecting market concerns about the

[26] Obstfeld and Taylor (2004) provide a lucid treatment of the issues related to comparing onshore to offshore interest rates with an empirical focus on historical data.

[27] The literature on asset mobility suggests that a "home bias" exists when it comes to the willingness of investors to exploit international investment opportunities (Lewis 1999).

future course of fiscal and monetary policy. On average, the spread should be lower when the government's position in office is more secure. The expectations variable, therefore, should have a positive parameter estimate.

The impact of an actual cabinet end on the spread will vary according to the degree to which markets anticipate the end. If a cabinet ends when markets have expected the event, the effect of the end on the spread will be relatively small. On the other hand, if the cabinet end surprises market actors, the spread will jump considerably.

Data and Sample

We construct a measure of the interest rate differential by comparing onshore interbank deposit (ask) rates obtained from Datastream to offshore (London) deposit rates as reported by the *Financial Times*. The reported rates are for three-month deposits in identical currencies.[28] We have comparable data for eleven countries: Britain, Belgium, Denmark, Germany, Italy, the Netherlands, Norway, Sweden, Japan, Australia and New Zealand. The daily series for these countries vary significantly: data from 1980 to the present exist for two countries (Britain and Norway); from 1987 on for four countries (Belgium, Denmark, Germany, and Italy); and from 1997 on for the remaining four countries. The sample contains 23,869 observations.

The average spread for our sample is 0.10 (10 basis points). Spreads did increase dramatically during the final two weeks of September in 1992 following the ERM crisis – on average, to 87 basis points. Nevertheless, the average spread is not overly influenced by this event.[29]

Table 5.8 contains descriptive statistics.

Control Variables and Method

The literature reaches no consensus on the set of explanatory variables required to explain variations in the onshore–offshore spread. Consequently, we draw on Arbitrage Pricing Theory to suggest appropriate controls (see Chapter 3 for a discussion). These variables include the daily return on gold prices, oil prices, and an aggregate index of global stock market performance. This set of variables captures global trends

[28] Using one-month deposit rates found almost identical results, although these data were available for only seven countries.

[29] We experimented with alternative codings of the ERM crisis. The results did not change appreciably.

Table 5.8. *Summary statistics for onshore–offshore interest rates*

Variable	Mean	Std. Dev.	Minimum	Maximum
Onshore–offshore spread	0.116	0.282	−3.752	9.5
Expectations	0.160	0.150	0.0007	1.427
Government end	0.002	0.041	0	1
Expectations*end	0.0006	0.018	0	1.427
EMS crisis	0.003	0.057	0	1
Capital Account liberalization	95.973	8.414	75	100
Government partisanship	0.218	0.320	0	1.27
EMS 1979–87	0.059	0.237	0	1
EMS 1987–92	0.252	0.434	0	1
EMS 1992–98	0.233	0.423	0	1
Euro	0.079	0.270	0	1
Fix	0.114	0.318	0	1
Return on gold price	−0.00008	0.008	−0.109	0.106
Return on Brent oil price	0.0003	0.023	−0.355	0.214
Return on global market index	−0.00007	0.006	−0.082	0.075
Exchange rate realignment	0.0003	0.018	0	1

N = 23,869.

that should, according to APT, largely drive returns on domestic financial assets.

To account for the relationship between exchange rate changes and the domestic interest rate, we include dummy variables for the country's exchange rate regime: a unilateral peg, participation in different stages of the EMS, and membership in the single-currency (Euro). We also include a variable for currency realignments and a separate variable for the EMS crisis of September 1992 (coded one from September 16, 1992 through September 30, 2002).

We include a measure of capital account liberalization from Quinn (1997)[30] and our measure of government partisanship.

We estimate a panel model using OLS with a set of country specific fixed effects (intercepts) to account for unmeasured heterogeneity, a time counter to capture unmeasured global cycles and a lagged

[30] Aliber (1973), Dooley and Isard (1980), Ito (1986), and Marston (1995) discuss the impact of capital controls on interest rate differentials.

endogenous variable to absorb country-specific serial correlation. We report Huber/White robust standard errors to deal with issues of potential heteroskedasticity.

Results

Column one in Table 5.9 contains a baseline model of the onshore-offshore interest rate differential. Parameter estimates for the fixed effects and the lagged endogenous variable are not reported for the sake of space. The expectations variable is positive and statistically significant: as the likelihood of a cabinet dissolution increases, so does the interest rate that domestic financial institutions have to pay relative to offshore institutions.[31] The impact is substantively significant as well: a one percent increase in the likelihood of a cabinet dissolution leads domestic banks to pay interest rates that are more than 11 basis points higher than offshore banks.

The economic controls fail to attain statistical significance. This is not all that surprising: while we found in Chapter 3 that these variables could account for changes in equity market performance, we did not find a similar pattern for long-term interest rates.

Exchange rate behavior, including the ERM crisis and periodic realignments within the EMS are associated with higher spreads. During these times of crisis, governments must increase interest rates to make domestic deposits more attractive.

The parameter estimates for participation in an exchange rate regime reveal interesting patterns. Countries that participated in the EMS or that pegged unilaterally had higher spreads when compared to those that allowed their exchange rate to float. Market actors likely feared the potential imposition of capital controls to maintain these exchange rate commitments. The parameter estimate for participation in the Euro lends credence to this interpretation. Adoption of the single currency – an arrangement where domestic governments could no longer implement capital controls – is associated with significantly lower spreads.

Unsurprisingly, the parameter estimate for capital account openness is negatively signed and statistically significant. Market actors require less compensation to keep their money in countries with few constraints on capital mobility.

On the other hand, the coefficient on the partisanship variable is somewhat unexpected – it is negative and statistically significant. Higher

[31] See note 24.

Table 5.9. *Model of onshore-offshore spreads*

Independent variables	A	B	C
Political expectations	0.116**	0.117**	0.117**
	(0.012)	(0.012)	(0.012)
EMS Crisis	0.724**	0.724**	0.725**
	(0.029)	(0.029)	(0.029)
Capital Account liberalization	−0.002**	−0.002**	−0.002**
	(0.000)	(0.000)	(0.000)
Government partisanship	−0.058**	−0.058**	−0.058**
	(0.007)	(0.007)	(0.007)
EMS 1979–87	0.097**	0.097**	0.097**
	(0.015)	(0.015)	(0.015)
EMS 1987–92	0.123**	0.123**	0.122**
	(0.010)	(0.010)	(0.010)
EMS 1992–98	0.082**	0.082**	0.081**
	(0.009)	(0.009)	(0.009)
Euro	−0.034**	−0.034**	−0.034**
	(0.010)	(0.010)	(0.010)
Fixed exchange rate	0.051**	0.051**	0.051**
	(0.009)	(0.009)	(0.009)
Return on gold price	−0.232	−0.232	−0.234
	(0.198)	(0.198)	(0.198)
Return on Brent oil price	−0.019	−0.019	−0.019
	(0.071)	(0.071)	(0.071)
Return on global economic index	−0.030	−0.030	−0.031
	(0.258)	(0.258)	(0.258)
Exchange rate realignment	0.858**	0.858**	0.858**
	(0.090)	(0.090)	(0.090)
Government end		−0.016	0.018
	(0.040)	(0.066)	
Expectations*end			−0.096
		(0.151)	
Constant	0.200**	0.200**	0.200**
	(0.041)	(0.041)	(0.041)
N	23869	23869	23869
R-squared	0.2055	0.2054	0.2054
Prob(F)	0.0000	0.0000	0.0000

$^{**}p < 0.05$.

levels of left party control are associated with lower interest rate differentials. One potential reason for the magnitude of this estimate is that Britain, Denmark, and Italy had right-wing governments during the ERM crisis – a period when spreads exceeded 500 basis points. Re-estimating the model while omitting the last quarter of 1992, however, provides the same result: left governments are still significantly associated with smaller spreads, although the size of the parameter estimate is cut in half.

The model in column two adds a dummy variable, end, for the actual end of a cabinet. This variable is not individually significant. End and expectations, however, are theoretically related and empirically correlated. An *F*-test rejects the null that they are jointly insignificant ($F=44.83$, $p=0.000$). End has negatively signed parameter estimate, suggesting that the date of a cabinet dissolution is associated with a smaller spread. Such an interpretation would be misleading. The average level of expectations when a cabinet comes to an end is 0.38, which substantively mitigates the negative impact of a cabinet end.

The model in column three evaluates our argument that the market impact of an actual cabinet dissolution depends on political expectations. We include expectations, end, and an interaction term, expectations*end. Expectations still has a statistically significant and positive impact on interest rate differentials. End and expectations*end are individually insignificant. The combination of expectations, end, and expectations*end is, however, jointly significant ($F=30.02$, $p=0.000$). The parameter estimate for end is positive, while the estimate for expectations*end is negative, suggesting that the impact of a cabinet end on the onshore–offshore spread is mitigated by the degree to which markets anticipate the event.

To see the substantive impact of these results, we graph the conditional impact of expectations and end on the interest rate differential in Fig. 5.2. The x-axis in the graph represents values of expectations. Toward the left, market actors expect the cabinet to continue in office. On the right, market actors anticipate that the cabinet will end soon. The y-axis is the predicted interest rate differential, holding all variables at their means.

The line with the circle symbols graphs the impact of the expectations variable on the interest rate differential when a cabinet end does not occur. The line is positive and statistically different from zero – just as one would expect from the parameter estimate. The line marked with the square symbol represents the predicted interest rate differential when a cabinet end does occur given differing levels of market expectations. When the

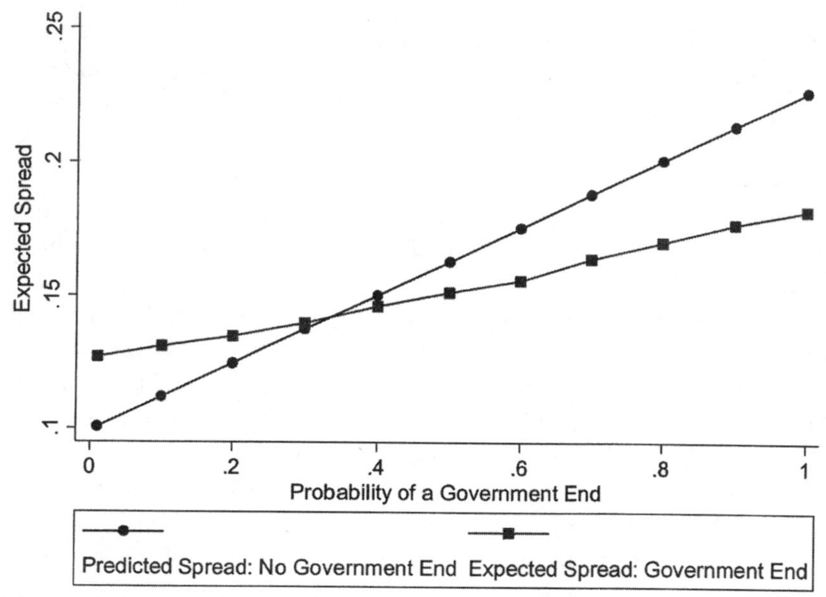

Figure 5.2. Impact of cabinet dissolutions on onshore–offshore spread.

expectations variable is low – that is, when market actors anticipate that the government will continue – the occurrence of a surprise cabinet dissolution sharply increases the onshore–offshore spread. The difference between the two lines is large and statistically significant. As the expectations variable increases – that is, as market actors anticipate a cabinet end – the impact of an actual end declines. The lines intersect when the expectations variable is around 0.35. At this point, an actual cabinet end has no effect on interest rate differentials. Market actors have already anticipated the event and adjusted their behavior accordingly. The results, therefore, underscore for the importance of taking market beliefs into account when attempting to estimate the impact of a political event.

CONCLUSION

In this chapter, the focus has been on two types of interest rates: those for government bonds and the onshore–offshore spread. We demonstrated that the probability of a cabinet end affects these interest rates. When cabinets are likely to dissolve, interest rates are higher. If a cabinet ends unexpectedly, surprising market actors, interest rates will increase more sharply than if markets anticipated the end of the cabinet. Expectations about political processes, therefore, affect market behavior.

Both these interest rates have implications for political outcomes. Higher interest rates for government debt make it more difficult for politicians to manage fiscal policy, limiting their ability to implement new programs or cut taxes. Higher interest rates also dampen economic activity in the private sector. Lower levels of investment and, in turn, overall growth, can hurt incumbents at the polls.

Higher interest rates, therefore, may have negative consequences for incumbent governments – either directly by increasing the costs of government borrowing or indirectly by slowing economic growth. Since interest rates respond to political processes, politicians may have incentives to change the configuration of political institutions that inform the political expectations of market actors.

6

Bargaining and Bonds: The Process of Coalition Formation and the Market for Government Debt in Austria and New Zealand

The previous chapters show that parliamentary political events affect market behavior. Where the outcome of those events is less predictable, market returns tend to be lower than in situations where the political result is anticipated. But the previous tests do not tap into the *process* of political events. Parties posture for influence; legislators make proposals and counter-proposals. The media covers politics closely, reporting on how parties are performing, what policies are on the table, and what the likely outcome will be. The information contained in these news reports conditions the expectations of market actors. We argue that the market impact of political news during these processes will vary according to the prior expectations of market actors about the likely outcome. If news items confirm the beliefs of economic actors, this information will have little effect on market behavior. In situations where the eventual outcome is less predictable, however, we anticipate that these news items will affect market performance as economic actors update their expectations based on the new information. In this chapter and the next two, we examine case studies of political events to investigate this argument, generating data that not only captures the exact timing of the arrival of information but also accounts for the prior beliefs of market actors.

We first analyze two specific coalition formations: Austria after the October 1999 elections and New Zealand after the October 1996 elections. Both negotiations proved contentious and lengthy. In each, the outcome appeared to be in doubt until the very end of the process. Yet, in both cases, market reaction to the coalition outcome was subdued, leading some to conclude that these processes did not affect markets. These claims, however, fail to incorporate how the prior beliefs of market actors condition the impact of new information. By measuring market beliefs, we show that these processes of cabinet negotiation did affect the market for government debt. To accomplish this task, we develop a measure of the political information available to markets based on news accounts of the process of party negotiation.

The next section details the process of cabinet formation in Austria and New Zealand. The second section reconstructs the ebb and flow of cabinet bargaining. The third section assesses the impact of cabinet bargaining on bond markets.

TWO CASES OF CABINET BARGAINING

In this section, we review the process of cabinet negotiations in Austria and New Zealand, highlighting the key players, major issues, and patterns of interaction.

Cabinet Negotiations after the 1999 Austrian Elections

The October 3, 1999 election stunned the Austrian political establishment. The success of the far-right Freedom Party, under the leadership of Joerg Haider, signaled voters' disapproval of the long-running coalition between the center-left Social Democrats, the SPO, and the center-right People's Party, the ÖVP. The two parties had cooperated in government throughout the post-war period, institutionalizing a norm of proportionality for the government, economy, and society. Although the SPO remained the largest party, it lost six seats in the election. The FPO and the ÖVP were in a dead heat for second place. Once the postal ballots had been counted, the FPO outpolled the ÖVP by slightly more than 400 votes, giving them both 52 seats in the parliament.

The incumbent SPO Chancellor Viktor Klima reacted initially by encouraging a continuation of the traditional SPO–ÖVP coalition and indicated an unwillingness to deal with Haider and the FPO. The FPO, buoyed by its electoral triumph, welcomed offers from all parties to form a government. Haider boldly claimed that the FPO would be a "strong player in the political game."

The ÖVP's incentives, however, were less clear. In one sense, the ÖVP enjoyed an enviable position in the negotiations. From a policy perspective, it was positioned between the SPO and the FPO on many issues. As the second largest party in parliament, its seats would be invaluable to form a majority coalition. In short, any coalition was likely to involve the ÖVP. Indeed, Laver and Sheple's winset program indicates that the ÖVP was a strong party. Political and market actors seemed to recognize the ÖVP's advantageous bargaining position. In personal interviews with central bank officials, they recalled a strong belief throughout the process that the ÖVP was likely to emerge as a governing party.

On the other hand, the ÖVP had lost the election, dropping 12 seats in the process. The ÖVP leader, Wolfgang Schuessel, had pledged not to participate in government if the ÖVP received fewer votes than the FPO. On October 13, a few days after the election, he stated, "I concluded from the results of the election that voters do not want a resumption of the governing coalition in the old style." Additionally, it was whispered that Schuessel and SPO leader Klima did not get along well personally. Clearly, the ÖVP was reluctant to form another coalition with the SPO.

In the Austrian political system, the president plays a role in the coalition process. He selects the party to form a government and, in turn, must approve any coalition agreement. Immediately after the election, President Thomas Klestil signaled his desire for a continuation of the SPO–ÖVP coalition. On October 14, Klestil asked the SPO to begin exploratory talks with all other parties, including the FPO. Even though SPO leader Klima had ruled out a coalition with the FPO, the two parties scheduled a meeting for November 15. In the meantime, the Green party indicated that it would not join any government and the ÖVP reiterated its refusal to deal with Klima and the SPO – a position it took even until December 2. On the weekend of December 4–5, however, ÖVP leader Schuessel indicated that he would be willing to negotiate with the SPO, although he attached some strict conditions to his announcement. On December 9, therefore, President Klestil formally requested that the SPO form a new government. The ÖVP's leadership endorsed the negotiations with the SPO on December 13 and negotiation between the SPO and the ÖVP commenced on December 17, a few days later.

Talks between the two parties dragged through mid-January. Nevertheless, on January 17, the outlines of an agreement appeared on the horizon. An ÖVP spokesperson said, "The chances are very good that we will find a solution in the next few days." And by January 19, a coalition agreement had been struck. Party leaders from both parties approved the agreement in principle, although the distribution of cabinet portfolios had not been determined. The political establishment breathed a sigh of relief that any deal to include the FPO in government had been avoided.

But, as in any agreement, the devil is in the details. The failure to agree on the distribution of portfolios proved to be the undoing of the potential

SPO–ÖVP coalition. In particular, the ÖVP insisted on the finance portfolio, a demand the SPO was unwilling to meet. By January 21, the deal was dead. In response, SPO leader Klima announced his intention to explore the formation of a minority government. President Kestil authorized him to examine the possibility and report back in one week.

The political wrangling between the SPO and the ÖVP increased public support for the FPO. Opinion polls indicated that in a new election, the public would support the far right party over the two established major parties. As Klima explored a minority government, the ÖVP and the FPO opened discussions even though they had not been authorized by the President. On January 22, Schuessel declared that he would "explore the possibility" of a coalition with the FPO. In turn, the FPO voted unanimously on the 24th to support talks with the ÖVP. As those talks began the following day, Klima abandoned his efforts to form a minority government. President Kestil, reluctant to accept the FPO into government, declined to ask the leaders of either the ÖVP or the FPO to form a government. Instead, he opted to wait for the "outcome of these talks before taking the next step in forming a government."

On February 1, the ÖVP and the FPO announced a coalition agreement, with Schuessel as Prime Minister. The two parties presented the proposed cabinet to President Kestil the following day. After delaying for two days and asking the FPO to drop two of its more controversial nominees for cabinet positions, Kestil accepted the coalition late on February 3. The new coalition was sworn in on February 4, touching off protests within Austria and formal complaints from the European Union.

The 1999 elections, therefore, altered the Austrian political landscape, shattering the traditional dominance of the SPO and the ÖVP. While voters did mark their ballots for change, few could predict how the new ÖVP–FPO coalition would perform in office. Despite initial cooperation, the new coalition failed to survive. To ease concerns about the FPO's radical agenda, Haider relinquished his position as party chairman in May 2000. Nevertheless, he remained the party's most popular politician. Free from the responsibilities of holding a cabinet portfolio, he openly challenged and criticized the government's policies, especially the performance of FPO ministers who had, in his view, compromised the party's ideals. Amid the FPO's divisions, Chancellor Schuessel called for new elections in November 2002. Although the ÖVP emerged as the largest party, its coalition options were limited. Consequently, despite its heavy electoral losses, the FPO was invited to re-form the coalition, further cementing the end of the old post-war party system.

Cabinet Negotiations After the 1996 New Zealand Elections

The October 1996 election in New Zealand inaugurated a new mixed majoritarian-proportional representation electoral system. Predictably, the new electoral system led to the proliferation of new parties and political personalities, a parliament where no party commanded a majority of seats, and lengthy party negotiations over the composition of the cabinet.

Prior to 1996, New Zealand – as with most former British colonies – possessed a typical "Westminster" political system. The single-member district first-past-the-post electoral rules produced a two-party system dominated by the Labour Party on the left and the National Party on the right. Through the 1960s, New Zealand enjoyed strong growth and excellent living standards. Indeed, New Zealand ranked among the wealthiest countries in the world during this period. But the global economic shocks of the 1970s hit New Zealand exceptionally hard, producing a combination of high inflation and stubborn unemployment that devastated New Zealand's economy. In reaction, voters in the early 1980s rejected the incumbent National government and installed a Labour administration to deal with the economic crisis. Despite their left-wing ideology and unionist constituents, the Labour government surprisingly adopted market-oriented structural reforms designed to reduce inflation, deregulate major industries, and open New Zealand to the world economy. These policies produced a dramatic economic revival. But the reforms also created resentment among constituents who believed the Labour party leadership had betrayed their interests, that the party's policy performance in office had not been faithful to the objectives stated in its campaign manifesto, and that the political system systematically excluded certain voices.

Seeking to capitalize on this disaffectation, the opposition National party pledged to hold a referendum on the electoral system. When the National party won the 1990 election, it honored its commitment (*The Economist*, 26 September 1992). In 1992, voters rejected the first-past-the-post electoral system, supporting a mixed majoritarian-proportional representation system.[1] Modeled after the German electoral system, the new system gave each voter two votes – one for a local representative elected in a single member district, and a second for legislative seats determined by proportional representation. The proportional representation vote totals would determine the overall proportion of seats allocated to each party, with the

[1] In 1993, the Citizen Initiated Referenda Act also gave voters the right to petition for a (non-binding) referendum to be held on a particular issue, another departure from traditional "Westminster" political institutions (Mulgan 1994).

seats first filled by the representatives selected in the single member districts and then completed by party lists. As with the German system, the New Zealand system also includes an electoral threshold: parties that do not garner at least five percent of the proportional representation vote do not win any seats (unless a party representative wins one of the single-member districts, in which case she will be seated). Proponents of the system argued that it would provide wider representation while maintaining a certain level of accountability.

With the real possibility of winning seats under the new electoral system, political leaders created new parties on the left (e.g., The Alliance) and the right (e.g., the Association of Consumers and Taxpayers-ACT, Christian Coalition). The most compelling of these new parties could not be classified as left or right: New Zealand First, led by the ex-National politician Winston Peters, a self-described nationalist. Running on a populist platform, Peters and NZ First tapped into the hostility toward immigration and globalization while at the same time calling for expanded social, environmental, and education policies. Since a falling out with the National Party leader Jim Bolger in the early 1990s precipitated Peters' departure from that party, many commentators assumed that Peters would prefer to enter into a coalition with the Labour party should no party command a majority of seats. But Peters would rule out no coalition deals prior to the election, leaving party leaders, pundits, and voters to guess at the eventual outcome.

In the run-up to the election, polls indicated that National was likely to lose support, but still remain the largest party. Commentators anticipated that Bolger would have to cobble together a coalition between National, ACT NZ, and the Christian Coalition in order to remain in office. A center-left coalition, dominated by the Labour Party under the leadership of Helen Clark and composed of some combination of Labour, Alliance, and NZ First, was judged a more likely outcome.

The combination of the new system, with its new alternatives, and its uncertain coalition possibilities contributed to a lively and confusing campaign. Many voters remained unsure how their vote choices would eventually affect the final composition of the government. Politicians, too, appeared puzzled about how to position themselves, caught between the need to appeal for votes in the election and the desire to jockey for negotiating power in its aftermath.

Turnout was high on election day, October 12. Over 90 percent of eligible voters cast ballots. As expected, National remained the largest party, polling 34 percent of the vote and winning 44 seats, 17 short of a majority in the 120-seat parliament. Labour came in second, with 28 percent of the vote and 37 seats; NZ First garnered 13 percent of the vote and 17 seats; Alliance 10 percent and 13 seats; ACT NZ six percent and 8 seats. (The Christian Coalition failed to meet the five percent threshold and was not awarded any seats.)

Clearly, both National and Labour would need some help in order to form a government. On the right, National could count on the support of ACT NZ, but the two parties still lacked a majority of legislative seats. The left-wing Alliance would likely support a Labour government (although they did not want to participate in it), but it did not bring enough votes for Labour to secure a majority. For both National and Labour, therefore, the support of Winston Peters and his NZ First party were necessary to form a majority government.

NZ First had bargaining power. (Laver and Shepsle's winset program labels it as a strong party.) And Winston Peters was determined to play kingmaker. Peters candidly stated that NZ First would enter into a coalition with the party that offered it the most policy concessions, rating both National and Labour as having equal chances at the outset. He further called for patience, suggesting that negotiations could drag on until the Christmas holiday. Finally, he requested both National and Labour to take a vow of confidentiality surrounding the coalition negotiations. The public was not to know what was discussed until after the new government had formed. On October 21, NZ First initiated talks with National. On October 23, NZ First leaders met with Labour. Negotiations continued in this parallel fashion throughout November and into December. NZ First would meet with National and then Labour, sometimes on the same day!

As the negotiations proceeded, the public became increasingly anxious about the eventual outcome. In late October, Peters was involved in a late-night bar fight, causing him to miss a round of negotiations the following day. In early November, Bolger's National government allocated $563,000 to assist the parties involved in the negotiations, including a $100,000 grant to NZ First, causing some observers to claim that National was attempting to buy NZ First's support. On November 19, Peters sought to reassure that Labour remained in contention after newspaper speculation that a deal with National was imminent.

Toward the end of November, negotiations became more serious as all the parties hoped to have a deal in place by the opening of parliament on December 13. NZ First modified its stance on the compulsory superannuation surtax, signaling compromise in the negotiations. On December 5, National Party MPs agreed to postpone tax cuts in order to enter into a coalition. The following day, National MPs approved a proposed coalition agreement with NZ First. On December 7, Labour party leaders hailed a "breakthrough" meeting with NZ First and, in turn, approved their own proposed coalition agreement with Peters and his party. Finally, on December 10, Peters took the agreements to the NZ First party caucus, where, after a nine-hour meeting, they chose to join with the National Party to form the government.

For everyone, the outcome had been in doubt until the very end. NZ First used its position to squeeze policies and portfolios from both National and Labour. For National, the price of remaining in power was high. Not only did they have to postpone tax cuts and increase spending on social policies, they also gave NZ First nine of the 20 cabinet portfolios, a figure that would increase to eleven after two years' time. Peters himself was to serve as Deputy Prime Minister and as Treasury Minister, a new position that was to be senior to the Minister of Finance.

For NZ First, the price of power was high too. Labour politicians were angry at being led on and vowed to bring down the government. In an effort to embarrass NZ First, Labour quickly released some of the policies it had offered. Although Peters secured both policy and portfolio concessions for his party, his negotiation style alienated public support. Many resented the fact that a party with only 13 percent of the vote could determine the new government's policy priorities. Others complained that parties put power over principles during the bargaining process.

The lengthy negotiation touched off renewed debate about the electoral system. While many were angry about the process, others noted that NZ First would never again be able to play one side off the other as it had done. And, in the meantime, New Zealand had largely gotten what it asked for with the new electoral system: a parliament with more parties, a more diverse set of MPs, and a centrist government based on compromise.

MEASURING THE NEGOTIATION PROCESS

We want to determine whether the process of cabinet negotiations affects asset markets. The first step is to develop an appropriate operationalization of party bargaining. Measuring a dynamic process like coalition bargaining can be difficult. A simple timeline of meetings between parties may provide little information about the tone, details, and context of cabinet negotiations – information that is likely to influence the perceptions of market actors. Instead, we rely on media accounts of the negotiation process to provide details about cabinet bargaining. National media cover the cabinet formation process closely, reporting on which parties are negotiating, what portfolios and policies are on the table, and what the likely outcome will be.

A team of research assistants performed a content analysis of news stories covering the party negotiations in both Austria and New Zealand. The team systematically recorded information contained in the articles of *der Standard*, one of the major Viennese dailies, collecting over 750 articles for the period October 1999 to February 2000. For the New Zealand case, we employed 141 articles from *The Dominion Post*, out of Wellington, for the period October to December 1996. The research assistants coded each paragraph of each article for the following information:

1. Source of the activity – which party or institution discussed the potential coalition;
2. The activity – whether the party participated in a meeting, made a formal offer, or made a public statement about a potential coalition;
3. The target of the activity – the coalition being discussed by the source;
4. An evaluation of whether the coalition is likely to form;
5. An evaluation of whether the coalition is positive or negative for the country.

Appendix 6.1 shows the coding instructions and appendix 6.2 indicates the coding scheme, both for the Austrian case. The New Zealand case was coded similarly. Tests of inter-coder reliability among the research team revealed high levels of agreement – the kappa coefficients for each category were above 0.9 (Brennan and Prediger 1981).

The content analysis provides us with an overwhelming amount of information about the bargaining process. We have a data set of daily frequency showing party activities, parties' evaluations of the negotiation process, and parties' evaluations of potential coalitions. Using that information, we can reconstruct the evolution of bargaining in the cabinet formation process.

As a first step, we tallied the number of mentions for each potential coalition that indicated whether that coalition was likely or unlikely, regardless of the source. We then subtracted the number of "unlikely" mentions from the number of "likely" mentions to generate a daily indicator of the net number of "likely" mentions.

Turning to the Austrian case first, Fig. 6.1 indicates the number of net likely mentions for each of the ÖVP–FPO, SPO–ÖVP, and SPO–FPO

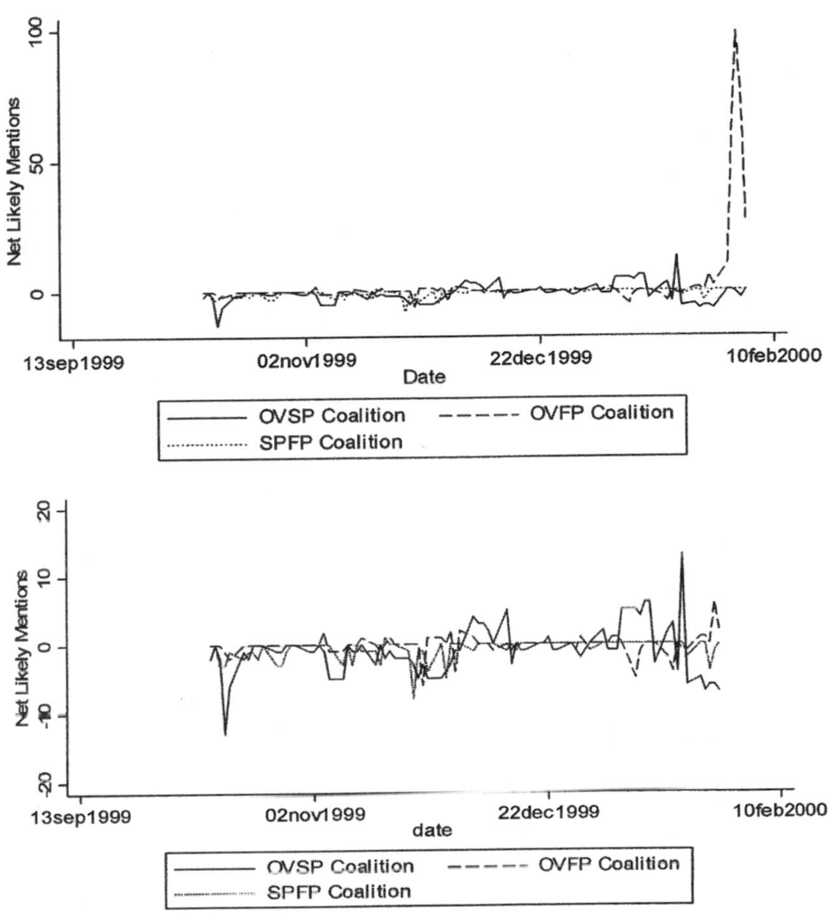

Figure 6.1. Net likely mentions for coalitions: Austria.

coalitions. (The reduced sample in the bottom panel of figure 6.1 omits the final days of the negotiations to clarify the variation during the bargaining process.) Shortly after the election, much of the press coverage of a potential SPO–ÖVP coalition views are unlikely. As negotiations continue, however, there is an uptick in the number of articles that see the traditional governing coalition as the likely result, reflecting renewed efforts at bargaining between the two parties in December and January. The collapse of the meetings between the SPO and the ÖVP, however, sends this measure sharply downward in mid January. The coverage for a potential ÖVP–FPO coalition is more mixed – a few days of positive coverage is followed by coverage that dismisses the possibility. It is not really until the very end of the period when the number of net "likely" mentions becomes consistently greater than zero. Finally, the content analysis indicates that an SPO–FPO coalition is unlikely, particularly early in the negotiation process. Indeed, after December, the coalition is rarely even mentioned. The content analysis, therefore, captures the ebb and flow of party negotiation: tremendous uncertainty just after the election, replaced by a sense that the SPO and ÖVP would patch up their differences, followed by a bargaining collapse that left Austria with the ÖVP–FPO coalition.

Figure 6.2 shows the number of net likely mentions for the National–NZ First and Labour–NZ First coalitions. With the information blackout about the coalition negotiations, fewer articles provide an analysis of the potential outcome. Shortly after the election, the Labour–NZ First coalition garners a slightly more positive evaluation, although the difference is not particularly striking. In mid-November, the National–NZ First coalition enjoys a slight uptick in the number of net likely mentions. In response to this speculation, Peters issued a public statement that a coalition with Labour was still a possibility. The number of likely mentions for National–NZ First spikes in early December as the National party caucus agrees to the policy concessions necessary to move forward with the coalition agreement. Again, the content analysis reflects the process of negotiation: a weak expectation shortly after the election that Labour and NZ First would coalesce, followed by a small shift toward a National–NZ First coalition in mid-November, with the uncertainty resolved only in early December.

Beliefs about Which Coalition Will Form

The raw data on the net number of "likely" mentions suggest that both coalition negotiations entailed long periods of political uncertainty. In Austria, the ÖVP–FPO coalition came as a surprise in the wake of the sudden collapse of SPO–ÖVP bargain. In New Zealand, Winston Peters and the NZ First party kept everyone guessing until the last moment. But just how unexpected were the eventual outcomes?

Market actors had prior beliefs about the probability of different coalition outcomes. The distribution of seats, party statements, and the negotiation process informed market actors about the likelihood of different outcomes. These prior beliefs, in turn, condition how the arrival of information affected the assessment of different coalition possibilities. Unexpected information may have caused market actors to update their beliefs about the eventual outcome. In other cases, information may have

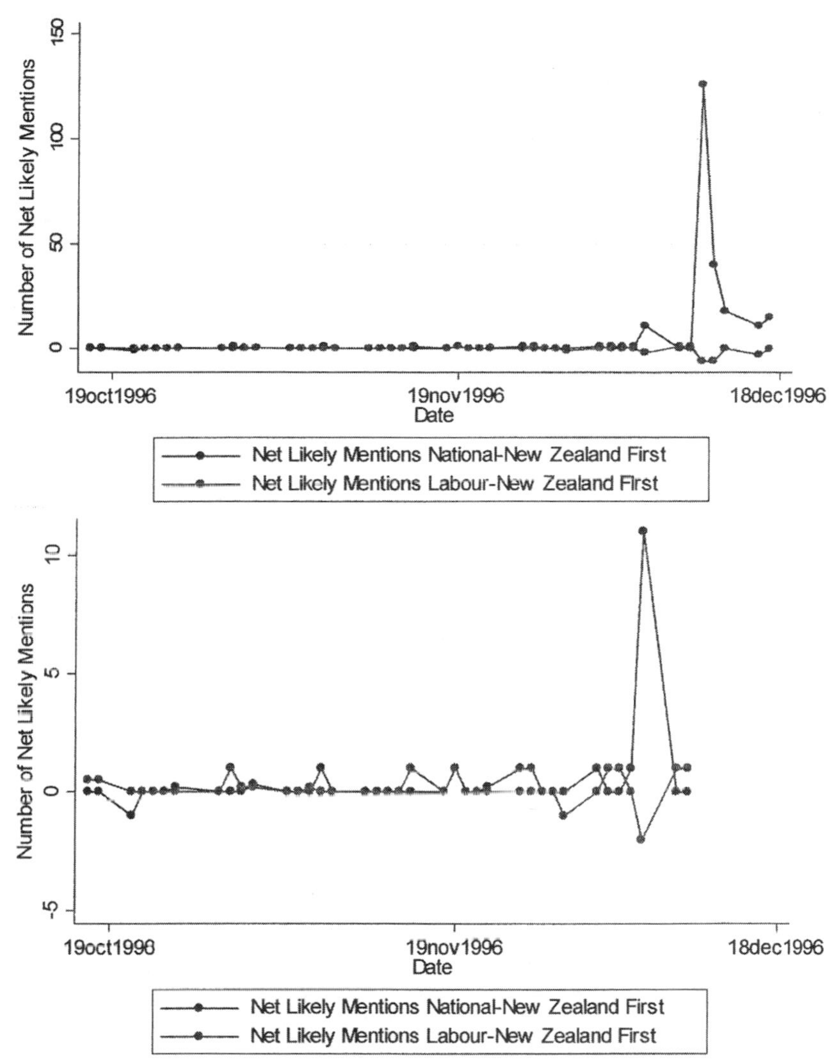

Figure 6.2. Net likely mentions for coalitions: New Zealand.

simply reinforced the market's prior beliefs. Without an understanding of how markets update and process political information, however, we may not be able to estimate accurately market reaction to a political event.

To measure the market's beliefs about the formation of different coalitions, we employ the data on the net number of likely mentions. For each coalition possibility, market actors estimate the probability that the net number of likely mentions will be greater than zero – i.e., whether there will be more "likely" mentions than "unlikely" mentions of that coalition.

On days when a coalition possibility is not mentioned, the data are coded as missing. While this is an imperfect measure of the probability of different coalitions, it does provide a way to estimate changes in the perceptions of market actors.[2]

The prior beliefs of market actors condition the effect of each day's news stories about coalition formation. We assume that the parameters that constitute the prior density function are normally distributed and informative. The posterior also follows a normal distribution. Market actors update beliefs about the probability of a positive net number of "likely" mentions using the data from news stories each day. We use Bayes' theorem to calculate this posterior probability (Granato 1996):

$$\theta_t = P(\theta_{t-1}|\text{Net Likely Mentions}) = L(\theta_t|\text{Net Likely Mentions})^* P(\theta_t).$$

Appendix 6.3 indicates the exact formulae used to calculate the posteriors.

Figure 6.3 indicates the evolution of the posterior beliefs concerning the probability of a positive number of likely mentions for the SPO–ÖVP, ÖVP–FPO, and SPO–FPO coalitions. Our measure captures the uncertainties about an SPO–ÖVP coalition, particularly just after the election. Indeed, the initial negativity about a potential SPO–ÖVP coalition depresses

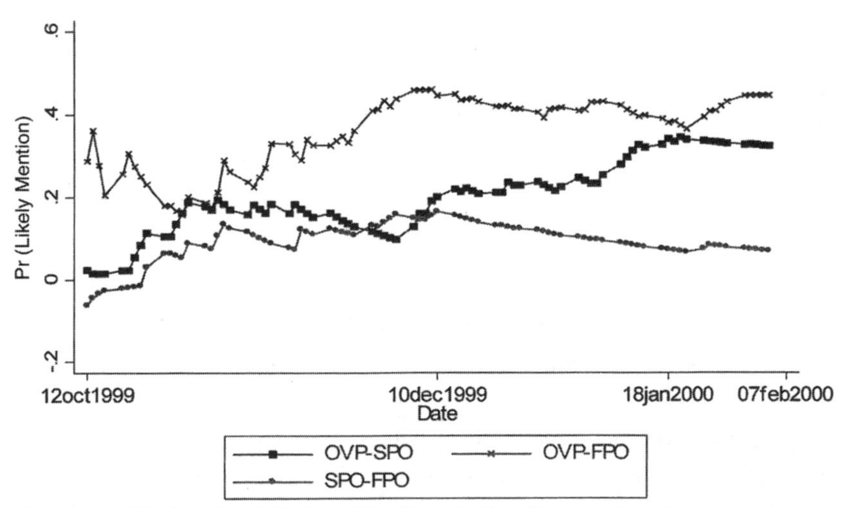

Figure 6.3. Updated beliefs about likelihood of coalitions: Austria.

[2] In particular, this measure does not account for the compositional nature of the coalition formation problem. That is, our measured probabilities for each coalition are independent of one another – an increase in one probability is not necessarily accompanied by a decrease in the other probabilities.

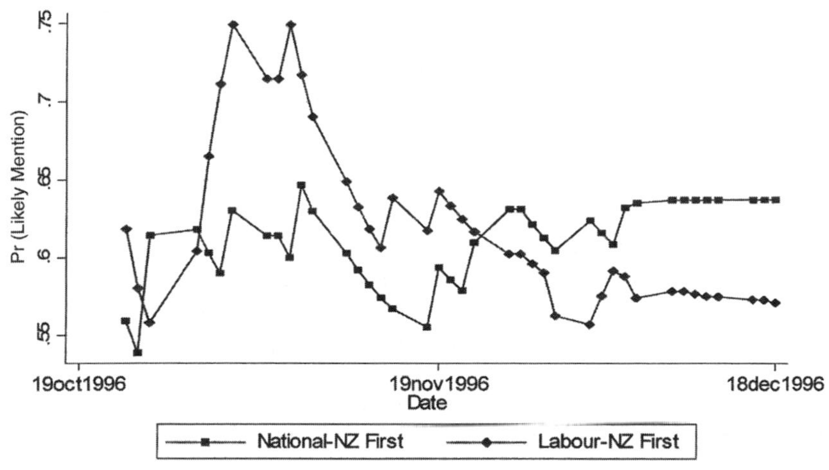

Figure 6.4. Updated beliefs about likelihood of coalitions: New Zealand.

the subsequent probabilities throughout much of the negotiation period. Instead, the probabilities of a likely mention are always highest for an ÖVP–FPO coalition. The pattern of posterior beliefs about the potential ÖVP–FPO coalition suggest that market actors anticipated the eventual partnership *much earlier* in the negotiation process than indicated by the narrative overview or the raw data. The probability of a positive mention for the ÖVP–FPO increases throughout the early part of the negotiation process, crossing the 0.4 threshold on November 29 and hovering there for the rest of the process. This analysis suggests that market actors were not surprised by the formation of an ÖVP–FPO coalition. Instead, they anticipated the result long before the collapse of the SPO–ÖVP negotiations.

Figure 6.4 shows the evolution of posterior beliefs for the New Zealand case. These probabilities again reflect the process of negotiation and media speculation. Shortly after the election, a Labour–NZ First coalition appears most likely. But, in mid-November, the probability of a positive number of net likely mentions for a National–NZ First begins to grow and quickly surpasses the potential Labour coalition. As with the Austrian case, the analysis suggests that market actors anticipated the eventual result well in advance of the end of negotiations.

THE TEST: PREDICTING SHORT-TERM INTEREST RATES FOR GOVERNMENT DEBT

We test whether information about the bargaining process affects interest rates on government bonds. We anticipate that news about bargaining will affect interest rates only when it affects beliefs of market actors about the relative likelihood of different coalition possibilities.

The Data

To assess the influence of cabinet bargaining on markets, we examine the behavior of market determined interest rates for government bonds in Austria and New Zealand during the respective coalition negotiation periods. Market data are the daily closing prices of government bonds issued at various maturities.[3] Table 6.1 provides descriptive statistics.

Table 6.1. *Descriptive statistics*

Austria

Variable	Mean	Std. Dev.	Minimum	Maximum
Δr_t (change in the short rate)	0.003	0.023	−0.106	0.089
S_t (spread between the long and short rate)	0.568	0.086	0.403	0.732
Net mentions SPO–ÖVP	−0.998	3.495	−13	13
Net mentions ÖVP–SPO	3.045	15.289	−6	99
Net mentions SPO–FPO	−1.263	1.232	−8	1
Posterior SPO–ÖVP	0.200	0.091	0.015	0.345
Posterior ÖVP–FPO	0.359	0.087	0.157	0.461
Posterior SPO–FPO	−0.005	0.395	−1.611	0.166

N = 84

New Zealand

Variable	Mean	Std. Dev.	Minimum	Maximum
Δr_t (change in the short rate)	−0.006	0.028	−0.117	0.102
S_t (spread between the long and short rate)	−0.248	0.069	−0.398	−0.063
Net mentions National–NZ First	5.818	20.843	0	126
Net mentions Labour–NZ First	−0.288	1.525	−6	1
Posterior National–NZ First	0.611	0.027	0.539	0.647
Posterior Labour–NZ First	0.620	0.054	0.557	0.749

N = 40

[3] We are grateful to Helmut Stix of the National Bank of Austria for generously providing the Austrian data.

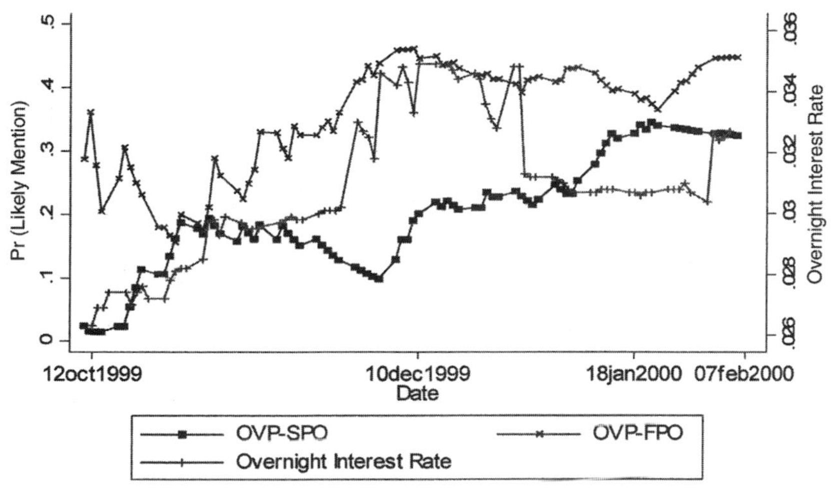

Figure 6.5. Coalition bargaining and interest rates: Austria.

Figure 6.5 shows the evolution of the probability that an ÖVP–FPO coalition and an ÖVP–SPO coalition would receive a net likely mention and the overnight interest rate on Austrian government debt during the negotiation period. Throughout the early part of the negotiations, both the probability for the ÖVP–FPO coalition and the short-term interest rates increase. Short term rates fall sharply at the end of December, after the resumption of SPO–ÖVP negotiations. But they jump right back up once an ÖVP–FPO coalition becomes a reality. One explanation of this pattern may stem from the unprecedented nature of an ÖVP–FPO coalition. Although market actors could foresee this coalition, they did not know what its policy program would entail. Short-term interest rate increases, therefore, might reflect this uncertainty about the coalition's policy priorities. A second interpretation rests on the disjuncture between market beliefs about which coalition would form and actual events. Interest rates peak just as the probability of a net positive likely mention for the ÖVP-FPO peaks – but it is also around this time that the ÖVP reverses field and begins negotiations with the SPO. Market actors could have responded to this unanticipated event by pushing up interest rates.

Figure 6.6 also shows how interest rates in New Zealand evolved during the negotiation period. Throughout most of the bargaining, interest rates hold steady, as if market actors are taking a "wait-and-see" attitude toward the coalition formation process. It is only after the National–NZ First coalition becomes apparent in early December that interest rates fall. Although the new coalition promised more spending, the fall in interest

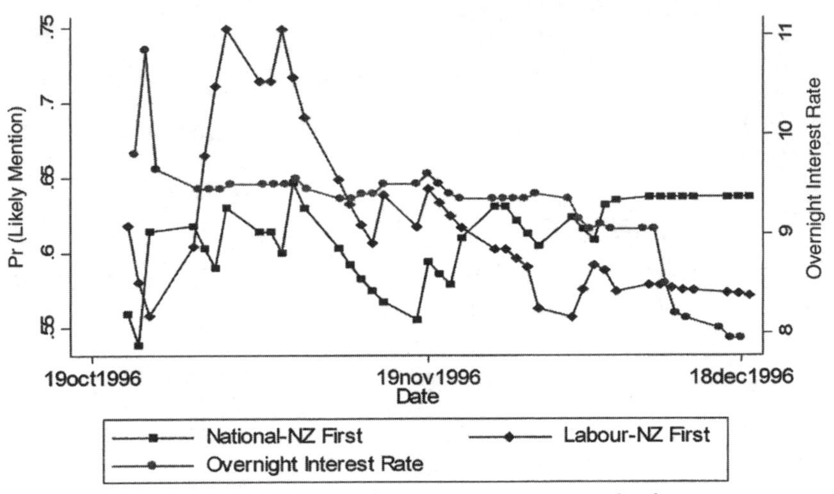

Figure 6.6. Coalition bargaining and interest rates: New Zealand.

rates could have reflected market relief at the continuation of a right government.

In both cases, short-term interest rates appear to respond to changes in posterior beliefs about the probability of a likely mention for different coalitions. We next describe a more formal test.

Explaining Changes in Short Term Interest Rates

An enormous literature from economics and finance models the level and change in interest rates. The dominant model of the term structure of interest rates – a model that links short-term to long-term interest rates – is the expectations theory. Derived from rational expectations and the efficient markets hypothesis, the expectations theory argues that the behavior of long-term interest rates is determined entirely by expected changes in short-term interest rates.[4] While there are a large number of different implementations of the expectations theory for the term structure (see Shiller 1990 and Cuthbertson 1996 for reviews), we use the model

[4] While a large empirical literature rejects the implications of the expectations hypothesis, it remains a valuable and essential tool in understanding how interest rates evolve. As King and Kurmann note: "While this [the expectations theory of the term structure] has strong implications that have been rejected in many studies, it nonetheless seems to contain important elements of truth. Therefore, many central bankers and other practitioners of monetary policy continue to apply it as an admittedly imperfect yet useful benchmark" (2002, p. 49).

developed by Shiller (1979) and implemented by Campbell and Shiller (1987) among others.[5]

Shiller's version of the expectations theory is based on the assumption that the yield expected by speculators holding long-term bonds is equal to a constant term premium plus a weighted average of current and expected future short rates.[6] Let R_t^L be the long-term rate of return and let r_t denote the one-period (or short-term) interest rate. According to Shiller (1979) the expectations theory of the term structure is a relationship between the long and short rate that satisfies:

$$R_t^L = k + \sum_{j=0}^{\infty} w_j E_t r_{t+j} \tag{6.1}$$

where k is a constant term premia, E_t is the expectations operator given time t information, and w_j are weights whose value are determined by the duration between the long and the short rate.[7]

The Campbell–Shiller (1987) approach to testing the expectations theory of the term structure relies upon the calculation of the theoretical spread between long and short-term interest rates. Following Campbell and Shiller, Eq. (6.1) is equivalent to

$$S_t^e = k + \sum_{j=1}^{\infty} \omega_j E_t \Delta r_{t+j}$$

where S_t^e is the theoretical spread $(R_t^L - r_t)$, $\omega_j = w_j + w_{j+1} + \ldots + w_{n-1}$, and Δ denotes the first difference operator. This equation implies that the spread between the long and short rate is equal to a constant plus a linear combination of expected changes in the short term interest rate. Campbell and Shiller test the expectations theory through a comparison of actual and theoretical spreads where the theoretical spreads are calculated from forecasts of the actual spread calculated from a bivariate vector autoregression (VAR) model. The VAR models the actual spread (S_t) and changes in the short rate (Δr_t) as functions of their own and each other's past values.

[5] One major advantage of choosing these models is that this version of the model uses a linear formula for long-term yields.

[6] This holding period return is not an integral part of the model; some models argue that it reflects a risk premia while others suggest that it reflects a liquidity premia.

[7] The weights satisfy $w_j = h^j(1-h)/(1-h^n)$ where $h \equiv 1/(1+\bar{R})$ and R is the average long-term yield over the sample period.

Implicit – and important – in the Campbell–Shiller approach is the underlying assumption that forecasts of short rate changes generated from a bivariate VAR accurately (or at the very least adequately) reflect the behavior of market participants. Since expectations theory implies that the spread is an optimal forecast of a weighted average of future short rates, Campbell and Shiller argue that it is a good proxy for the wide array of information available to economic agents at time *t*.

In the test, we do not exploit the distinction between the theoretical and actual spread; rather, we take the VAR based on expectations theory as our analytical anchor and add political variables to this very simple specification. If all the information necessary for predicting future changes in interest rates is contained in the present (and lagged) values of the actual spread, then our variables of interest should not be statistically significant. If, on the other hand, political information matters, then it should have a statistically significant influence on changes in the short rate.

Results

Our implementation of the Campbell–Shiller methodology uses the overnight interest rate as the short-term rate and the interest rate on the 10-year bond as the long-term rate; the actual spread is the difference between these two rates. The substance of the results we report below does not change if we use either the 20-year or the 30-year bond as the long-term rate. We estimate a bivariate VAR where the dependent variables are, as suggested by the expectations theory, the change in the short rate and the long-short spread. Included in the VAR, and determined by likelihood ratio tests, are two lags of each dependent variable. We also include exogenous variables measuring changes in the underlying performance of 16 industrial sectors, the price of gold, the price of Brent crude and the return on the U.S. ten-year government bond. Estimated quantities for these variables are not reported for ease of presentation.

To assess the influence of news about cabinet bargaining on interest rates, we proceed in three steps. First, we include in our VAR model dates of events that are considered – ex-post – to be important during each cabinet negotiation. In a second specification, we measure political information using the net likely mentions for each pair of potential coalition partners. The third specification includes our measure of market beliefs about the probability that each coalition would get a net number of likely mentions.

We first consider the results of the Austrian case. Our initial specification of the VAR model includes dummy variables for important events in the bargaining process (results not presented). In neither the short-rate or in the spread equations are any of these variables statistically significant.[8] These events did not appear to have any effect on the market for government bonds.

Table 6.2 contains the results of the other two VAR models.[9] For ease of presentation, we show only the coefficients and standard errors for the variables measuring political information and suppress the coefficients for the lagged endogenous variables. Column 1 includes the number of net likely mentions for potential coalition partners for the model of changes in the short-term interest rate (top panel) and the spread (bottom panel). Surprisingly, none of the three political variables is statistically significant in either equation. We checked to see if this result was due, at least in part, to collinearity by examining the correlations between the measures (never greater than 0.3) and, in alternative specifications, by dropping one of the measures from the model. No test revealed collinearity as a culprit; raw measures of information arrival into the market do not cause traders to bid up short-term interest rates.

If information arrival does alter the behavior of market participants – information above and beyond that captured in the actual spread – that information will be conditioned by their prior expectations. We examine this idea by including the measures of market beliefs about the ÖVP–FPO, SPO–ÖVP, and SPO–FPO coalitions (results in column 2). In the short-rate model, these measures are all statistically significant, indicating that they provide information about interest rate movements. The ÖVP–FPO measure is positive, as suggested by Fig. 6.3 – as markets came to believe a potential ÖVP–FPO would get more favorable media coverage, short term interest rates increase. In contrast, the estimate for the SPO-ÖVP measure is negative – as their assessment of this coalition improved, short-term interest rates declined. (The ÖVP–FPO measure and the SPO–ÖVP measure are essentially uncorrelated ($r = 0.06$).) In alternative specifications, we included the dummy variables for important dates (not reported).

[8] If these dummy variables are lagged then the variables for December 5 and December 9 are statistically significant and are positive for the short-rate equation and negative for the spread equation. Lagging these variables, however, does not seem appropriate in that the news stories appear in the morning paper and the interest rates – being closing prices – reflect the behavior of speculators during the trading day.

[9] Diagnostic tests show that the residuals from these models pass tests for residual normality, serial correlation, and heteroscedasticity.

Table 6.2. *Vector autoregression results: Austria*

Δ Overnight Rate (Δr_t)	I	II
Net mentions SPO–ÖVP	–0.000	
	(0.001)	
Net mentions ÖVP–FPO	0.000	
	(0.000)	
Net mentions SPO–FPO	0.002	
	(0.002)	
Posterior SPO–ÖVP		–0.078**
		(0.034)
Posterior ÖVP–FPO		0.086**
		(0.042)
Posterior SPO–FPO		0.316**
		(0.102)
Constant	–0.021	–0.175**
	(0.016)	(0.053)
Spread (s_t)		
Net mentions SPO–ÖVP	–0.000	
	(0.001)	
Net mentions ÖVP–FPO	–0.000	
	(0.000)	
Net mentions SPO–FPO	–0.001	
	(0.002)	
Posterior SPO–ÖVP		0.084**
		(0.036)
Posterior ÖVP–FPO		–0.093**
		(0.045)
Posterior SPO–FPO		–0.380**
		(0.108)
Constant	0.027	0.208**
	(0.017)	(0.056)
N	84	84

Both models include two lags of the endogenous variables and a set of exogenous variables comprised of the change in the price of gold, the change in the price of Brent crude and the change in the 10-year U.S. treasury bond rate.

The models pass diagnostic tests for residual serial correlation, normality and heteroscedasticity at the 0.05 level.

*$p < 0.10$.

**$p < 0.05$.

The inclusion of these variables did not affect the significance of the belief measures. None of the dummy variables was ever significant with one exception: December 9, the day President Kestil formally asked the SPO to form a coalition. The estimate of the December 9 dummy variable was negative. These results suggest that markets bid up interest rates in response to the policy uncertainty of an ÖVP–FPO coalition. When the traditional SPO–ÖVP coalition – with a more predictable policy outcome – appeared more likely, interest rates dropped.

It is possible that market behavior may have influenced the negotiation process. Politicians might have altered their bargaining strategies based on the response of the markets to alternative coalition possibilities. That is, changes in either the short term (overnight) interest rate or the interest rate spread could have influenced the probability that a particular coalition will form. In the language of vector autoregression, the measures of posterior beliefs may not be strictly exogenous to movements in government determined interest rates. To evaluate this possibility, we estimate an additional VAR model that includes the interest rates (the change in the short rate and the long-short spread) as well as the three posterior beliefs as endogenous variables. The model includes two lags of these five variables as well as the battery of control variables. The results, not reported, provide no support for the conjecture that the posterior probabilities of different coalitions are a function of interest rate changes.

Granger causality tests (Table 6.3) show that neither the change in the overnight interest rate nor the spread between the long and short term rate have a statistically significant impact on any of the three posterior beliefs about which coalition will form. Market behavior, therefore, appears to not to have influenced the process of coalition formation in Austria. This null result is plausible: politicians caught up in the process of cabinet bargaining must already balance a variety of interests and concerns. Unless there is a large and unanticipated shift in asset prices, they are unlikely to pay attention to routine market fluctuations. Alternatively, the null result may reflect the limitations of our simple measure of cabinet negotiations. That is, our constructed probabilities may not pick up how politicians subtly respond to market behavior during the bargaining process.

We performed a similar exercise with the New Zealand case. In the first specification of the VAR model, we included dummy variables for "important" dates in the negotiation process (results not reported). As before, none of these dummy variables achieved statistical significance in either the short-term interest rate or spread equations. By themselves, these events do not appear to have an impact on the bond market.

Table 6.3. *Granger causality tests, Austria*

Equation	Excluded	$\chi 2$	Prob
Δ Overnight rate (Δr_t)	Spread (s_t)	10.307	0.006
Δ Overnight rate (Δr_t)	Posterior SPO–ÖVP	5.492	0.064
Δ Overnight rate (Δr_t)	Posterior ÖVP–FPO	3.598	0.165
Δ Overnight rate (Δr_t)	Posterior SPO–FPO	7.189	0.027
Δ Overnight rate (Δr_t)	ALL	12.042	0.149
Spread (s_t)	Δ Overnight rate (Δr_t)	1.354	0.508
Spread (s_t)	Posterior SPO–ÖVP	6.574	0.037
Spread (s_t)	Posterior ÖVP–FPO	3.653	0.161
Spread (s_t)	Posterior SPO–FPO	10.272	0.006
Spread (s_t)	ALL	14.572	0.068
Posterior SPO–ÖVP	Δ Overnight rate (Δr_t)	2.007	0.367
Posterior SPO–ÖVP	Spread (s_t)	2.482	0.289
Posterior SPO–ÖVP	Posterior ÖVP–FPO	3.822	0.148
Posterior SPO–ÖVP	Posterior SPO–FPO	3.434	0.180
Posterior SPO–ÖVP	ALL	13.223	0.104
Posterior ÖVP–FPO	Δ Overnight rate (Δr_t)	2.317	0.314
Posterior ÖVP–FPO	Spread (s_t)	2.748	0.253
Posterior ÖVP–FPO	Posterior SPO–ÖVP	2.827	0.243
Posterior ÖVP–FPO	Posterior SPO–FPO	0.212	0.899
Posterior ÖVP–FPO	ALL	9.984	0.266
Posterior SPO–FPO	Δ Overnight rate (Δr_t)	3.703	0.157
Posterior SPO–FPO	Spread (s_t)	3.332	0.189
Posterior SPO–FPO	Posterior SPO–ÖVP	1.739	0.419
Posterior SPO–FPO	Posterior ÖVP–FPO	4.331	0.115
Posterior SPO–FPO	ALL	14.437	0.071

Granger causality test is based on a VAR with variables (and two lags) included as endogenous variables. A set of exogenous variables comprised of the change in the price of gold, the change in the price of Brent crude and the change in the 10-year U.S. treasury bond rate are also included.

Table 6.4 reports the results of the VAR models for the New Zealand case. Columns 1 and 2 include the number of net likely mentions for potential coalition partners for the model of changes in the short-term interest rate and the spread, respectively. The net number of likely mentions for the National–NZ First coalition has a small, negative impact on interest rates. The other variables fail to attain statistical significance.

Table 6.4. *Vector autoregression results: New Zealand*

Δ Overnight Rate (Δr_t)	I	II
Net mentions National–NZF	−0.001**	
	(0.000)	
Net mentions Labour–NZF	−0.000	
	(0.004)	
Posterior National–NZF		−0.435**
		(0.134)
Posterior Labour–NZF		0.113*
		(0.062)
Constant	−0.016	0.194**
	(0.018)	(0.098)
Spread (s_t)		
Net mentions National–NZF	0.000	
	(0.000)	
Net mentions Labour–NZF	−0.006	
	(0.005)	
Posterior National–NZF		0.512**
		(0.148)
Posterior Labour–NZF		−0.122*
		(0.069)
Constant	0.023	−0.231**
	(0.022)	(0.108)
N	40	40

Both models include two lags of the endogenous variables and a set of exogenous variables comprised of the change in the price of gold, the change in the price of Brent crude and the change in the 10-year U.S. treasury bond rate.
The models pass diagnostic tests for residual serial correlation, normality and heteroscedasticity at the 0.05 level.
*$p<0.10$.
**$p<0.05$.

Columns 3 and 4 report the results of including the measures of market beliefs for the two main coalition possibilities. As in the Austrian case, these measures are statistically significant in the short-rate model, indicating that they provide information about interest rate movements. The probability of a net likely mention for National–NZ First has a negative parameter

Table 6.5. *Granger causality tests, New Zealand*

Equation	Excluded	χ^2	Prob
Δ Overnight rate (Δr_t)	Spread (s_t)	5.706	0.058
Δ Overnight rate (Δr_t)	Posterior National–NZF	3.374	0.185
Δ Overnight rate (Δr_t)	Posterior Labour–NZF	4.324	0.079
Δ Overnight rate (Δr_t)	ALL	14.847	0.021
Spread (s_t)	Δ Overnight rate (Δr_t)	13.105	0.001
Spread (s_t)	Posterior National–NZF	3.801	0.149
Spread (s_t)	Posterior Labour–NZF	4.908	0.086
Spread (s_t)	ALL	24.110	0.000
Posterior National–NZF	Δ Overnight rate (Δr_t)	1.585	0.453
Posterior National–NZF	Spread (s_t)	0.109	0.947
Posterior National–NZF	Posterior Labour–NZF	3.642	0.162
Posterior National–NZF	ALL	12.861	0.045
Posterior Labour–NZF	Δ Overnight rate (Δr_t)	0.691	0.708
Posterior Labour–NZF	Spread (s_t)	0.171	0.918
Posterior Labour–NZF	Posterior National–NZF	2.396	0.302
Posterior Labour–NZF	ALL	9.729	0.137

Granger causality test is based on a VAR with variables (and two lags) included as endogenous variables. A set of exogenous variables comprised of the change in the price of gold, the change in the price of Brent crude and the change in the 10-year U.S. treasury bond rate are also included.

estimate: interest rates fall as this coalition appears more likely. In contrast, interest rates are higher as the probability of a likely mention for the Labour alternative increases.

As with Austria, we also evaluated whether interest rate changes influenced the posterior probabilities of alternative coalition possibilities. Granger causality tests (Table 6.5) also yield no evidence that interest rate movements affect the posterior belief regarding the likelihood of which coalition will form.

CONCLUSION

In attempting to assess the impact of democratic political events on financial markets, it is important not only to consider the information available to market actors, but also how they process that information. The prior beliefs of market actors will condition the response to information arrival. News that causes market actors to change their expectations of political outcomes is more likely to lead to a change in behavior. In contrast, asset owners will not shift their portfolios in response to information that reinforces expectations.

In this chapter, we investigated two episodes of cabinet formation. By focusing on these two specific events, we were able to develop measures that accurately reflected both the information available to market actors and the timing of when that information became available. Further, we employed a Bayesian transformation of the data to capture the prior beliefs of market actors. The results indicate that the process of forming and updating beliefs do strongly influence how markets respond to political events. In the next chapter, we perform a similar test on a different political event: the 2000 U.S. Presidential election.

APPENDIX 6.1: CODING INSTRUCTIONS

GENERAL INSTRUCTIONS

Instructions for filling in each category in the coding sheet are outlined below. The articles need to be coded by paragraph. For each source, code each coalition discussed in the paragraph.

Every paragraph mentioning a potential coalition should be coded.

Quotes from the past or about the past should be coded as if mentioned or discussing the present. It doesn't matter if the statements are about what happened last week, that day, or tomorrow as long as it is about the current government building process.

Don't use the later contextual clues to code earlier parts of the article. Code only by information in that particular sentence or what has come before. If something is a quotation, however, then later information identifying the speaker of the quotation can be used.

Finally, if you can‘t decide if a statement has something to be coded, then code as 999 if it takes more than 30 seconds to make the choice.

LINE BY LINE INSTRUCTIONS

Source: This category captures all sources who discuss the various possible coalitions among the political parties. The source is the organizational affiliation of the person discussing the potential coalition rather than the person/organization conducting the action. For example, a sentence that reads "ÖVP and SPO are meeting today" should be coded as media, because the source here is the journalist explaining what is happening, not the ÖVP or SPO; they are participants, not sources in this case. But indirect quotations should be coded according to attribution. For example, "ÖVP and SPO are meeting today" should be coded 170. But "An ÖVP spokesperson announced that ÖVP and SPO are meeting today" should be coded as 111.

Action: This category captures the action discussed by the source. The source could give conditional statements about coalitions, definitive statements about coalitions, or could participate in informal or formal meetings or make actual formal offers to join a coalition. The difference between conditional and definitive statements is that conditional statements assert that the action will take place only if some conditions are met. The key is to distinguish between signals of what might or might not happen and clear statements of what will happen. Definitive statements are like lines in the sand, whereas conditional statements suggest that there are multiple possible options in the future. If the statement is just the opinion of the source, code it as 210. If the source is discussing what happened in a meeting, code it 230 or 240 as appropriate. Finally, if a source suggests that one party would like to make a formal offer to another, code it as 250, even if the offer hasn't happened yet. The suggestion that a formal offer might be on the table is a serious claim, and should be coded as an actual offer.

Examples:

Conditional: "ÖVP would like to rejoin the SPO coalition, but there are issues that need to be resolved" or "ÖVP and FPO could still work out an agreement."

Definitive: "ÖVP will decide next week whether to withdraw its promise to go into the opposition" or "SPO cannot accept Haider as a participant in the government."

Coalition: The category codes the coalition being discussed by the source. When the party of the potential Prime Minister is given, use the more specific codes, otherwise just use the general code. If the story talks about a party choosing to go into opposition, rather than entering a coalition, code it as the party in opposition code. But the choice under discussion must be about the party itself choosing to go into opposition, not ending up in opposition because two other parties decide to form a coalition. For example, "ÖVP is thinking about whether to go into opposition after the election results" would be coded as 311. But "SPO may end up in opposition because ÖVP and FPO are close to agreement" should be coded as 330. There is also a general code for any coalition. Use this code for statements that discuss either the need for any government to form or speculation that no government may be possible, which will often be framed as a sense that new elections will be necessary.

Potential for success of coalition. This category codes for the potential of the coalition to work out. If the source thinks the coalition will happen, then code positive; if the source thinks the coalition will not work out, negative. If the source is ambivalent or does not make a particular claim about the potential of success, code mixed. The question to ask is "Will this coalition happen?".

Evaluation of coalition. This category codes the source's evaluation of the coalition's ability to govern Austria well. The question to ask in this category is "Does the source think the coalition ought to govern Austria?"

The previous category codes for whether or not the coalition will happen; this category codes for whether or not it should happen. If the source thinks the coalition would be good for Austria, code 510. If the source thinks it would be detrimental for Austria, code 520. If the source thinks the effects would be mixed or that the coalition needs some changes to work well, code 530. If the source is neutral, code 540.

APPENDIX 6.2: CODING CATEGORIES

100 Source

110 ÖVP Party Leader (Schüssel)
111 ÖVP Party Other
120 SPO Party Leader (Klima)
121 SPO Party Other
130 FPO Party Leader (Haider)
131 FPO Party Other
140 Green Party Leader (Van der Bellen)
141 Green Party Other
150 Austrian President (Klestil)
160 European Union (Not specific)
161 European Council/Council of Ministers
162 European Parliament
163 European Commission
164 Specific Member State
170 Media: Journalistic commentary on coalitions
171 Austrian Business Leaders
172 Public, including polls on various coalitions
173 Other Austrian elites
180 Other sources, including American and Israeli responses

200 Action

210 Conditional statement: party might enter this coalition, if conditions are right; a testing of the waters approach; or actions conditional on those of other actors in the process

220 Definitive statement: party definitely wants to enter this coalition, party will pursue this course of action, no conditions on action

230 Informal meetings between parties, past or present
240 Formal meetings between parties, past or present (with formateur)
250 Formal offers

300 Coalition under discussion

302 New elections
305 All party government
310 ÖVP minority
311 ÖVP in opposition
320 ÖVP–SPO (unclear who is PM)
321 ÖVP–SPO (with ÖVP as PM)
322 ÖVP–SPO (with SPO as PM)

330 ÖVP–FPO (unclear who is PM)
331 ÖVP–FPO (with ÖVP AS PM)
332 ÖVP–FPO (with FPO as PM)
340 ÖVP–Green (unclear who is PM)
341 ÖVP–Green (with ÖVP as PM)
342 ÖVP–Green (with Green as PM)
344 ÖVP with any other party
345 "Best heads" government SP–VP–Green (excludes FPO)
350 SPO Minority
351 SPO in opposition
360 SPO–FPO (unclear who is PM)
361 SPO–FPO (with SPO as PM)
362 SPO–FPO (with FPO as PM)
370 SPO–Green (unclear who is PM)
371 SPO–Green (with SPO as PM)
372 SPO–Green (with Green as PM)
374 SPO with any other party
380 FPO Minority
381 FPO in opposition
390 FPO-Green (unclear who is PM)
391 FPO–Green (with FPO as PM)
392 FPO–Green (with Green as PM)
394 FPO with any other party
396 Green with any other party
399 Green minority

400 Potential success of the coalition
410 Positive potential for coalition: coalition is likely to happen
420 Negative potential for coalition: coalition not likely to happen
430 Mixed potential for coalition: coalition may or may not happen
440 Neutral on potential; purely evaluative

500 Evaluation of the coalition
510 Positive evaluation of the coalition: The coalition would be good for Austria and should be pursued
520 Negative evaluation of the coalition: The coalition would be bad for Austria and should not be pursued
530 Mixed evaluation of the coalition: The coalition has its good and bad sides or needs work to become good governing coalition
540 Neutral evaluation of the coalition: Does not provide an evaluation of the coalition

999 No data

APPENDIX 6.3: UPDATING BELIEFS ABOUT "LIKELY" MENTIONS FOR EACH COALITION

The data on market beliefs was constructed using formulae from Granato (1996). The standard Bayesian updating formula to calculate the posterior mean, θ_t, for a normal prior distribution with informative priors is:

$$\theta_t = \frac{(1/\sigma_{t-1}^2)\theta_{t-1} + (N\mu/\sigma_t^{*2})}{(1/\sigma_{t-1}^2) + (N/\sigma_t^{*2})} \tag{A6.3.1}$$

where

θ_{t-1} = mean of prior probability that the net number of likely mentions > 0

σ_{t-1}^2 = prior variance

μ = data based probability that the net number of likely mentions > 0

σ_t^{*2} = data based variance

N = sample size at time t.

The formula to calculate the prior variance is:

$$\sigma_t^2 = \frac{1}{1/\sigma_{t-1}^2 + N/\sigma_t^{*2}}. \tag{A6.3.2}$$

In order to calculate μ, we convert the net number of likely mentions to a probability using the simple formula for z-scores:

$$z^* = \frac{-(\text{net likely mentions})}{\sqrt{\sigma_t^*/N}} \tag{A6.3.3}$$

and

$$\mu = \text{normprob}(z^*). \tag{A6.3.4}$$

7

Time, Shares, and Florida: The 2000 Presidential Election and Stock Market Volatility

Modern presidential elections tend to be predictable: the winner is known long before election day. With the combination of lop-sided vote totals and sophisticated voter surveys, television news reports can confidently predict a winner even before polls close on the west coast. The 2000 contest between the Democratic candidate, Vice President Al Gore, and Republican George Bush, Governor of Texas, however, did not conform to this pattern. Throughout the campaign, polls had the candidates running close. The unpredictability of the race made markets jittery. One portfolio manager commented, "The election is so important and the outcome is so unknown and the effect of it is so unknown that things are on knife edges out there."[1] Despite the closeness of the race, most Americans assumed that they would quickly learn the identity of the next president on the evening of November 7th, thanks to the wonders of exit polling. But the actual vote totals were so close that television analysts could not conclude who would win the majority of electoral college votes. Indeed, the news anchors were embarrassed when, after calling Florida as a Gore state early in the evening, they had to switch their call, classifying it as a toss-up an hour later. The media then called Florida for Bush later in the night, prompting Gore to call Bush to concede. But a few hours later, it was still not certain how Florida would vote, and news organizations took Florida out of the Bush column. Gore called Bush back. The night ended without a clear winner.

Presidential elections affect stock market performance. Most studies look at how markets behave in the days and months prior to an election or focus on how markets respond to the selection of a Democrat or

[1] Alan Kral, Portfolio Manager, Trevor Stewart Burton (CNNFN, 3 November 2000).

Republican.[2] We, too, are interested in how presidential elections affect stock market performance but, in this chapter, we take advantage of the unique circumstances of the 2000 presidential race. We examine how the announcement of state-level election results during the night of November 7–8, 2000 affected asset price behavior in overnight trading markets.

We expect that the prior beliefs about the likely election winner will condition how these markets respond to the announcement of projected election results. Information that confirms market beliefs will have little or no effect on market behavior. The announcement that Gore carried Massachusetts came as no surprise to anyone. In contrast, information that creates a major change in the probability of winning is likely to affect how traders evaluate the future policy environment. Network projections about the race in Florida, therefore, are likely to generate price changes as traders adjust their expectations. Using state-level polling data, we develop a unique measure of the probability that Gore will win a majority of electoral college votes. We update this measure as states are called to reflect the changing beliefs of market participants. We examine minute-by-minute transactions data for trading on two major futures prices, the NASDAQ 100 Index and the S&P 500 Index, and the U.S. Dollar-Japanese Yen exchange rate. That is, we can ascertain how the announcement that California went for Gore or that Iowa voted for Bush affected these markets.

By focusing on overnight returns, we isolate the effect of political information on market behavior. Since campaigns or cabinet negotiations occur over a period of days, one might argue that changes in market behavior during these processes reflect changes in economic fundamentals rather than political developments. But during the night of November 7–8, no macroeconomic announcements were made; no earnings were reported; interest rates did not change. The only information that mattered centered on who was likely to become the next President of the United States.

In this chapter we also introduce a concern with financial market volatility. In financial markets, the variance around the evolution of asset prices represents the notion of volatility. Volatility serves as an indicator for uncertainty surrounding the future path of asset prices. Indeed, the anticipated (or implied) volatility of an asset is one of the key factors

[2] For example, see Herron 2000; Herron et al. 1999; Roberts 1994; Leblang and Mukerhjee 2004; Gemmill 1992, 1995; Lin and Roberts 2001.

that traders use to price options, making it of particular concern. We discuss the motivation for this focus and also a variety of methodological tools to estimate volatility.

MEASURING THE OVERNIGHT ELECTION RETURNS

The 2000 election reminded Americans of a fact they learned in high school civics classes: the President is not directly elected. Instead, a winning presidential candidate must capture a majority of votes in the electoral college. Electoral college votes are determined by the presidential votes cast in each particular state. With two exceptions (Maine and Nebraska), the race for electoral votes is a winner-take-all proposition – that is, the winning candidate in each state is entitled to one hundred percent of the state's electoral college votes.

Polls indicated that the 2000 race would be close in terms of popular vote, so the logic of the electoral college became an overriding concern for those who wished to predict the outcome of the presidential election. As the polls closed on the night of November 7, the initial results indicated that the race would not produce a decisive win for either candidate, but rather come down to how a few key swing states voted, notably Florida with its 25 electoral college votes.

We measure the arrival of electoral information on the night of November 7–8 by constructing a variable that estimates the probability that Gore will win a majority of electors in the electoral college and, thus, become the 43rd President. Following the logic of the electoral college, this measure is based on state level polls for each of the 50 states and exploits the fact that these polls contain a degree of sampling uncertainty. As each state is called over the evening of November 7th and into the morning of November 8th, we update this measure and then employ it as a proxy for how traders update their priors regarding the likelihood of a Gore victory.

Table 7.1 reports the last poll for each state prior to the election, including the sample size of the poll, the percentage of respondents responding with a preference for Gore (Gore%), for Bush (Bush%), and the share of the two-party vote for Gore (Gore/(Bush + Gore)).[3] Using this information we test the null hypothesis that, in the population, Gore's share of the two party vote is greater than or equal to 0.50001 against the

[3] We are grateful to Charles Franklin and Chris Wlezien for sharing these data; see Franklin (2001) and Wlezien (2001).

Table 7.1. *State polls and priors*

State	Sample size	Gore %	Bush %	Gore/ (Bush + Gore)	*p*-value	Electoral votes	Time called by CNN (EST)
Alaska	400	26	47	0.356	0.000	3	12:00 a.m. (B)
Alabama	625	38	55	0.409	0.000	9	8:00 p.m. (B)
Arkansas	286	44	47	0.484	0.287	6	12:12 a.m. (B)
Arizona	423	39	49	0.443	0.010	8	11:51 p.m. (B)
California	600	45	44	0.506	0.607	54	11:00 p.m. (G)
Colorado	400	38	47	0.447	0.017	8	11:41 p.m. (B)
Connecticut	447	48	32	0.600	1.000	8	8:00 p.m. (G)
Delaware	625	42	46	0.477	0.127	3	8:00 p.m. (G)
Florida	600	48	46	0.511	0.697	25	see below
Georgia	512	37	53	0.411	0.000	13	7:59 p.m. (B)
Hawaii	261	50	31	0.617	1.000	4	11:00 p.m. (G)
Iowa	603	44	43	0.506	0.609	7	5:00 a.m. (G)
Idaho	633	30	56	0.349	0.000	4	10:00 p.m. (B)
Illinois	600	50	42	0.543	0.983	22	8:00 p.m. (G)
Indiana	600	30	53	0.361	0.000	12	6:00 p.m. (B)
Kansas	600	32	55	0.368	0.000	6	8:00 p.m. (B)
Kentucky	625	41	51	0.446	0.003	8	6:00 p.m. (B)
Louisiana	660	38	46	0.452	0.007	9	9:21 p.m. (B)
Massachusetts	401	52	30	0.634	1.000	12	8:00 p.m. (G)
Maryland	627	52	38	0.578	1.000	10	8:00 p.m. (G)
Maine	400	47	36	0.566	0.996	4	10:10 p.m. (G)
Michigan	600	51	44	0.537	0.964	18	9:24 p.m. (G)
Minnesota	1015	47	37	0.560	1.000	10	10:25 p.m. (G)
Missouri	600	46	46	0.500	0.498	11	10:47 p.m. (B)
Mississippi	625	41	52	0.441	0.002	7	8:00 p.m. (B)
Montana	628	37	49	0.430	0.000	3	10:00 p.m. (B)
North Carolina	625	41	48	0.461	0.024	14	8:14 p.m. (B)
North Dakota	586	35	47	0.427	0.000	3	9:00 p.m. (B)
Nebraska	1007	31	56	0.356	0.000	5	9:00 p.m. (B)
New Hampshire	801	39	45	0.464	0.021	4	12:07 a.m. (B)
New Jersey	843	41	36	0.532	0.970	15	8:00 p.m. (G)
New Mexico	425	45	45	0.500	0.498	5	not called*
Nevada	625	43	47	0.478	0.132	4	1:31 a.m. (B)

(*continued*)

Table 7.1. *(continued)*

State	Sample size	Gore %	Bush %	Gore/ (Bush + Gore)	*p*-value	Electoral votes	Time called by CNN (EST)
New York	700	54	37	0.593	1.000	33	9:00 p.m. (G)
Ohio	600	43	50	0.462	0.032	21	9:19 p.m. (B)
Oklahoma	625	39	54	0.419	0.000	8	8:00 p.m. (B)
Oregon	600	45	44	0.506	0.607	7	not called*
Pennsylvania	600	50	42	0.543	0.983	23	9:24 p.m. (G)
Rhode Island	370	47	29	0.618	1.000	4	9:00 p.m. (G)
South Carolina	625	38	53	0.418	0.000	8	7:00 p.m. (B)
South Dakota	300	33	51	0.393	0.000	3	9:00 p.m. (B)
Tennessee	500	46	51	0.474	0.124	11	11:03 p.m. (B)
Texas	625	30	64	0.319	0.000	32	8:00 p.m. (B)
Utah	914	27	59	0.314	0.000	5	10:00 p.m. (B)
Virginia	625	41	49	0.456	0.013	13	7:33 p.m. (B)
Vermont	400	52	36	0.591	1.000	3	7:00 p.m. (G)
Washington	500	50	42	0.543	0.974	11	12:08 a.m. (G)
Wisconsin	400	39	44	0.470	0.113	11	6:21 a.m. (G)
West Virginia	536	39	41	0.488	0.280	5	10:46 p.m. (B)
Wyoming	412	32	57	0.360	0.000	3	9:00 p.m. (B)

Florida

Time	Event
7:52 p.m.	Called for Gore
8:55 p.m.	Toss-up (taken away from Gore)
1:18 a.m.	Called for Bush
2:58 a.m.	Toss-up (taken away from Bush)

* New Mexico and Oregon were not called before markets closed on November 8, 2000.

alternative hypothesis that Gore's share is less than 0.50001. The *p*-values for rejection of the null are also listed in Table 7.1. Higher *p*-values indicate the probability of making an error by rejecting the null that Gore will win the state.

For example, Gore's share of the two-party vote in Massachusetts was 63.4 percent. The *p*-value for rejection of the null that Gore would get

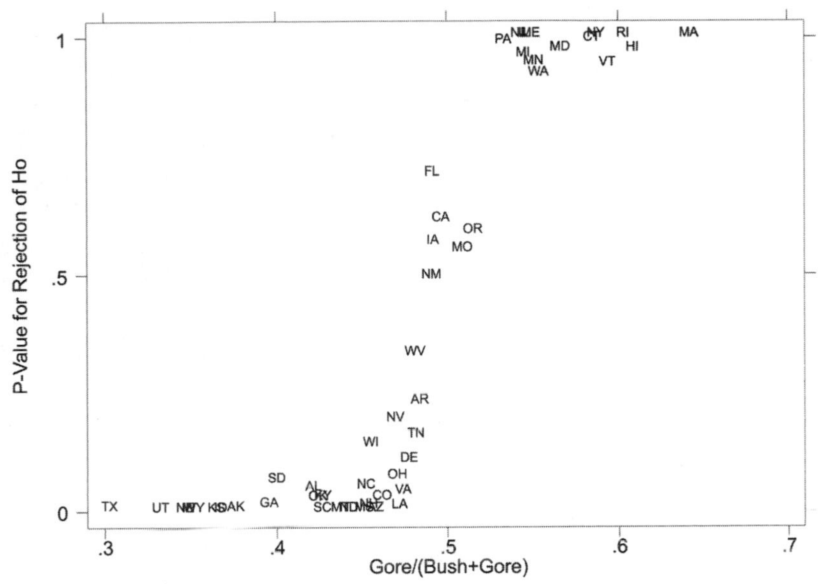

Figure 7.1. Vote shares and p-values.

at least 50 percent and win the state is 1.00, indicating that it is certain that an error will be made if that state's electoral votes are given to Bush. Likewise, the p-value for rejection of the null for Texas is 0.000, meaning that there is zero chance out of a thousand that Gore will win that state. The p-values for each state are graphed in Fig. 7.1. As one would expect, there is an S-shaped relationship between the share of the two-party vote for Gore and the p-value for rejecting the null. The states in the middle are those considered to be "toss-ups" – states that are too close to call.

Since the polls contain sampling uncertainty, there is a probability that an error will be made in rejecting the null hypothesis. The second step in variable construction exploits this uncertainty. We randomly draw a number from a uniform [0,1] distribution and create a variable Q with observations for each state. We then compare the random variable Q with the p-value for rejection of the null hypothesis. If Q is less than the p-value, then Gore wins state i and gets all of state i's electoral college votes. If Q is greater than the p-value, then Bush wins the state and its electoral college votes. We do this for each state. If Gore wins sufficient states to give him more than 270 electoral college votes, then he wins the election.

This simulation process described in the previous paragraph is repeated 1000 times. The proportion of Gore victories out of these 1000 trials represents the probability that Gore receives the 271 votes needed to win the presidency. Based on the final state polls, Gore wins in 378 out of the 1000 replications. That is, at the beginning of the evening (3:45 p.m. EST), the probability of Gore winning the electoral college vote was 0.378.

We recorded the exact time when each state was called by CNN. This information is also contained in Table 7.1. As each state is called over the course of the election night, Gore's probability of winning an electoral college victory is updated. Once a state is called, the probability of winning that state goes to either zero or one, depending on whether the state is called for Bush or for Gore. With this updated probability for a particular state, we then repeat the simulation process, giving us a variable that measures the probability of a Gore victory to the minute.

The probability that Gore wins the electoral college is graphed in Fig. 7.2. The probability of a Gore victory increases dramatically at 7:52 p.m. when Florida is called for Gore and then declines at 8:55 p.m. when CNN takes Florida from Gore's win column. The probability that Gore wins nosedives when Florida was called for Bush at 1:18 a.m., but then increases when Florida was once again labeled a "toss-up" at 2:58 a.m. At 6:21 a.m. November 8th, when Wisconsin was called, there is no still no winner, but the probability of a Gore victory has increased to around 0.65.

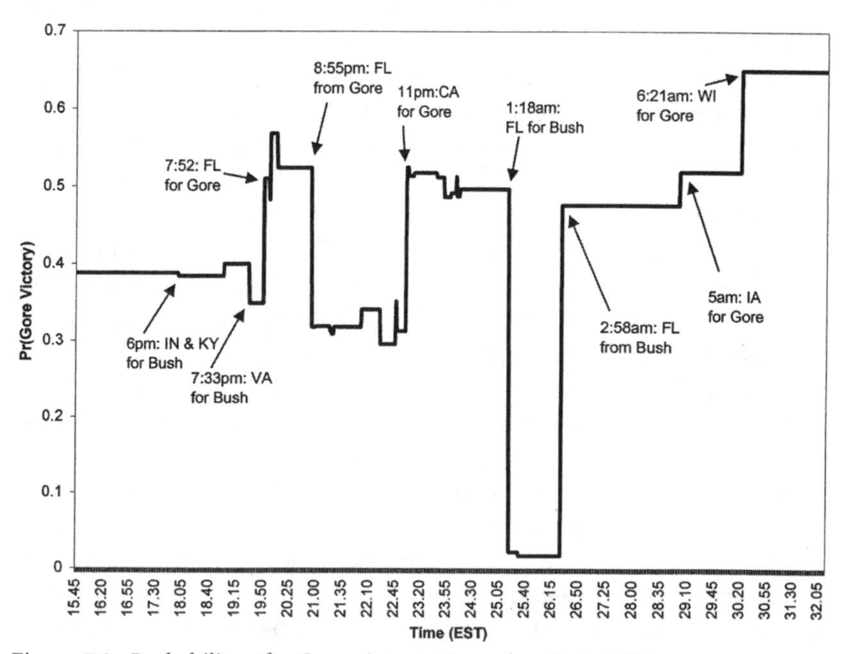

Figure 7.2. Probability of a Gore victory, November 7–8, 2000.

This measure captures the prior beliefs that market actors were likely to have about the eventual election outcome. It allows us to gauge how the calling of specific states affected those beliefs. And it allows us to have an exact time when this information became available to market actors. We use this variable to evaluate the behavior of overnight traders.

THE OVERNIGHT MARKET FOR STOCK FUTURES

The New York Stock Exchange is open for trading between the hours of 9:30 a.m. and 4:30 p.m. eastern time. It closes for the night prior to the reporting of election results. After hours, traders can trade options and futures contracts through the GLOBEX electronic trading system. GLOBEX, developed by Reuters and the Chicago Mercantile Exchange, is an automated system that provides information about trades (bid and ask prices), routs orders, and executes trades. Using the GLOBEX system, individuals can trade a wide variety of futures, options and interest rates.

The GLOBEX system reports information on the price and volume for every individual transaction during the trading session. We use this "tick" data to track the movements of two major futures[1] prices: the NASDAQ 100 Index and the S&P 500 Index.[5] These tick data were aggregated to provide the average price and total volume of trades for each minute during the trading session. To avoid overlap with the NYSE, and because we use a five minute lag in some of the models, the sample period is 4:35 p.m. (EST) on November 7th through 8:59 a.m. on November 8th. Figures 7.3 and 7.4 graph price and volume data for these two indices. Descriptive statistics for these two indices are contained in Table 7.2.

THE U.S. DOLLAR-JAPANESE YEN EXCHANGE RATE

Tokyo is home to the third largest foreign exchange trading market in the world, after markets in New York and London. The Tokyo market for the U.S. Dollar–Japanese Yen market is extraordinarily deep – average

[4] A future is a legally binding agreement to buy or sell the cash value of the asset at a specific future date. In the case of these two futures, the maturity date was November 15, 2000.

[5] Unfortunately, futures for the Dow Jones Industrial Average were not traded during November 2000.

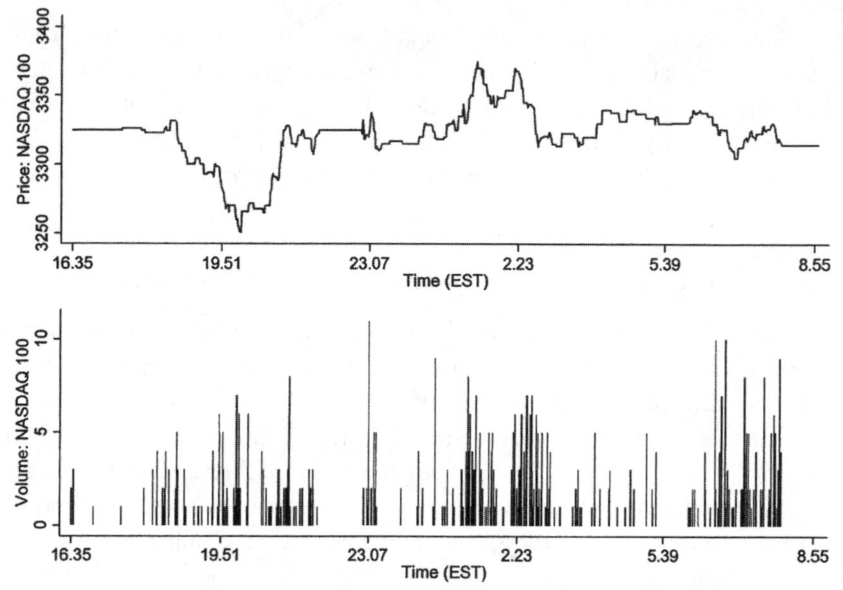

Figure 7.3. Overnight markets for NASDAQ futures.

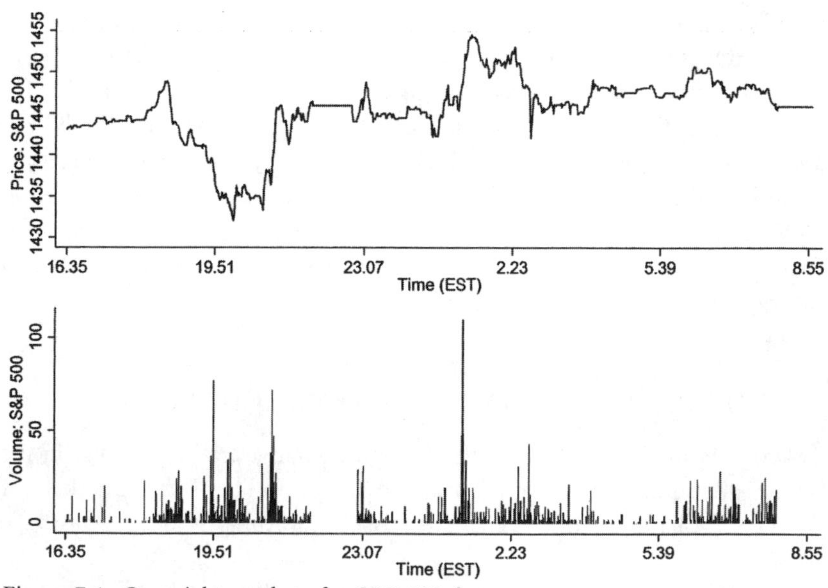

Figure 7.4. Overnight markets for S&P 500 futures.

Table 7.2. *Summary statistics and correlation for overnight models (N = 1030)*

Variable	Mean	Std. Dev.	Minimum	Maximum
D(log(SP))*100	0. 0002	0. 031	−0.296	0.199
D(log(NP))*100	−0.0002	0. 069	−0.421	0.466
Expected duration (SP)	0. 056	1. 292	−6.941	2.204
Volume SP	3.738	8. 128	0	110
Expected duration (NQ)	−1.385	0.925	−5.286	−0.183
Volume NQ	0. 646	1. 529	0	11
P(electoral victory Gore$_{t-5}$)	0. 441	0. 155	0. 021	0.657
Entropy	0.889	0.228	0.082	0.999
Summary statistics for USD/JYP (*N* = 721)				
D(log(USD/JPY))	−5.60e − 07	0.0002	−0.0007	0.001
P(electoral victory Gore$_{t-5}$)	0.398	0.142	0.021	0.55
Expected duration	0.815	0.502	0	1.792

* Correlation significant at the 0.05 level.

daily spot trades amounted to almost 9 billion dollars in 2000.[6] Normal trading hours in Tokyo occur after markets close in the United States. Consequently, trading in Tokyo on November 8 occurred as the overnight drama of U.S. Presidential election unfolded.

Figure 7.5 shows the closing price (or price at the last trade) as aggregated by minute of the dollar−yen exchange rate during the evening of November 7th (i.e., the next day in Tokyo).[7] The dollar−yen spot exchange rate traded between 107.3 to 107.8 yen per dollar. Table 7.2 contains descriptive statistics.

We examine how political information affects both the prices movements and the volatility of these on the NASDAQ futures, the S&P 500 futures, and the dollar−yen exchange rate. The next section discusses the motivation for this focus and describes the appropriate methodological tools.

[6] In 2000 the combination of voice and electronic trades for the USD−JPY exchange rate totaled 2,234,469 *million* dollars (Ueda Harlow Ltd, Currency Traders, http://www.ueda-net.co.jp/hb/eindex.html).

[7] We obtained tick data for the USD−JYP exchange rate from Snapdragon Systems Ltd, a foreign exchange trading firm located in London. We thank Adam Hartley, President of Snapdragon, for helping us obtain these data.

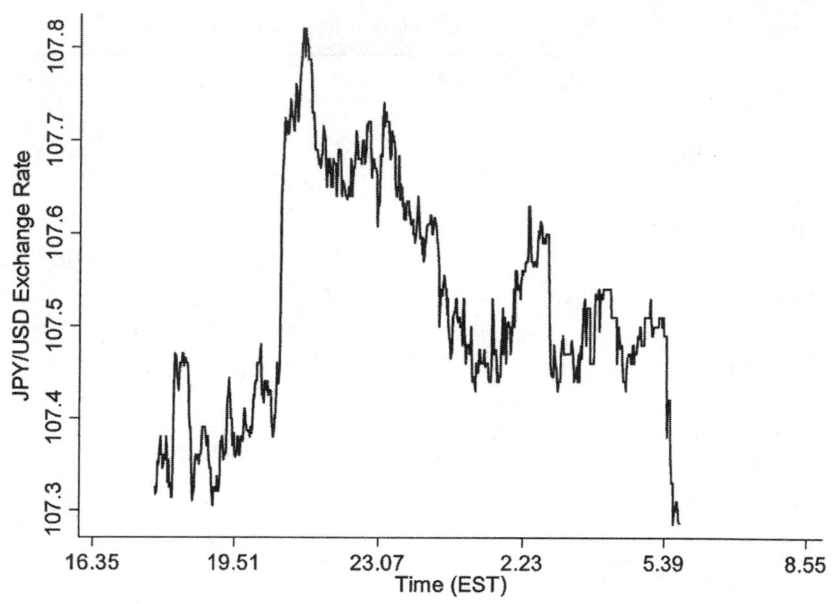

Figure 7.5. U.S. Dollar–Japanese Yen exchange rate.

ASSET PRICE VOLATILITY

High frequency data on asset prices exhibit some empirical regularities, including fat tailed distributions and volatility clustering.[8] The presence of fat tailed distributions signals the frequent occurrence of extreme swings in the asset price. That is, large price changes – events which we would expect to be rare if price changes were drawn from a normal distribution – occur more frequently than predicted by the normal distribution (Fig. 7.6). Volatility clustering simply means large changes in prices are often followed by other large price changes – in either direction; small changes tend to follow small changes (Fig. 7.7). As a result, the variance of financial asset returns often cluster over time, giving rise to what has been termed autoregressive conditional hetero-skedasticity or ARCH.

The presence of fat-tailed distributions and the occurrence of volatility clustering does not necessarily imply anything about the mean performance of financial assets that exhibit these characteristics. Positive and negative shocks tend to negate each other in terms of mean behavior – that is,

[8] Dacorogna et al. (2001) provides a useful introduction to the theory, modeling, and empirics of high frequency data.

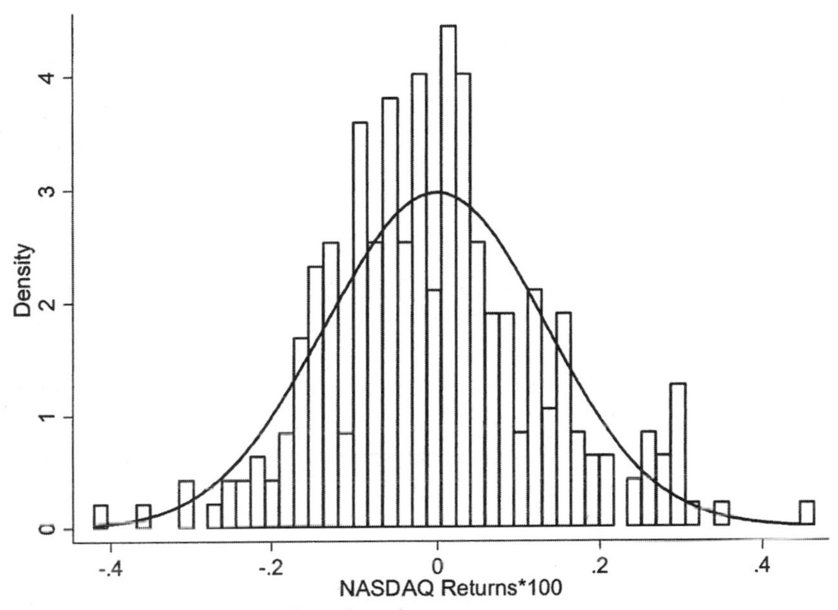

Figure 7.6. The non-normality of stock returns.

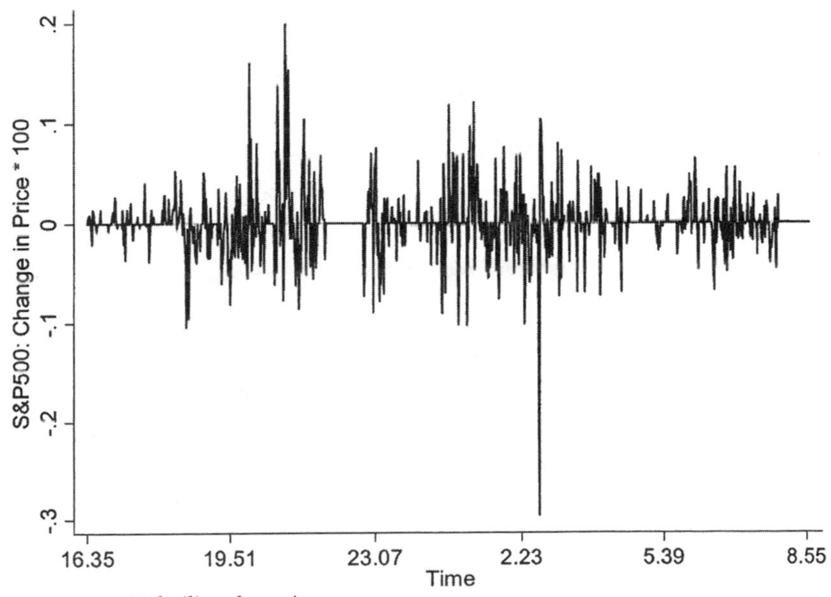

Figure 7.7. Volatility clustering.

under the assumption of efficient markets, equilibrium prices fully reflect all available (and relevant) information. Consequently, all information available to agents at time *t* is incorporated in past prices and "the current price is a sufficient statistic for the distribution of future price movements" (Baillie and Bollerslev 1989, p. 298). Put simply the best predictor of an asset's value tomorrow is its value today.

But this result does not hold for the variance of asset price movements. Although price forecasts will, on average, remain unbiased, the variance of those forecasts will vary over time. In some periods, traders will have a precise forecast of what the asset price will be. In other periods, those forecasts may be less precise. (In a statistical sense, these forecasts will be unbiased, but less efficient.) As we discuss below, the GARCH model allows us to estimate the conditional variance of the price forecasts or, in other words, the asset price volatility.

While the efficient markets hypothesis (EMH) describes how unexpected information can cause a change in the *mean* price of an asset, it says nothing about how information influences the *variability* of an asset price. In this section we describe a model based on the mixture of distributions hypothesis that not only provides a framework whereby information arrival influences the variability of an asset price but which also accounts for the volatility clustering and excess kurtosis often observed in financial time series.[9] We argue that the arrival of political information can affect asset price volatility. We then review a variety of ARCH and GARCH models, which are designed explicitly to model both the mean behavior of an asset and its conditional variance – or volatility. In the final section, we discuss how we specifically use these models to test whether the calling of specific states on election night affected the volatility of these futures prices in overnight trading.

Mixture of Distributions Hypothesis

Imagine a market populated by *J* active traders. During the course of a trading day (or any other period of time) the price of a given asset moves through a number of distinct Walrasian equilibria: a set of prices such that there is no asset for which there is excess supply or demand. As information – about employment, earnings, or elections – arrives into

[9] A number of studies of financial markets draw upon the mixture of distributions hypothesis (MDH) to link the behavior of traders, with the volatility clustering and kurtosis observed in asset price returns (e.g., Clark 1973; Tauchen and Pitts 1983; Melvin and Yin 2000).

the market, traders adjust their long or short positions for particular assets. In general, the mixture of distributions hypothesis shows how the arrival of information leads markets to shift from one equilibria to another. If these shifts (changes in the equilibrium price) are normally distributed, then aggregating them over the course of a trading day leads to a sequence of price changes that exhibit a fat tailed distribution and volatility clustering.

Let the desired position of the *j*th trader during the *i*th within period equilibrium be expressed as $Q_{ij} = \alpha[P^*_{ij} - P_i]$. Here α is a positive constant, P_i is the current market price and P^*_{ij} is the *j*th trader's reservation price given by her perception of the "true" value of the asset.[10] A positive value for Q_{ij} reflects that trader j holds a long position in the asset (their reservation price is greater than the current market or spot price) and that they expect it to appreciate. In this case trader j will buy the asset. If, on the other hand, Q_{ij} is negative then trader j holds a short position, believes that the spot price exceeds their reservation price, and will sell the asset.

At any moment during the trading period, equilibrium conditions require the total of all J traders' (long and short) positions sum to zero: $\sum_{j-1}^{J} Q_{ij} = 0$. This implies that the average of all reservations prices $P_i = \frac{1}{J}\sum_{j=1}^{J} P^*_{ij}$ clears the market. As information arrives in the market, traders reevaluate their reservation prices. This reevaluation may lead some traders to lower (or raise) their reservation price by some increment. The result is a new equilibrium. The average change to the traders' reservation prices changes the market price of the asset from the $(i-1)$th to the *ith* within-day equilibrium. This can be expressed as:

$$\Delta P_i = \frac{1}{J}\sum_{j=1}^{J} \Delta P^*_{ij} \tag{7.1}$$

where ΔP_i is the change in spot price of the asset and $\Delta P^*_{ij} = P^*_{ij} - P^*_{i-1,j}$. If the individual increments that make up ΔP^*_{ij} are normally distributed then $\Delta P_i \sim N(0, \sigma_i^2)$ and ΔP_i is said to be drawn from a mixture of normal distributions.

The movement from one equilibria to another is caused by the arrival of new information which causes traders to revise their reservation rate.

[10] We ignore transaction costs and assume that traders differ only in terms of their reservation price. The variance in reservation prices across traders is based on differences in (i) expectations regarding the future value of the asset and/or (ii) private information regarding the performance or value of the asset.

To find the daily (or any other period) change in the price of an asset, we sum the within day changes. Since these within day changes are normally distributed and depend upon the arrival of new information, the daily price change is a mixture of normals with mixing variable *I*:

$$\Delta P = \sum_{i=1}^{I} \Delta P_i \tag{7.2}$$

where $\Delta P \sim N(0, \sigma_i^2 I)$ and I is a random variable measuring the number of within-period information events. I is referred to as the "mixing" variable.[11] Lamoureux and Lastrapes (1990) and Laux and Ng (1993) show how a mixture of distributions model can provide the rationale for a GARCH type model. Denoting a time period with the subscript t and assuming that information arrival is time dependent (serially correlated), we have:

$$I_t = a + bI_{t-1} + u_t \tag{7.3}$$

where a is a constant, b is the serial correlation parameter and u is an error term. Innovations to the information flow (the mixing variable) are a function of b. If the mixture of distributions model is valid then $h_t = \sigma^2 I_t$. Substituting Eq. (7.3) into this expression for the variance gives:

$$h_t = \sigma^2 a + bh_{t-1} + \sigma^2 u_t \tag{7.4}$$

which indicates that the daily variance of asset price returns is conditional upon the arrival of information (I_t).

The expression in Eq. (7.4) shows that the variance of an asset can be influenced by the arrival of information into the market and is consistent with the assumptions of the efficient markets hypothesis. In fact, Eq. (7.4) has been used as the basis for a number of studies of stock price volatility (e.g., Lamoureux and Lastrapes 1990; Bollerslev, Chou, and Kroner 1992; Laux and Ng 1993; Tauchen and Pitts 1983). Since information (I) is usually not directly observed, the mixing variable is operationalized in

[11] The motivation for a mixture of distributions model such as this one builds upon the notion of a subordinated stochastic process. In the present context the random variable I is the mixing variable representing the random rate at which information flows into the market. Using the language of a subordinated stochastic process, ΔP_i is subordinate to ΔPi^* and I is the directing process. See Mandelbrot and Taylor (1967), Clark (1973), Westerfield (1977), and Lamoureux and Lastrapes (1990).

terms of trading volume, which these authors argue is a proxy for the amount of daily information that flows into the market.[12] But other measures of information exist. For instance, Melvin and Yin (2000) measure information related to the Deutschmark directly by counting the number of news stories about Germany that appear on the Reuters screen during a trading period.

Generalized Autoregressive Conditional Heteroscedasticity (GARCH) Models

A large literature finds evidence of conditional heteroscedasticity in daily asset price returns (e.g., Lobo and Tufte 1998; Theodossiou 1994; Koutmos and Theodossiou 1994). While the martingale property states that mean return (R_{t+1}) is unpredictable, it says nothing about the variance (conditional second moments) of price changes. It is possible, therefore, that asset price changes exhibit time varying variability. Consequently, we need to model not only the conditional mean of asset price returns, but also the conditional variance or volatility.

Autoregressive Conditional Heteroscedasticity (or ARCH) (Engle 1982) and Generalized Autoregressive Conditional Heteroscedasticity (or GARCH) (Bollerslev 1986) models were developed to deal with the temporal dependence that exists in the second moments of many economic and financial series.[13] GARCH models are often used to analyze financial time series because it is assumed that economic agents form expectations about this period's variance based on the long term mean of the variance, the forecasted variance from the prior period, and new information about volatility gleaned in the prior period.

A GARCH model is comprised of two equations: one for the conditional mean and the other for the conditional variance. In the GARCH (p, q) specification, the conditional mean can be written as:

$$\begin{aligned} y_t &= x_t\gamma + \varepsilon_t \\ \varepsilon_t &\sim V(0, \sigma_t^2) \end{aligned} \tag{7.5}$$

[12] The use of volume as the mixing variable has some theoretical justification. Epps and Epps (1976) and Howison and Lamper (2000) explicitly formulate models where volume is the mixing variable. Karpoff (1987) is a survey of the literature that uses trading volume to account for the mean and variance of asset price changes.

[13] Excellent textbook treatments of ARCH and GARCH processes include Tsay (2002), Brooks (2002), Franses and van Dijk (2000) and Enders (2004). For applications, see Lobo and Tufte (1998) and Koutmos and Theodossiou (1994).

where y_t is the dependent variable observed at time t, x is a matrix of independent or exogenous variables hypothesized to effect the conditional mean of y, and is an error term that follows some distribution V with mean zero and variance σ_t^2. Usually V is the standard normal distribution, but the Student-t, power exponential, and the generalized error distribution are also used. Given that returns from tick data exhibit significant leptokurtosis, we assume that V is the Student-t distribution.

The unique feature of GARCH models is that we can specify how the conditional variance evolves (σ_t^2) over time in response to both past values and to exogenous shocks. The conditional variance for the standard GARCH (p, q) model is:

$$\sigma_t^2 = \omega + \sum_{i=1}^{q} \alpha_i \varepsilon_{t-i}^2 + \sum_{i=1}^{p} \beta_i \sigma_{t-i}^2. \tag{7.6}$$

Using the lag or backshift operator,[14] Eq. (7.6) can be rewritten as:

$$\sigma_t^2 = \omega + \alpha(L)\varepsilon_t^2 + \beta(L)\sigma_t^2. \tag{7.7}$$

In most cases there is one ARCH and one GARCH term.

The conditional variance for the standard GARCH (1,1) model with exogenous variables is:

$$\sigma_t^2 = \omega + \alpha\varepsilon_{t-1}^2 + \beta\sigma_{t-1}^2 + \pi p_t.$$

The variance σ_t^2, called the conditional variance, is the one-period ahead forecast variance based on all information available at time $t-1$. The conditional variance is a function of three terms: the constant (ω), the ARCH term (ε_{t-1}^2), and the GARCH term (σ_{t-1}^2). The ARCH term can be interpreted as news about volatility (or volatility shocks) from prior periods. The GARCH term represents the variance from $t-1$. The GARCH setup also allows the conditional variance to be influenced by exogenous variables (p_t).[15] We exploit this feature to investigate how political events impact asset price volatility.

[14] The backshift operator can be represented as: $\alpha(L) = \alpha_1 L + \cdots + \alpha_q L^q$ and $\beta(L) = \beta_1 L + \cdots + \beta_p L^p$.

[15] The set of exogenous variables contained in the conditional variance (p) can be identical to the set of exogenous variables contained in the mean equation (x) without encountering problems of identification.

A limitation of this standard GARCH model, however, is that it treats errors or innovations (ε_t^2) symmetrically. That is, GARCH models assume both positive and negative innovations have the same effect on the conditional variance. While this simplifies the analysis, the direction of the innovation may actually determine its effect on the conditional variance. For instance, a positive (negative) shock or innovation may have a larger effect on the conditional variance than a negative (positive) one. This phenomena is quite common in the analysis of stock returns where investors engage in herding behavior: a negative shock leads to larger volatility than a positive shock. Similarly, if a currency begins to depreciate unexpectedly it is likely that speculators will jump on the bandwagon. It is common for stocks and currencies to experience greater volatility when there are unanticipated depreciations than when there are unanticipated appreciations (e.g., Zakoian 1990; Glosten, Jaganathan, and Runkle 1993). Nelson (1991) developed an Exponential GARCH (EGARCH) model to deal with this problem in a parsimonious manner. The EGARCH model relaxes this assumption of symmetric effects.

The EGARCH (1,1) model with exogenous variables specifies the conditional variance as:[16]

$$\log(\sigma_t^2) = \omega + \alpha z_{t-1} + \beta \log(\sigma_{t-1}^2) + \delta(|z_{t-1}| - E|z_{t-1}|) + p_t\pi$$

where z_t represents standardized innovations (ε_t/σ_t), p_t is a matrix of exogenous variables influencing the conditional variance and E is the expectations operator. In this specification, the conditional variance is a function of four terms (aside from p_t): the constant (ω), the GARCH term (σ_{t-1}^2) and two ARCH terms – an asymmetric component (z_{t-1}) and a symmetric component ($|z_{t-1}| - E|z_{t-1}|$).

Consider first the symmetric component of the ARCH term, ($|z_{t-1}| - E|z_{t-1}|$). This component measures deviations between the realized and expected innovations and is designed to capture how unexpected innovations affect conditional volatility. According to the literature, δ should be greater than zero. Therefore, standardized innovations that are larger in absolute magnitude than the expected absolute value ($|z_t| > E|z_t|$) will increase future volatility above its average level. On the other hand, if $|z_t| < E|z_t|$, then future volatility will be lower than average.

[16] Most statistical software implements Nelson's (1991) EGARCH model using $\sqrt{2/\pi}$ in the parenthetical expression rather than $E|z|$.

The αz_{t-1} term provides for the asymmetric effect of the standardized innovations. Assuming δ is positive, then a positive (negative) value for α implies that positive (negative) shocks (e.g., unexpected currency depreciations) will have a larger effect on future volatility than negative (positive) shocks. That is, an unexpectedly large innovation will increase the future volatility more than an unexpectedly small innovation will decrease the future volatility.

GARCH models are often used to evaluate the impact of risk on return. Some models in finance assume that asset holders will be compensated for holding riskier assets while others suggest that increased risk will drive investors to diversify their portfolios (see the discussion of the CAPM in Chapter 3). Since GARCH models estimate the conditional variance, they can examine whether the variance of an asset return influences the level of the return. Following Engle, Lilien, and Robins (1987) we operationalize the notion of risk by including the conditional variance in the mean equation.[17] Specifically we use the log of the variance at time $t-1$ as a regressor in the mean equation; we rewrite the mean equation from Eq. (7.5) as:

$$y_t = x_t\gamma + \rho\log(\sigma^2_{t-1}) + \varepsilon_t.$$

In this set-up, ρ measures how the log of the conditional variance influences the value of stock market returns.

THE TEST: OVERNIGHT MARKET VOLATILITY AND THE NOVEMBER 2000 ELECTION

We use a GARCH set-up to investigate asset price behavior and volatility during the night of the 2000 Presidential election. The mean equation includes an AR(1) term to account for serial correlation. We measure the arrival of new political information in two ways. First, we include a dummy variable for the time when CNN called each "toss-up" state – that is, states where the share of the two party vote for Gore was between 0.4 and 0.6. As these variables do not take into account the political expectations of market actors, we expect that most will have no statistical

[17] In addition to the log of the variance, researchers have used the standard deviation of the conditional variance and the conditional variance itself in the mean equation. The choice between these specifications is usually driven by the value of the conditional variance as compared to the mean of the dependent variable.

effect on asset prices. Second, we include the change in the probability of a Gore victory, *Change in Gore Probability.* Since this variable captures how market actors update their expectations of the political outcome, it should affect the mean behavior of these assets. A negative parameter estimate indicates that increases in the probability of a Gore victory produce a drop in the price.

The conditional variance is modeled as a GARCH(1,1) process and includes exogenous variables measuring the expected duration between trades (*Expected Duration*) and the volume of trades (*Volume*).[18] Previous studies of stock market volatility argue that total volume and the amount of time that has passed since the last trade are important exogenous variables. O'Hara (1995) argues that "if market participants can learn from watching the timing of trades, then the adjustment of prices to information will also depend on time" (p. 169). Engle (1996) empirically implements this idea and argues that the expected duration between trades should have a statistically significant effect on the variance of price changes.

In alternative specifications, we also include two measures designed to capture information about electoral results as components of the matrix p_t in the equation for the conditional variance. The first measure is the probability of an electoral victory for Gore lagged five minutes, *Probability of a Gore Victory.*[19] A negative parameter estimate indicates that volatility is lower as the probability of a Gore victory is higher.

The second measure, *Entropy*, captures the uncertainty surrounding the electoral outcome. Denote the probability of an electoral victory by Gore by p; the entropy measure takes the highest value (equal to 1) when p is closest to 0.5 (a situation when the outcome is truly a toss-up) and takes the value of zero when p is equal to either zero or one.[20] Following Freeman, Hays, and Stix (2000), we expect that this entropy measure to increase the conditional variance: when the outcome is most uncertain, market volatility should be highest.

[18] Unfortunately, given the depth of currency markets, it is not possible to obtain data on the number of trades or on the volume of currency traded during each transaction for the U.S. Dollar–Japanese Yen exchange rate. Consequently, we omit these variables from the dollar–yen models.

[19] The five minutes because that is the average amount of time it takes for a trade to be executed by the GLOBEX system. Changing the lag from between one and ten minutes did nothing to alter the results.

[20] The entropy measure is constructed as $E = 1 - 4(p - 0.5)^2$.

We estimate several different models including a simple GARCH model, an EGARCH model, and an EGARCH-in-Mean model. We distinguish between alternative techniques and specifications by performing a number of diagnostic tests for serial correlation in the residuals, serial correlation in the squared residuals (ARCH), and normality of the residuals. We report three additional measures to help determine the most appropriate specification: the Akaike information criterion (AIC), Schwarz's Bayesian information criterion (BIC), and the final likelihood. Information criteria remove a degree of subjectivity when it comes to evaluating competing models. These measures are comprised of two components: one that is a function of the residual sum of squares and another that adds a penalty for the loss of degrees of freedom associated with the inclusion of additional parameters.[21]

RESULTS

Table 7.3 contains the results for the models of Standard and Poors (S&P 500) futures and NASDAQ futures. The estimates for both series are remarkably similar. Hence, we restrict the discussion to the results of the S&P 500 models.

We first ran a GARCH model including dummy variables for when "toss-up" were called in the mean equation. Only two calls have a statistically significant effect on the price of the S&P futures: the initial Florida to Gore call at 7:52 p.m. (negative estimate) and the call to take Florida out of the Gore column at 8:55 p.m. (positive estimate). The other state-call variables did not achieve statistical significance (results not reported). The failure to attain significance should not be surprising – these simple dummy variables did not take into account market expectations about the overall probability of a Gore victory. Since it is impossible to tell whether these calls confirmed market expectations or forced economic actors to recalculate their election night predictions, we should observe no systematic effect on the price behavior.

Next we included the Change in the Gore Victory variable in the mean equation of a series of GARCH models. The first column reports the results of a simple GARCH(1,1) model. In the mean equation, the AR(1) term is statistically significant. Changes in expectations of a Gore Victory have no effect on the market behavior. The Change in the Gore Victory

[21] Brooks (2002) provides a discussion.

Table 7.3. *Results*

	S&P 500 Futures				NASDAQ Futures			
Mean	I	II	III	IV	V	VI	VII	VIII
Constant	−0.0007	0.0001	0.0001	−0.0009	0.0012	−0.0002*	0.00003*	−0.0004
	(0.0005)	(0.0002)	(0.0003)	(0.002)	(0.0017)	(0.0000)	(0.0000)	(0.0003)
ΔP [Electoral victory $Gore_{t-5}$]	−0.0719	−0.049*	−0.049*	−0.049*	0.121	−0.009*	−0.021*	−0.007*
	(0.0855)	(0.023)	(0.023)	(0.023)	(0.108)	(0.004)	(0.0037)	(0.0038)
Log $(\text{variance})_{t-1}$				−0.0002*				−0.0002*
				(0.0001)				(0.0001)
AR(1)	0.201*	0.163*	0.163*	0.165*	0.052	0.031*	0.042*	0.0456*
	(0.033)	(0.015)	(0.015)	(0.016)	(0.075)	(0.003)	(0.002)	(0.0032)
Variance								
Constant	0.0001*	−0.451	−0.441	−0.462	0.0005*	−0.46*	−0.138*	−0.229*
	(0.0000)	(0.837)	(0.807)	(0.737)	(0.0000)	(0.09)	(0.025)	(0.042)
Arch	0.0914*	1.208	1.198	1.179	0.098*	1.276*	1.652*	1.869*
	(0.0098)	(7.629)	(7.389	(6.273)	(0.009)	(0.557)	(0.278)	(0.427)
Asymmetric component		0.136*	0.148*	0.145*		−0.016	0.119	0.080
		(0.098)	(0.105)	(0.080)		(0.059)	(0.124)	(0.089)
Garch	0.7910*	0.934*	0.935*	0.931*	0.790*	0.903*	0.944*	0.924*
	(0.009)	(0.011)	(0.011)	(0.012)	(0.011)	(0.009)	(0.006)	(0.008)
Expected duration	0.0001*	0.039*	0.0373*	0.046*	0.0001*	0.044*	0.007	0.018*
	(0.000)	(0.011)	(0.010)	(0.013)	(0.0000)	(0.015)	(0.007)	(0.011)

(*continued*)

Table 7.3. *(continued)*

	S&P 500 Futures				NASDAQ Futures			
Mean	I	II	III	IV	V	VI	VII	VIII
Volume	0.0001*	0.010*	0.0102*	0.010*	0.0003*	0.242*	0.109*	0.159*
	(0.000)	(0.003)	(0.003)	(0.003)	(0.0000)	(0.017)	(0.011)	(0.014)
P [Electoral	−0.0014*	−0.063*		−0.077*	−0.0003*	−0.187*		−0.136*
victory $Gore_{t-5}$]	(0.0000)	(0.037)		(0.053)	(0.0000)	(0.052)		(0.041)
$Entropy_{t-5}$			−0.038				−0.022	
			(0.037)				(0.021)	
Student-t		2.008*	2.008*	2.008*		2.001*	2.000*	2.0003*
distribution		(0.1031)	(0.0979)	(0.090)		(0.0001)	(0.0000)	(0.0000)
Diagnostics								
LB Q(12) Test (χ^2) *p*-value	0.8018	0.6755	0.6718	0.676	0.4225	0.2303	0.2138	0.2197
LB Q^2 (12) Test (χ^2) *p*-value	0.0004	0.9993	0.9998	0.9964	0.785	0.1117	0.0057*	0.5262
ARCH−LM (12) (*F*) *p*-value	0.0141	0.9999	0.9998	0.9962	0.791	0.1748	0.0039*	0.5044
AIC	−4713	−5356	−5353	−5334	−2836	−5989	−5503	−5592
BIC	−4670	−5302	−5299	−5257	−2792	−5935	−5450	−5533
Likelihood	2366	2689	2687	2679	1427	3005	2763	2808

* p < 10.

is negative but not significant. The conditional variance is modeled as a GARCH(1,1) process. All three exogenous variables are statistically significant at the 0.05 level. Increases in volume and longer periods between trades are both associated with higher volatility while an increase in the probability that Gore wins the electoral college is associated with lower volatility.

The results from column one, however, should be viewed with caution. A glance at the diagnostics reported in the bottom panel of Table 7.3 reveals problems with this specification. While the Ljung-Box test does not allow us to reject the null of no serial correlation in the residuals, the Ljung-Box test for serial correlation in the squared residuals and the ARCH LM test both strongly reject the null of homoscedastic disturbances. There is also evidence that the residuals are more leptokurtotic than the standard normal distribution.

To remedy these problems we adopt an EGARCH(1,1) model with a student-t distribution (column two). The EGARCH specification captures the likely asymmetry in the conditional variance that may contribute to the findings of persistent ARCH. The student-t distribution provides a better fit when residuals have fatter tails. Indeed, the parameter for the student-t distribution is statistically significant beyond the 0.0001 level. The diagnostic tests for the model in column two confirm our modeling decision: there is no evidence of serial correlation in the residuals or the squared residuals. The information criteria statistics also support the EGARCH specification.

It is one thing to have a model that passes diagnostic tests; the proof of the pudding, however, is how well the parameter estimates square with theoretical expectations. In the case of the EGARCH (1,1) model the estimates are consistent both with our hypotheses and with the findings of prior research. In the mean equation, the Change in Gore Victory variable is negative and statistically significant. As market actors believe that the probability of a Gore victory is more likely, the price of the S&P futures decreases. A one percent increase in the probability of a Gore victory translates into a market expectation that the S&P index will decline by 1.05 percent over the next month (at maturity of the futures contract).

Turning next to the conditional variance, the GARCH term is positive and statistically significant, indicating that the variance at time t is a function of the variance one minute ago. While the ARCH term is not significantly different from zero, the asymmetric component of the conditional variance is significant and positively signed, indicating that negative shocks at time $t-1$ are associated with a larger conditional variance at time t.[22]

The exogenous variables in the conditional variance equation are all statistically significant. Greater volume and a longer expected duration between trades are associated with greater volatility in S&P returns. The probability of Gore victory is negative and statistically significant. The greater the probability that Gore will win the 2000 election, all other things being equal, the lower is stock market volatility.

Column three includes the entropy measure in the conditional variance rather than the probability of a Gore victory. The parameter estimates in mean equation remain unchanged. Increases in the probability of a Gore victory cause price decreases. In the conditional variance equation, substituting the entropy variable is not statistically informative. While all the other variables remain in their predicted directions, the entropy variable is not statistically significant and incorrectly signed. The information criteria also point to the model in column two as the preferred specification.

Column four reports the results from the EGARCH-in-mean specification. Recall that this technique includes the (lagged) log of the conditional variance as one of the regressors in the mean equation. Based on the results in columns two and three, we include the probability of a Gore Victory variable rather than the entropy measure in the conditional variance equation. In the mean equation, the change in Gore Victory remains negative and statistically significant, with a parameter estimate consistent with previous models. The log of the conditional variance is statistically significant and negative. As the volatility of the S&P futures contract (as measured by the log of the variance) increases, the return on the asset falls.

We next evaluated how the dollar–yen exchange responded over the course of election night. As in the previous tests, our first step was to include a dummy variable when each toss-up state was called in the mean equation of a GARCH model. In the case of the exchange rate,

[22] When GARCH or EGARCH models are fit to high frequency data (as we do here), it is not unusual for the conditional variance parameter estimates (α and β) to be close to a unit root (Bollerslev and Rossi 1996; Bollerslev, Chou, and Kroner 1992). Bollerslev and Rossi (1996, p. xii) point out that "[T]he first finding of unit roots caused a good deal of confusion in the early ARCH literature," but we know now that "the behavior of a martingale can differ markedly from the behavior of a random walk." Other work reports that "standard asymptotically based inference procedures are generally valid even in the presence of IGARCH (integrated GARCH) effect" (Bollerslev, Chou, and Kroner 1992, p. 15; Lumsdaine 1991). The literature is not clear about which coefficients (or combination of coefficients) – α, β, δ – constitute the long-run effect.

none of these dummy variables approached conventional levels of statistical significance. (Results not reported.) Again, since these dummy variables do not capture the political expectations of market actors, these null results are unsurprising.

Next we included the change in the probability of a Gore victory in the mean equation for the dollar–yen exchange rate (Table 7.4).[23] Consider the model in column one. The coefficient on the change in the probability of a Gore electoral victory is negative and statistically significant. As traders anticipate that Al Gore will claim a majority in the electoral college, the dollar appreciates relative to the yen.

In the model of the conditional variance, both the ARCH and GARCH coefficients are statistically significant, indicating that past shocks and variances have a positive impact on the conditional variance at time *t*. The duration between trades contains information valuable to asset traders: the longer the period of time between trades, the higher is subsequent volatility. Finally, the coefficient on the probability of an electoral college victory for Gore has a negative and statistically significant impact on the volatility of the USD–JPY exchange rate – expectations of a Gore victory lead to lower volatility. The residuals from this model are well behaved; there is no evidence of serial correlation in either the errors or squared errors.

The model in column two substitutes the measure of entropy for the probability of a Gore victory in the conditional variance. As with the analyses of the S&P 500 and NASDAQ futures, there is no evidence that overall uncertainty affects the conditional volatility of assets.

Column three reports the results of a GARCH-in-MEAN specification to see if the conditional variance of the USD–JPY exchange rate affects price changes. While the parameter estimate for the log of the variance is positive, it is far from statistically significant. Using either the variance or the standard deviation in the place of the log variance does not change the results.

Discussion

An increase in the probability of a Gore victory decreases stock market futures and leads to an appreciating dollar. Substantively, these results reflect market evaluations of the economic policies of the two candidates. As the incumbent Vice President, a Gore victory would have implied policy

[23] In results not reported here we experimented with an EGARCH specification but found no evidence of asymmetric volatility for the dollar–yen exchange rate.

Table 7.4. *Results for USD/JPY*

	USD/JPY		
Mean	I	II	III
Constant	$-4.29e^{-6}$	$-5.14e^{-6}$	$2.98e^{-5}$
	$(3.25e^{-6})$	$(5.76\ e^{-6})$	$(4.09e^{-5})$
ΔP [Electoral victory Gore$_{t-5}$]	$-5.03e^{-4}$*	$-6.54e^{-4}$*	$-6.23e^{-4}$*
	$(3.79e^{-3})$	$(3.90e^{-4})$	$(3.35e^{-4})$
Log (variance$_{t-1}$)			$1.44e^{-6}$
			$(2.14e^{-6})$
Variance			
Constant	$6.81e^{-9}$*	$2.84e^{-9}$	$-2.08e^{-9}$
	$(1.60e^{-9})$	$(6.40e^{-11})$	$(9.28e^{-10})$
Arch	0.145*	0.149*	0.1499*
	(0.027)	(0.029)	(0.030)
Garch	0.599*	0.599*	0.599*
	(0.035)	(0.039)	(0.038)
Expected duration	$5.99e^{-9}$*	$7.22e^{-9}$	$8.378e^{-9}$
	$(6.76e^{-10})$	$(8.89e^{-10})$	$(1.045e^{-9})$
P[Electoral victory Gore$_{t-5}$]	$-1.45e^{-8}$*		$4.35e^{-9}$*
	$(3.35e^{-9})$		$(1.99e^{-9})$
Entropy$_{t-5}$		$-2.91e^{-9}$	
		$(5.88e^{-9})$	
Student-t distribution	20.00*	20.00*	20.00*
	(3.56)	(4.26)	(4.831)
Diagnostics			
LB Q (12) Test (χ^2) *p*-value	0.547	0.520	0.472
LB Q^2 (12) Test (χ^2) *p*-value	0.114	0.101	0.174
ARCH–LM (12) (*F*) *p*-value	0.133	0.114	0.220
AIC	−14.786	−14.804	−14.810
BIC	−14.735	−14.753	−14.735
Likelihood	5331	5337	5340

* $p < 10$.

continuity after the Clinton administration, a period of monetary and fiscal responsibility that had seen the budget deficits of the 1980s become surpluses in the late 1990s. Bush's campaign, on the other hand, centered on a stimulus package financed through tax cuts. In at least the short-term, therefore, markets seemed to anticipate that a Gore victory would result in interest rates that would be higher than interest rates under a potential Bush administration. Higher interest rates tend to dampen stock market performance and lead to a currency appreciation. Lower interest rates make equities a more attractive investment option and contribute to a depreciating currency. Further, the volatility of all three series is lower when the probability of Gore victory is high, suggesting that market actors perceived that Gore would continue the status quo policies and that Bush represented a more uncertain economic future.

CONCLUSION

Along with the results of the previous chapter, this chapter reinforces the claim that the prior beliefs of market actors strongly condition market responses to the arrival of political information. To evaluate this argument, we again examined a specific political event: the 2000 U.S. presidential election. Only at this level can we develop measures that capture the beliefs of market actors and the times at which they receive new information. Moreover, by focusing solely on election night, we discount the influence of other potential factors on markets and, as a result, we can isolate the importance of political information.

As in the previous chapter, the announcement of specific information had no systematic relationship with market behavior. Concluding that market actors do not respond to political events, however, would not be incorrect. Only by accounting for the beliefs of market actors can we accurately gauge the market impact of news about political processes. By calculating and updating the probabilities of a Gore victory, we were able to show that the calling of states that altered the potential electoral outcome actually did influence prices of different assets.

Our analyses of coalition formation in Austria and New Zealand and the 2000 U.S. election are events that have a limited duration. This allows us to assume reasonably that asset market behavior does not influence political processes. But we know that market events do have the potential to shape political outcomes. A financial market crisis may damage the incumbent government's popularity or precipitate a new election. Accounting for this endogeneity between political processes and market behavior is the task of the next chapter.

8

Polls and Pounds: Exchange Rate Behavior and Public Opinion in Britain

To this point, we have investigated how political events shape asset market behavior. We have shown that less predictable events often lead to shifts in asset market behavior or increases in market volatility. But what are the political consequences of this asset market volatility? In this chapter, we examine how asset market volatility can affect government popularity.

One issue in measuring the impact of asset market behavior on political outcomes is that neither "markets" or "politics" is exogenous. If we take asset markets as exogenous to political factors, we discount the possibility that politics affects market behavior. On the other hand, if we assume that political events are exogenous, we ignore the possibility that market activity can precipitate a cabinet dissolution or affect an electoral outcome. An accurate assessment of how markets and domestic politics affect each other, therefore, requires an analysis of how both evolve together.

We examine the relationship between government popularity and exchange rate movements in Britain between 1987 and 2001. We argue that unexpected drops in the government's public support will lead to currency depreciations and increased exchange rate volatility. In turn, unanticipated depreciations hurt the government's public support.

We estimate separate models of exchange rate volatility and government voting intention iteratively and recursively. At each iteration, we use estimates from each model to generate measures of exchange rate and public opinion shocks. These generated variables are then employed in the next iteration of the estimates, including measures of political shocks in the model of exchange rate volatility and measures of exchange rate behavior in the model of voting intention. We are able, therefore, to determine more accurately the political costs of currency depreciation and the exchange rate consequences of political competition.

FOREIGN EXCHANGE, GOVERNMENT POPULARITY AND EXPECTATIONS

We begin with the assumption that economic and political agents employ available information to make decisions. This information can come from a variety of economic (e.g., data regarding unemployment or inflation) or political (e.g., the timing of elections or the policy preferences of governing parties) sources. Currency behavior and government popularity ratings, therefore, reflect the information currently available to economic and political agents.

Agents use this information to forecast currency prices and popularity ratings, making predictions about the evolution of these variables. The realization of information that does not fit with those expectations, however, will compel them to change their behavior. If government popularity shifts unexpectedly, currency traders quickly adjust to the new situation. Similarly, if exchange rate movements substantially deviate from currency forecasts, that deviation should affect the government's popularity rating.

Opinion Polls and Exchange Rate Volatility

Foreign exchange markets are among the deepest and widest financial markets in the world. The size and technological efficiency of currency markets mean that they quickly incorporate available and relevant information into the price of the currency. On average, therefore, the best predictor of a currency's value tomorrow is its value today. In other words, exchange rate levels move according to a random walk. Only news or unanticipated events affects the exchange rate.

We argue that news about politics, particularly the government's popularity, affects the exchange rate. As currency traders buy and sell foreign exchange, they gauge the government's commitment to the exchange rate. Traders must determine the probability of a change in economic policy that would affect the exchange rate. A key piece of information for currency traders in calculating this probability is the government's public standing.[1] Opinion polls about "voting intention" and "government approval" provide convenient summary statistics not just of the government's overall policy performance, but also of the potential for future policy change.

[1] The literature on voting behavior distinguishes between the concepts of public popularity, vote intention, and government approval. For data reasons, we rely on the vote intention as the key indicator of the government's popular support.

First, opinion polls indicate the ability of the incumbent government to press its policy agenda. Strong approval ratings for the government increase the incentives for backbench legislators (and coalition partners) to support the government's agenda. A popular government, therefore, is more likely to win support for its legislation or respond decisively to a shock than a government that does not enjoy public support. On the other hand, backbench legislators often attempt to distance themselves from an unpopular government by voting against or delaying the government's program. Weak popularity can also embolden the opposition (or coalition partners) to challenge government policies (Martin 2000; Huber 1996a).

Second, the government's popularity ratings can also provide information about the timing of a cabinet dissolution or election – events where the composition of the government may change, leading to different economic priorities for the government. Martin (2000) shows that public opinion shocks can alter the calculations of parties in a coalition government, leading them to precipitate a cabinet dissolution by withdrawing their support. In parliamentary systems with endogenous electoral timing, governments may also attempt to use opinion polls to strategically call of an election (Smith 2004; Huber 1996b). In Britain, for example, John Major put off elections until the last moment in both 1992 and 1997 because opinion polls earlier in the term did not favor the Tories.

Finally, opinion polls also provide clues to the future partisan composition of government. Opinion polls often indicate which parties stand to benefit and which will lose at the next election. Currency traders, therefore, can anticipate a partisan change in government long before an election.

The government's standing in the polls is a simple measure, easily monitored by currency traders. At the same time, it allows currency traders to extrapolate a great deal of information about the possibility of partisan and policy change, shaping their expectations about the government's commitment to the exchange rate. Consequently, the information contained in opinion polls conditions the policy expectations of currency traders. Unanticipated shocks to the government's approval will cause traders to update their expectations and, therefore, may affect exchange rate behavior. In particular we expect an unanticipated drop in support to lead to currency depreciation.

The government's popular standing also conditions the precision of currency forecasts. Although the forecasts of currency traders will, on average, remain unbiased, the variance of those forecasts – or what financial economists call the "volatility" of the exchange rate – may vary over time. In some periods, traders have precise forecasts of the exchange rate. At other times, those forecasts are less precise – in other words, exchange rate volatility may be high. Estimating the volatility accurately conditions the frequency and size of unanticipated depreciations and depreciations that, in turn, influence approval.

Both the level of the government's popularity and changes in the government's popular standing affect exchange rate volatility. If the government enjoys strong public support, economic actors can be confident that the current government is likely to win the next election and existing economic policies will remain in place. On the other hand, if polls indicate that the government would decisively lose an election, currency traders can infer that the opposition will form the government and that policy would change. In both situations, the political future and exchange rate policy are predictable.

In contrast, if opinion polls do not indicate which party would decisively win an election, currency traders cannot predict the composition of future governments and, in turn, the government's commitment to the exchange rate. This political uncertainty increases the variance of currency forecasts. When polls indicate that the government and opposition have similar levels of popular support, therefore, we expect higher levels of exchange rate volatility.

A change in the government's support – especially an unanticipated change – provides new information about the government's prospects and the implications for policy. The level of government support conditions how the market responds to an opinion shock.

Consider the situation where a government enjoys solid public support. A positive shock to the government's poll numbers is unlikely to affect markets. Since the government is popular, currency traders already assume that the government will remain in office. An increase in the government's popularity will not change their expectations about the government's exchange rate policy. A negative shock, however, increases uncertainty about the future composition of the government. Since the governing and opposition parties are running closer, currency traders are less able to forecast future economic policy precisely. As a result, a negative shock increases exchange rate volatility.

Similarly, if the government's popularity is low, an unanticipated negative shock to public opinion will not change the forecasts of currency traders. They already expect the government to lose the next election and have made adjustments based on the projected policies of an opposition government. As a result, a negative shock to public opinion should not affect exchange rate volatility. An unanticipated positive shock to the government's popularity, however, will change expectations. A positive shock indicates that the government's political fortunes are rising, making any upcoming election less predictable. That increased political uncertainty will result in higher levels of exchange rate volatility.

Finally, in situations where the opinion polls do not indicate that the government or opposition have a distinct advantage, we expect a positive shock to the government's popularity to decrease market volatility, and a negative shock to increase volatility.

Currency Markets and Government Popularity

Currency market turmoil can also affect the government's standing. With increasing trade and ever larger international capital markets, exchange rate politics have become highly salient at the domestic level. First, movements in the exchange rate have distributional consequences, often pitting actors in the tradeables and non-tradeables sectors against one another (Frieden 1991; Frieden 1999). A depreciated currency, for instance, makes exports more attractive on international markets, but raises the price of imports. As a result, certain sectors may blame the government for exchange rate movements that hurt their economic fortunes.

The British experience in the EMS highlights some of these distributional dilemmas. Exchange rate stability within the EMS helped sectors involved in international trade and finance. But to maintain the pound's parity with the German mark, the government had to keep interest rates high. Since home-ownership is widespread in Britain and mortgages tied to current interest rates, this policy hurt many home-owners, especially working-class home-owners who had just purchased their homes under Thatcher's privatization program (Clarke and Stewart 1995; Garrett 1992). Once grateful to the Conservative party for allowing them to purchase their own homes, these working-class constituents soon turned against the Major government as high mortgage payments placed them in financial straits.[2]

Further, with the increased volume and pace of international capital flows, the collective impact of decisions by currency traders can place tremendous pressure on a country's exchange rate and, in turn, government policy. Large and/or persistent exchange rate movements can compel a government to tighten both monetary and fiscal polices, to ease

[2] In the late 1990s, the Labour government experienced considerable tension in attempting to balance the conflicting policy demands of the (exposed) manufacturing sector with the (largely insulated) service sector.

market pressure. Exchange rate movements may signal that the government will be unable to follow through on its political agenda.

Finally, a sharp depreciation might serve as a focal point for the public, causing people to reevaluate their assessments of the government's economic performance and their future voting intentions (Bernhard 2001). A depreciation also damages the government's credibility with markets and constituents, especially if the government had publicly pledged to maintain the exchange rate.

Unanticipated changes in the level of the exchange rate, therefore, are likely to hurt the government's public support. Unanticipated movements may magnify the distributional consequences. They are also likely to generate news stories in the media that call attention to the government's economic record. Moreover, we expect that unanticipated depreciations will have a larger negative effect on government popularity than unanticipated appreciations. The public is more likely to interpret a depreciation as a signal that market actors lack confidence in the government's economic management and that a weakening economy is on the horizon.

BRITAIN

We focus on the British experience to examine the relationship between currency markets and government popularity. Britain's Westminster system provides clear lines of political accountability for economic policy (Powell 2000; Lijphart 1999). The majoritarian system usually "manufactures" a clear legislative majority for one party, allowing the formation of a single-party majority government. As a result, opinion polls represent a (relatively) direct indicator of the government's policy performance and electoral prospects.

Further, Britain is an open economy. Since 1979, there have been few, if any, restrictions on capital movements in or out of Britain (Quinn and Inclan 1997). Trade also accounts for a significant portion of economic activity. In the 1990s, imports and exports totaled about 50 percent of GDP. That trade is diversified between the Europe, United States, and the Commonwealth countries. With these levels of economic openness, therefore, the exchange rate should be a salient factor in British politics.

Indeed, the exchange rate has been a point of controversy throughout the post-World War II period. In the 1950s and 1960s, British policymakers sought to maintain the pound's postion as a major reserve currency. Balancing this external goal with domestic objectives, however, contributed to a stop-go pattern of macroeconomic policy: the government would pursue expansionary policies to maintain employment levels, but then quickly slam on the brakes due to balance of payments pressures (Britton 1991; Kavanaugh 1987; Scharpf 1987; Hall 1986; Alt 1979).

During the stagflation of the late 1970s, the pound came under heavy attack in international financial markets, forcing the Labour government to turn to the IMF for access to a special long-term loan. This humiliation exacerbated the Labour government's unpopular public standing. By the end of the 1970s, the pound played a diminished role as an international reserve currency.

In the 1980s and 1990s, debates about the exchange rate became intertwined with arguments about Britain's relationship with the European Community. In 1979, the new Conservative government declined to join the exchange rate mechansim (ERM) of the European Monetary System (EMS), preferring to let the pound float and allowing monetary policy to focus on domestic objectives. Thatcher's economic program did reduce inflation rates, but contributed to the appreciation of the pound, which wiped out Britain's export industries.

By the late 1980s, however, inflation once again approached 10 percent. With the success of the EMS member states in maintaining price stability, discussion in Britain soon centered on the question of British participation in the ERM. Thatcher steadfastly refused to join, arguing that it was dangerous to sacrifice policymaking autonomy. Under pressure from her party, however, she finally agreed to join the ERM in October 1990. Her belated acceptance of the EMS, however, was not enough to maintain the Conservative party's support after the disastrous attempt to institute the poll tax. In November 1990, party MPs replaced her with John Major.

British participation in the EMS, however, came at an inopportune time. In an effort to enhance the anti-inflation credibility of its commitment, the government entered the system at a parity higher than what many economists contended was justified by economic fundamentals. With the tightening of German monetary policy after German re-unification, the British government had to maintain high interest rates to sustain the pound's value, prolonging a recession long after inflation had been controlled. Then, in September 1992, amid concerns about the disparity of economic fundamentals across Europe and the ratification of the Maastricht Treaty, currency traders attacked the EMS, forcing the pound and the Italian lira to leave the system. The Major government, who had issued public assurances about the pound's value prior to the crisis, was forced to backtrack, losing credibility with the public and the markets.

After the crisis, the economy recovered quickly. Nevertheless, the Conservative party struggled through its term, divided over the question of Europe (e.g, Clarke, Stewart, and Whiteley 1998). Unsurprisingly, the Conservatives lost badly to the Labour party in the May 1997 election.

The question of British relationship to the European Union, especially whether to participate in the single currency (EMU), however, remained a controversial topic. Tony Blair, the Labour leader, sought to head off divisions within his own party about Europe by promising a referendum on the issue in a second Labour term – a referendum that has been repeatedly postponed. The Conservatives became increasingly vocal in their opposition to the Euro – a position that did not appear to help them in the 2001 election, even though opinion polls at that time showed the public strongly against British participation in EMU. These debates about the international role of the pound and participation in European monetary institutions have helped focus public attention on exchange rate movements and currency markets.

DATA AND METHODOLOGY

We estimate the relationship between exchange rate movements and opinion polls in Britain from the June 11, 1987 election until June 21, 2001, just after the 2001 election.

Exchange Rate Data

Exchange rate data consist of weekly spot prices of the pound denominated in U.S. dollars (Fig. 8.1).[3] The prices are from the Wednesday close to avoid problems associated with bank/national holidays and increased volatility on Mondays and Fridays (Baillie and McMahon 1989). The data are from the Federal Reserve Bank of Chicago.[4]

Exchange rate levels tend to be nonstationary data series (e.g., Diebold and Nerlove 1989, DeVries 1992, Taylor 1995). Indeed, both Phillips–Perron and Augmented Dickey–Fuller tests fail to reject the null hypothesis that the pound/dollar series contains a unit root. Consequently, we convert the exchange rate data into weekly percentage changes using the formula $R_t = \log(s_t) - \log(s_{t-1})$, where s_t denotes the

[3] As a robustness check, we also performed the analyses with the weekly spot prices of the British pound denominated in German marks and a trade-weighted exchange rate. The results, not reported, were quite similar.

[4] http://www.chicagofed.org/economicresearchanddata/data/index.cfm.

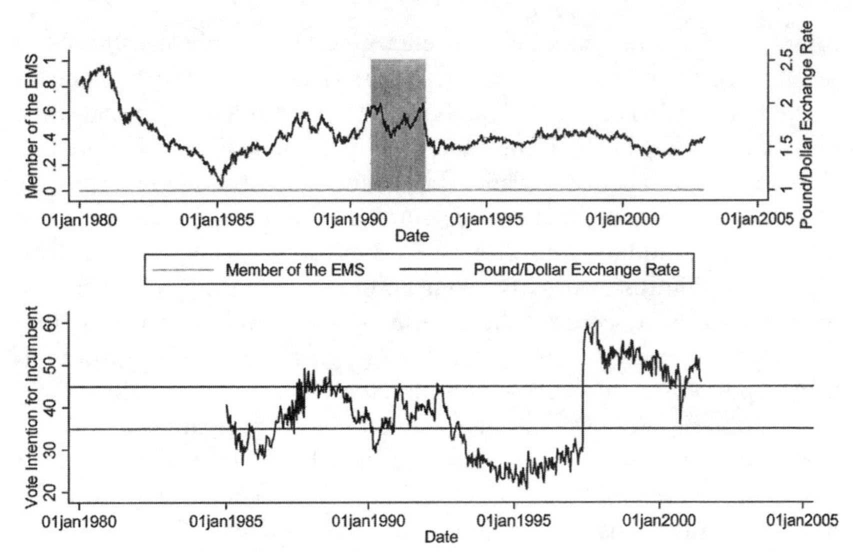

Figure 8.1. The data series. Horizontal lines indicate 35% and 45% levels of government popularity.

Table 8.1. *Summary statistics*

	ΔPound/Dollar exchange rate	ΔVote intention for government
Mean	0.00024	0.00791
Std. deviation	0.0137	1.6868
Minimum	−0.0452	−6.4200
Maximum	0.0864	19.44
Phillips–Perron#	−859.69*	−777.15*
Augmented Dickey-Fuller#	−28.88*	−30.01*

Test statistic from hypothesis test that the series contains a unit root.
$*p < 0.01$.

pound-dollar exchange rate. This differenced series is free from unit root problems (Table 8.1).

Polling Data on Vote Intention

To measure the government's popular standing, we employ data on vote intention. Opinion polls ask the question, "How would you vote if a General Election were held tomorrow?" Respondents then identify which party they would choose to support. Typically, polling houses in Britain ask this question each month. Monthly series on government popularity, therefore, are easily available. But given the size and technological sophistication of currency markets, currency traders are likely to respond to political information more quickly. Consequently, we need a measure that will track voting intention more frequently.

Fortunately, three major polling houses – Market and Opinion Research International (MORI), ICM Research, and Gallup – ask essentially the same question on voting intention at different times during each month (and more frequently as elections approach).[5] We merged the monthly results from the three polling houses into a weekly series on voting intention from 1985 until mid-June 2001.[6]

We created two data series on vote intention: one for the Conservatives and one for the Labour party. To combine the results across the different polling houses, we used the Kalman filtering and smoothing algorithm (Green, Gerber, and DeBoef 1999; Gerber and Green 1998). The procedure weights each observation (according to sample size, sampling error, and poll date) in order to smooth the series and interpolate missing observations (with standard errors).[7] The procedure, therefore, can help distinguish between random sampling error and true opinion

[5] In the 1990s, MORI polls were usually published in *The Times*, ICM polls in *The Guardian*, and Gallup polls in *The Daily Telegraph*. The MORI poll results are available from early 1979 to the present at http://www.mori.com. MORI supplied us with the fieldwork dates and sample sizes from 1983 on. From ICM, we have monthly results from 1984 on. Much of the data is available at http://www.icmresearch.co.uk. ICM provided us with fieldwork dates and sample sizes from 1989 on. Where unavailable, we assumed that ICM polls were conducted in the second week of the month with a sample size of 1000. (This sample size represents substantially fewer respondents than reported by ICM after 1989. We used this figure in order to be as conservative as possible in estimating the standard errors surrounding the interpolated poll numbers). Gallup has published monthly data on voting intention throughout much of the post-war period (King with Wybrow 2001; Butler and Butler 2000). Fieldwork dates and sample sizes are from King with Wybrow 2001. In addition, MORI's website contains the results, fieldwork dates, and sample sizes for irregular political polls on voting intention since 1992 (http://www.mori.com/polls/trends/voting-allpub.shtml). We included this information in our estimate of weekly voting intention.

[6] The sample period covers a major change in the methodology of many British opinion polls. Prior to 1992, most polling organizations used quota sampling (Jowell et al. 1993). Most polls, however, substantially mispredicted the 1992 election results, projecting a Labour victory. As a result, polling organizations switched to methods more consistent with a random sampling approach (King with Wybrow 2001).

[7] The correlation between the observed and smoothed opinion series is 0.998.

change.[8] Calculations were implemented using Samplemiser 4.0 (Green and Gerber 2000).[9]

With the (filtered and smoothed) measures of vote intention for the Conservatives and for Labour, we created a weekly series of voting intention for the incumbent government party (Fig. 8.1). From January 1985 through the 1997 election, this series is based on voting intention for the Conservative party. From May 1, 1997 to the end of the sample, the series represents voting intention for Labour.

We performed tests for stationarity on the voting intention series and could not reject the null hypothesis of a unit root.[10] As with the exchange rate series, therefore, we work with differenced data on voting intention. The differenced series passes all tests for the presence of a unit root (Table 8.1).

Table 8.1 provides summary statistics for the exchange rate and vote intention series.

METHODOLOGY

Our argument about the relationship between currency markets and government popularity presents a number of methodological challenges. First, exchange rates changes and voting intention affect one another, creating potential endogeniety problems. Estimating individual models for each dependent variable, therefore, will produce biased estimates and lead to incorrect inferences.

[8] It is possible that the poll results from polling houses systematically differ across polling houses. As a check, we regressed the generated data series on dummy variables for the three major polling houses. (The omitted category is polls from miscellaneous houses). With the differenced data series for voting intention for the incumbent party, none of the dummy variables were significantly different from zero, nor were they significantly different from one another.

[9] Available at http://statlab.stat.yale.edu/~gogreen/samplemiser.html. According to Green, Gerber, and DeBoef (1999), the key advantage of this program is its ability to accommodate observations that are unevenly spaced in time.

[10] In addition to standard Phillips–Perron and augmented Dickey–Fuller tests, we also implemented the Perron (1989) test for a unit root in the presence of a structural break. Perron (1989) argues that many findings of a unit root are caused by the occurrence of a single structural break in the data and, as a result, are spurious. Using this test, we still cannot reject the null hypothesis of a unit root. This test is not without controversy. Zivot and Andrews (1992), for example, argue that it is inappropriate to specify the date of the breakpoint because that choice of date is not known independently of the data (see Hansen 2001 and Patterson 2000). In our case, however, we know, even prior to examining the approval series, that there will be a structural break when a new party comes into power. We also implement these tests for the exchange rate series as a structural break may have occurred when Britain left the ERM. None of these tests reveal a unit root.

A second challenge arises from our assumption that economic and political actors make decisions at time t based on information available through time $t-1$. Measuring expectations based on estimates from the full sample, therefore, would not be accurate since those estimates incorporate information that occurred after time t.

Finally, we contend that surprises – or unexpected changes – in the exchange rate and/or government popularity influence the behavior of economic and political actors. To generate measures of surprises, we need to generate measures of expectations – baseline predictions and standard errors for time t based on information available through time $t-1$.

To meet these challenges, we estimate separate models of exchange rate volatility and government voting intention iteratively and recursively. By estimating each model iteratively, we circumvent problems associated with the endogeneity of the dependent variables. With recursive estimation, the parameter estimates are based on information available only in prior periods. In order to measure political and economic shocks, we use our estimates to generate a one-period ahead forecast and then compare the forecast to the realized variable. We then include those generated variables in the next iteration of the estimates. Consequently, we are able to follow the evolution of the relationship between the exchange rate and government popularity over time.

This section describes the specific process in detail. We first discuss the model to estimate exchange rate behavior and how we measure surprises in currency markets. We next describe the voting intention model and the measurement of public opinion shocks. Finally, we discuss the procedure for linking the two models.

Estimating Exchange Rate Behavior

Most studies of exchange rate movements employ random-walk models to explain short-term changes in spot prices. Although there is some evidence that exchange rates exhibit mean-reverting behavior, random walk models tend to outperform all other models in predicting out-of-sample exchange rate changes (Mussa 1984; Meese and Rogoff 1987; Meese 1990; Rogoff 1990; Taylor 1995).[11]

Taking these findings as a point of departure, we first model the evolution of the exchange rate, R_t, as a random-walk with a drift (results

[11] These conclusions are not necessarily applicable across exchange rates measured at different levels of aggregation (Dacorogna et al. 2001).

not reported). Diagnostic tests on the residuals from this model found no evidence of serial correlation (Ljung-Box Q statistic with 40 lags and LM tests with one and two lags). However, tests for temporal dependency in the conditional second moments (variance) of the residuals were not able to reject the null hypothesis of no conditional heteroscedasticity (Ljung-Box Q^2 statistics with 40 lags and ARCH–LM tests with one and two lags). Additionally, Jarque–Bera and associated tests reveal that the residuals suffer from both skewness and highly significant kurtosis.

This finding of conditional heteroscedasticity and fat tails (kurtosis) in the residuals is consistent with a large literature from financial economics (e.g., Lobo and Tufte 1998; Theodossiou 1994; Koutmos and Theodossiou 1994). Consequently, we employ a GARCH model to account not only for the time-varying volatility but also for the kurtotic (non-normal) nature of the residuals (Franses and van Dijk 2000; Nelson 1991; Bera and Higgins 1993; Baillie and McMahon 1989).[12]

In the GARCH (1,1) specification, the conditional mean can be written as:

$$\begin{aligned} R_t &= \zeta + m_t\eta + \varepsilon_t \\ \varepsilon_t &\sim N(0, \sigma_t^2) \end{aligned} \tag{8.1}$$

where R_t is the change in the log pound-dollar exchange rate at time t, ζ is a constant, η is a vector of parameters related to the set of m variables thought to affect R_t and ε_t is an error term that is distributed normally with mean zero and variance σ_t^2. In m we include a number of control variables, including lagged values of R_t, lagged changes in vote intention for the incumbent, lagged changes in unemployment and inflation, a dummy variable for British participation in the EMS (coded one from October 1990 through September 1992), and a dummy variable, *Crisis*, to control for the weeks following the pound's exit from the EMS (coded one from mid-September 1992 through the end of December 1992).

With GARCH models, the researcher can specify how the conditional variance (σ_t^2) evolves over time in response to past values, shocks, and exogenous variables. The conditional variance for the standard GARCH (1,1) model is:

$$\sigma_t^2 = \omega + \alpha\varepsilon_{t-1}^2 + \beta\sigma_{t-1}^2 + \pi x_t. \tag{8.2}$$

[12] A number of political economists have used variants of ARCH models to capture how democratic political events affect currency markets (Leblang and Bernhard 2006; Lobo and Tufte 1998).

The conditional variance, σ_t^2, is the one-period ahead forecast variance based on all information available at time $t-1$. The conditional variance is a function of four terms: a constant (ω), the ARCH term (ε_{t-1}^2), the GARCH term (σ_{t-1}^2), and a set of exogenous variables (x_t). The ARCH term can be interpreted as news about volatility (or volatility shocks) from prior periods. The GARCH term represents the variance from $t-1$. GARCH models, therefore, reflect the assumption that economic agents form expectations about this period's variance based on the long term mean of the variance (ω), the forecasted variance from the prior period (σ_{t-1}^2), and new information about volatility gleaned in the prior period (ε_{t-1}^2).

The GARCH setup also allows the conditional variance to be influenced by exogenous control variables (x_t). We include several variables in x_t to capture the influence of British participation in the EMS.

Generating exchange rate expectations and surprises

We use the predicted change in exchange rate changes, $\hat{R}_t$, to measure appreciation and depreciation surprises. From Eq. (8.1), we calculate both $\hat{R}_t$ and its standard error and generate a 95 percent confidence interval around the prediction. We then determine whether the realized value of the actual exchange rate was within that interval, above it, or below it. The variable, *Unanticipated Depreciation,* is equal to the actual residual if there is an unanticipated depreciation – i.e., if the actual value was greater than the upper bound of the confidence interval – for three weeks in a row.[13] This variable equals zero otherwise. The actual values for the Depreciation variable, therefore, are always non-negative (i.e., bounded below by zero). Similarly, the variable *Unanticipated Appreciation* is equal to the actual

[13] Although the three-week requirement is arbitrary, there are both theoretical and practical reasons for choosing it. From a theoretical perspective, it is unlikely that a single unexpected observation would generate enough media attention to affect public opinion. A series of unexplained exchange rate movements in the same direction, however, would be more likely to warrant news stories. (One can envision headlines: "Pound continues to slide.") These news stories are an important transmission mechanism connecting currency market behavior and public opinion (Sanders, Marsh, and Ward 1993). The practical reason is that the mean model of exchange rate behavior does a relatively poor job of predicting exchange rate movements. If we counted single observations outside the 95 percent confidence interval as unexpected movements, only a small fraction of exchange rate changes could be classified as "anticipated." By requiring three observations in a row to have large residuals, we are more likely to measure accurately the idea of an "unanticipated" change in exchange rates. We also experimented with two-week and four-week requirements. The results were similar, although at lower levels of statistical significance.

residual if the actual value was less than the lower bound of the confidence interval for three weeks in a row. It is coded zero otherwise.

We include these variables in the model of voting intention. We expect Depreciation and Appreciation to have negative effects on voting intention for the government. (Note that since the unanticipated values for Appreciation are always non-positive, a positive parameter estimate indicates a negative effect on government voting intention.)

Estimating Voting Intention for the Government

Estimating a voting intention model is fairly straightforward; the differenced series is well behaved and we use ordinary least squares with robust standard errors as our modeling strategy. The model is:

$$y_t = \tau + \theta z_t + u_t \tag{8.3}$$

where y_t is the differenced voting intention series, τ is a constant, z_t is a set of control variables thought to influence voting intention, θ are parameters to be estimated, and u_t is an error term.

Following the literature on voting behavior in the UK (e.g., Lewis-Beck 1988; Lewis-Beck, Norpath, and Lafay 1991; Clarke and Stewart 1995; Nadeau, Niemi, and Amato 2000; Sanders 2000; Clarke, Stewart, and Whiteley 1998), we include a variety of variables as controls in z_t to account for movements in the opinion polls: lagged vote intention;[14] election dates; a dummy variable to capture honeymoon effects, coded one for six weeks after an election;[15] and weekly changes in unemployment and inflation;[16,17]

[14] In alternative specifications, we included up to five lags of the differenced voting intention series as exogenous variables.

[15] A point of controversy in the British electoral literature is the degree to which the popularity of party leaders influences vote intention (Clarke, Ho, and Stewart 2000; Clarke and Stewart 1995; Stewart and Clarke 1992; Clarke, Stewart, and Whiteley 1998; Nadeau, Niemi, and Amato 1996; Jones and Hudson 1996). This research shows that the correlation between vote intention and prime ministerial approval is generally quite high. We do not include prime ministerial approval ratings due to difficulties associated with collecting this information on a weekly basis and differences in question wording across polling houses.

In alternative specifications, we included dummy variables for a series of political events: Major's selection as conservative party leader (the last three weeks in November 1990); the stock market crash of 1987 (October 1987); the petrol crisis of September 2000; the foot and mouth disease crisis (March 2001); the initial EU ban on British beef (March 18, 1996); the Gulf War (August 1990–March 1991); the end of the poll tax (March 1991); votes on the Maastricht treaty (various dates in 1992 and 1993); "critical" legislative votes; and budget announcements (Butler and Butler 2000). The inclusion of these variables did not change the substantive results.

Generating Public Opinion Shocks

We generate public opinion shocks in a manner similar to the measurement of economic expectations. After estimating Eq. (8.3), we obtain a predicted value for the differenced voting intention series, $\hat{y}_t$, and its associated standard error. We then construct a 95 percent confidence interval for $\hat{y}_t$ and determine whether the realized value falls above the interval, within it, or below it. We create two variables, *Positive Intention Shock* and *Negative Intention Shock*, to measure unanticipated movements in public support for the government. We code Positive Intention Shock as the value of the residual if the actual value of public support series lies above the upper bound of a 95 percent confidence interval surrounding the predicted value for three weeks in a row. The variable is coded zero otherwise. We code Negative Intention Shock as the value of the residual if the actual value of public support series lies below the lower bound of a 95 percent confidence interval surrounding the predicted value for three weeks in a row. The variable is coded zero otherwise. (Note, again, that values of Negative Intention Shock are always non-positive.) We include these shocks to the government's standing in the polls in the mean model of exchange rate behavior. Since these shocks are unanticipated, they represent new information about the government's commitment to the exchange rate. As such, we expect them to affect the exchange rate directly.

We also argue that the level of political uncertainty will condition the effect of an opinion shock on exchange rate volatility. We code a dummy variable, *Consequential*, as equal to one if voting intention for the governing party lies between 35 percent and 45 percent. In this range, it is not clear exactly which party would win an election.[18] Since traders are uncertain about future economic policies, we expect higher conditional

[16] We interpolated the weekly values of inflation and unemployment from monthly values. According to the British Office of National Statistics, the Consumer Price Indices (RPI) are usually released on the second Tuesday of the month. Unemployment data are released the second or third Wednesday of the month. While many studies model British public opinion using direct measures of inflation and unemployment, the Essex model argues that these macroeconomic conditions affect governing party support indirectly through subjective economic evaluations (Clarke, Stewart, and Whitely 1998; Sanders 1999, 2000). We do not include such subjective evaluations due to limitations in data availability.

[17] We performed the analyses without dummy variables to capture these specific events. In this specification, the effect of these specific events is picked up solely as shocks to public opinion. The results, not reported, are substantially similar to the models that include the dummy variables for the specific events.

[18] The selection of these cut-off points is based on the translation of votes into seats in the British electoral system (Monroe 2001). In the presence of a three-party system, the winning party need not capture 50 percent of the vote in order to secure

volatility. We include a second dummy variable, *Weak*, coded one when the voting intention for the governing party is less than 35 percent. (The omitted category is when voting intention for the governing party is greater than 45 percent).

We interact the surprise terms with the level of government support: *Positive Intention Shock* ∗ *Consequential*, *Negative Intention Shock* ∗ *Consequential*, *Positive Surprise* ∗ *Weak*, and *Negative Intention Shock* ∗ *Weak*. When the government's popularity is high, we expect negative shocks to increase exchange rate volatility. When the government's popularity is low, positive shocks will increase exchange rate volatility. (Note that values of Negative Intention Shock are always non-positive, so a positive parameter estimate indicates lower exchange rate volatility.)

Connecting the Models

We estimate both the exchange rate and vote intention models recursively and iteratively. Recursive estimation requires the use of an initial sample of data with which to calculate initial estimates. First, we use 102 weekly observations for the period January 2, 1985 through December 17, 1986 to estimate Eqs. (8.1), (8.2), and (8.3). With these estimates, we obtain initial measures of exchange rate shocks (Unanticipated Appreciation, Unanticipated Depreciation) and public opinion shocks (Negative Intention Shock and Positive Intention Shock).

Next, we include these variables in the exchange rate and government approval models. With the political variables, therefore, Eq. (8.1) becomes:

$$R_t = \zeta + m_t\eta + \varsigma P_{t-1} + \iota N_{t-1} + \varepsilon_t \tag{8.1'}$$

where P is a positive shock to vote intention and N is a negative shock to vote intention, both lagged one period.

Eq. (8.2) becomes:

$$\begin{aligned}\sigma_t^2 = \omega &+ \alpha\varepsilon_{t-1}^2 + \beta\sigma_{t-1}^2 + \pi_1 crisis_t \\ &+ \pi_2 P_{t-1} + \pi_3 N_{t-1} + \pi_4 C_{t-1} + \pi_5 W_{t-1} \\ &+ \pi_6 P_{t-1}C_{t-1} + \pi_7 P_{t-1}W_{t-1} + \pi_8 N_{t-1}C_{t-1} + \pi_9 N_{t-1}W_{t-1}\end{aligned} \tag{8.2'}$$

a legislative majority. Indeed, parties have secured sizable majorities by winning just 42–44 percent of the vote. We experimented with slightly different cut-off points. The results (not reported) were similar.

where P is positive intention shock, N is negative intention shock, C is consequential, W is weak, PC is positive intention shock∗consequential, PW is positive intention shock∗weak, NC is negative intention shock ∗consequential and NW is negative intention shock∗weak, all lagged one period.

Similarly, we take the estimates of unanticipated depreciation and unanticipated appreciation from estimating Eq. (8.2) and modify Eq. (8.3):

$$y_t = \tau + \theta z_t + \lambda_1 A_{t-1} + \lambda_2 D_{t-1} + u_t \qquad (8.3')$$

where A is an unanticipated appreciation and D is an unanticipated depreciation, all lagged one period.

We then estimate Eqs. (8.1′), (8.2′), and (8.3′) adding one observation to the original sample (i.e., for the time period January 2, 1985 through December 17, 1986. The sample includes 102 observations). From these estimates, we calculate an additional observation for positive intention shock, negative intention shock, unanticipated appreciation, and unanticipated depreciation. (Note that as we add observations, we do not re-estimate the entire series of generated variables. We only add a single new observation for each variable. The existing values of these variables remain unchanged). We then add another observation and re-estimate Eqs. (8.1′), (8.2′) and (8.3′) (i.e., the next sample includes January 2, 1985 through December 24, 1986, for a total of 103 observations). From those estimates, we obtain an additional observation for our generated variables. We continue this process – recursively and iteratively estimating Eqs. (8.1′), (8.2′) and (8.3′) and adding observations for the generated variables – until we have estimated each model on a total of 856 observations (January 2, 1985–June 21, 2001).

In order to obtain a sample that is based on the most accurate operationalizations of the generated variables, we exclude the initial 102 observations from the final analysis. The final models of both exchange rate volatility and government approval, therefore, are based on 754 observations.[19]

[19] We discuss three important econometric issues associated with our approach. First, the models do not suffer from problems of endogeneity. The measures of political shocks in Eqs. (8.1′) and (8.2′) and the indicators of economic performance in Eq. (8.3′) are at least weakly exogenous to their respective dependent variables. A variable, x, is weakly exogenous if current values of y do not explain current values of x (Kennedy 1998). Since the variables of interest on the right hand sides of Eqs. (8.1′), (8.2′), and (8.3′) are lagged, the models satisfy weak exogeneity. We employed a formal test for weak exogeneity as suggested by Hausman (1978) and Engle (1984) and described by Charemza and

RESULTS

Table 8.2 reports the results of the models. Figure 8.2 shows the frequency and magnitude of the generated variables. Unanticipated appreciations occurred 9 times in the sample; unanticipated depreciations 5 times. Positive public opinion shocks occurred 62 times; negative shocks 69 times.

The results of the voting intention model are located at the top of Table 8.2. The residuals pass diagnostic tests for serial correlation (Q and LM), ARCH (Q^2 and LM) and misspecification (RESET). The Jarque–Bera test, however, indicates that the residuals are not normally distributed. This is not surprising given the presence of a structural break in the raw data series when Labour is elected. In fact, if we estimate the Conservative government and Labour government samples independently, the residuals are normally distributed.

For ease of presentation, we do not show the parameter estimates for the control variables. The dummy variables for the 1987, 1992, 1997, and 2001 elections (and honeymoon periods) are statistically significant. The lagged change in unemployment has a significant negative effect on voting intention. Inflation does not attain conventional levels of statistical significance. Note, also, that lagged values of the change in exchange rate are not statistically significant. Anticipated exchange rate changes simply do not have any effect on vote intention for the government.

The parameter estimates for appreciation and depreciation square with our expectations. The estimate for unanticipated appreciations is positive,

Deadman (1992, p. 255–65). The test proceeds as follows: (i) estimate GARCH model (8.1′) and (8.2′), (ii) compute the residuals, (iii) include the residuals in model (8.3′), (iv) use t and likelihood ratio tests to test the significance of the generated residuals (the null being that the variable is weakly exogenous). Repeat this procedure, generating residuals from model (8.3′) and including them in GARCH model (8.1′) and (8.2′). In neither case were the residuals statistically significant; as a result, we conclude that the generated independent variables are (at least) weakly exogenous to the dependent variables in their respective models.

Second, we checked to see if Eqs. (8.1′), (8.2′), and (8.3′) could be estimated more efficiently in a simultaneous system. The correlation between the error terms of the two is statistically significant but weak (−0.07, $p = 0.04$). Finally, the measures of political expectations and economic information could be considered to be valid instruments in the sense that they are uncorrelated with the error terms in both equations (since they are measured at time $t-1$ and the errors are at time t). As a check, we adjust the standard errors for the generated variables using the degrees-of-freedom adjusted mean squared error from the equation of interest (Oxley and McAleer 1993). The results of this procedure did not differ from what is presented.

although statistically insignificant. The estimate for unanticipated depreciations is negative and statistically significant. In order to interpret this coefficient, recall that the depreciation measure is bounded below by zero. A negative estimate, therefore, implies a negative effect on voting intention for the incumbent party.[20]

What is the substantive impact of depreciations on predicted voting intention? The baseline is the situation where no unanticipated depreciation occurs. Holding all other variables at their means, an average unanticipated depreciation (0.007) reduces voting intention for the incumbent by 0.73 points. The largest depreciation (0.01; February, 1988) reduced government popularity by 0.91 points. These are substantively important numbers, especially if the parties enjoy similar levels of popularity.

Turn next to the GARCH model of exchange rate volatility, located on the bottom half of Table 8.2. The model passes tests for residual serial correlation (Q) and remaining ARCH (Q2). The Jarque–Bera test indicates that the residuals are not normally distributed; as a result, we utilize Bollerslev–Wooldridge robust standard errors. The ARCH(1) term is not statistically significant, suggesting that volatility shocks (i.e., last period's squared residuals, ε_{t-1}^2), do not influence current volatility, σ_t^2. The GARCH(1) term is statistically significant, indicating that last period's variance (σ_{t-1}^2) has a large impact on current volatility. The combination of the ARCH and GARCH terms are statistically less than one. The conditional variance, therefore, is mean-reverting and not long-memoried.

Again, we do not report the parameter estimates for the control variables in the conditional mean equation. The EMS crisis variable is, unsurprisingly, positive and significant. The pound depreciated by 7.6 per cent during the crisis. Additionally, the post-EMS dummy variable is also significant and positive, indicating that the pound depreciated slightly during this period. Other controls, including variables for membership in the EMS, change in unemployment, change in inflation, are not statistically significant. Lagged values of changes in the exchange rate were not individually or jointly significant.

[20] As a check on the robustness of the results, we estimated the models for only the post-EMS crisis period. We used observations from 1993 and 1994 to establish starting values and then estimated the full model on observations from the first week of January 1995 through June 2001. The results from this reduced sample are broadly consistent. The parameter estimates and significance of the key variables are largely unchanged. The coefficient for unanticipated depreciations in the opinion model remains statistically significant and positive but its parameter estimate decreases.

Table 8.2. *Models of voting and exchange rate volatility*

Variable	Coefficient	Robust SE	*p*-value
Dependent variable: Δ voting intention[a] model (estimated via OLS)			
Δ Vote intention (t–1)	−0.06	0.05	0.210
Δ Vote intention (t–2)	−0.19*	0.06	0.001
Δ Exchange rate (t–1)	−2.56	4.19	0.542
Δ Exchange rate (t–2)	−1.63	3.35	0.626
Unanticipated depreciation (t–1)	−90.36*	37.06	0.015
Unanticipated appreciation (t–1)	38.80	36.73	0.291
Constant	−0.046	0.053	0.387
Dependent variable: Δ exchange rate[a] estimated via GARCH			
CONDITIONAL MEAN			
Δ Vote intention (t–1)	0.000	0.0002	0.666
Δ Vote intention (t–2)	−0.000	0.0002	0.493
Δ Exchange rate (t–1)	−0.023	0.039	0.554
Δ Exchange rate (t–2)	0.036	0.036	0.325
Positive intention shock (t–1)	−0.000	0.001	0.904
Negative intention shock (t–1)	−0.002*	0.001	0.092
Constant	−0.002*	0.001	0.046
CONDITIONAL VARIANCE			
Positive intention shock (t–1)	0.077	0.99	0.938
Negative intention shock (t–1)	−0.447*	0.179	0.012
Consequential (t–1)	1.776*	0.241	0.000
Consequential ∗ positive intention shock (t–1)	−8.43*	3.43	0.014
Consequential ∗ negative intention shock (t–1)	0.277	0.185	0.134
Weak	0.095	0.192	0.621
Weak ∗ positive intention shock (t–1)	−0.02	1.27	0.988
Weak ∗ negative intention shock (t–1)	−0.193	0.282	0.493
Constant	−11.63*	0.377	0.000
GARCH TERMS			
ARCH(1)	0.006	0.025	0.821
GARCH(1)	0.803*	0.099	0.000

Joint tests	Chi^2	p-value
Consequential terms[b]	63.13	0.0000
Weak terms[c]	1.43	0.6994
Strong terms[d]	6.26	0.0438

$*p < 0.10$.
[a]Parameter estimates for control variables not shown for ease of presentation.
[b]Test joint significance of Consequential $_{t-1}$, Consequential $_{t-1}$ $*$ Positive Shock $_{t-1}$, Consequential $_{t-1}$ $*$ Negative Shock $_{t-1}$.
[c]Test joint significance of Weak $_{t-1}$, Weak $_{t-1}$ $*$ Positive Shock $_{t-1}$, Weak $_{t-1}$ $*$ Negative Shock $_{t-1}$.
[d]Test for joint significance of Positive Intention Shock $_{t-1}$ and Negative Intention Shock $_{t-1}$.

Interestingly, lagged values of changes in vote intention had no statistically significant impact on the exchange rate. As expected, anticipated changes in the government's public standing have no effect on exchange rate changes. Negative intention shocks to public opinion, however, are associated with currency depreciation. The parameter estimate is negative and statistically significant. The average negative shock to vote intention (−1.40) caused the pound's value to drop by 0.28 percent. The largest negative shock to vote intention (− 6.83, during the September 2000 petrol crisis) led to a depreciation of about 1.4 percent. The arrival of unexpected negative information about the government's public standing, therefore, clearly contributed to a weaker pound on international currency markets.

The conditional variance component of the table reports the effect of the political variables on the conditional volatility. The control variables are, again, omitted for ease of presentation. Unsurprisingly, the crisis variable is positive and statistically significant, indicating a much higher level of exchange rate volatility during the period.

The variables Consequential and Weak represent the level of the government's popular support. The positive and statistically significant parameter estimate for Consequential indicates that, as expected, exchange rate volatility is substantially higher when electoral outcomes are uncertain than when either the government or the opposition enjoys a decisive lead in public support. The parameter estimate for Weak indicates that exchange rate volatility is slightly higher when the government is very unpopular

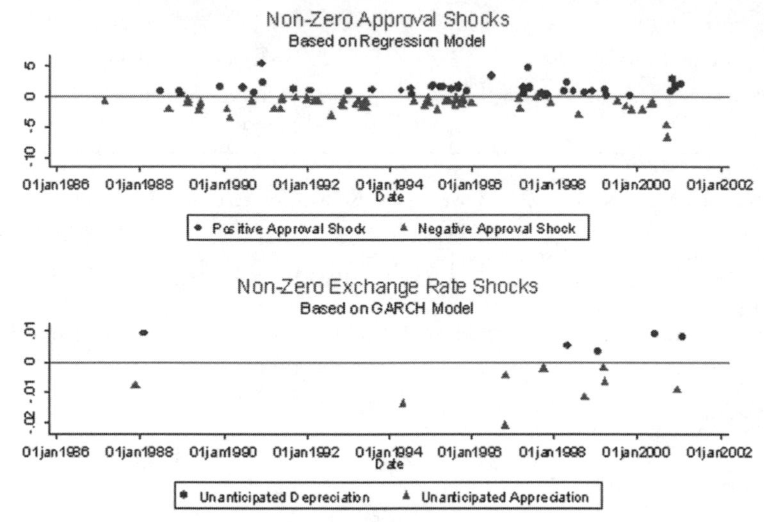

Figure 8.2. Public opinion and exchange rate shocks. See text for information on variable creation. Shocks are shown only when they are non-zero.

than when the government is popular, although this difference is not statistically significant.

We also include variables designed to measure the effect of positive and negative public opinion shocks on exchange rate volatility. We argued that the effect of those shocks would be contingent on the government's level of support. Table 8.3 reports the overall effects of positive and negative public opinion shocks on exchange rate volatility. Because the "dependent variable" in the conditional variance does not have a natural metric, cell entries are the expected changes in the conditional volatility compared to the baseline category where the government enjoys a large lead in the polls and there is no public opinion shock. We calculated the effects using the mean values of the type of shock.

Consider first the impact of a shock when the government's public support is weak. A positive or negative shock does not change the conditional volatility – the expected volatility does not statistically differ between the situations of "No Shock" and "Positive Shock."

If popularity levels for government and opposition are close (the Consequential category), a positive intention shock sharply decreases the conditional volatility. Presumably, a positive shock may make future elections more predictable. A negative shock, however, has no statistically discernible effect on the conditional volatility as compared to a situation when there is no shock.

Table 8.3. *Impact of vote intention shock on conditional variance of the exchange rate*

Level of government support	Intention shock		
	No shock	Positive shock	Negative shock
Strong	**0.35**	0.447	**0.975**
	(0.04, 0.66)	(−1.90, 2.80)	**(0.42, 1.53)**
Consequential	**2.12**	**−8.56**	**2.39**
	(1.41, 2.84)	**(−16.51, −0.62)**	**(1.66, 3.13)**
Weak	**0.34**	0.51	**1.34**
	(0.04, 0.67)	(−0.69, 1.72)	**(0.68, 1.99)**

Estimates and 95% confidence intervals based on estimates from the bottom panel of table 8.2.

Finally, in the situation where the government's popularity level is strong, a negative shock to public opinion increases the conditional volatility. As the electoral outcome becomes less predictable, exchange rate volatility increases.

Discussion

The results indicate that currency markets and opinion polls affect one another in a manner that largely matches our predictions. Unexpected depreciations decrease the government's support, while unanticipated negative intention shocks lead to currency depreciation. Further, exchange rate volatility is highest when opinion polls indicate that electoral outcomes are unpredictable.

But how does the argument compare to the actual performance of exchange rates and public opinion polls? To illustrate the importance of exchange rate and opinion shocks, we discuss the 2000 petrol crisis.

The Labour party entered office in 1997 with a moderate agenda under Tony Blair, who sought to complete the transformation of the party from a union-based machine to a mainstream social democratic party with a middle-class constituency. Coming after the tired Major government, Blair's early policy successes helped maintain high levels of political popularity throughout the first three years of its term. During this time, Labour's standing in the polls never dropped below 45 percent. With the Conservatives in disarray, a second term for Labour seemed a sure bet as elections were widely anticipated to occur at some point in 2001.

In summer 2000, however, a sudden series of oil price hikes sent the cost of gasoline soaring. Fed up with fuel prices, a grassroots movement quickly developed in early September to protest the government's response to the price shocks. Protesters, including farmers and truck drivers, blockaded refineries for eight days to demand a reduction in taxes on gasoline. (About 75 percent of the gasoline price paid by British motorists goes to fund government programs.) The Blair government initially mishandled the protests. Images of Mr. Blair sporting about in a luxury sedan while motorists could not find gas turned public opinion sharply against the Labour government. Within a month, Labour's support dropped 14 percentage points into a dead heat with the Conservatives. Almost just as quickly, however, the protest fizzled. With many citizens viewing the protesters as an inconvenience, the government recovered its standing in the polls.

According to the argument, the dramatic shock to public opinion should result in a depreciating currency and an increase in exchange rate volatility. The bottom panel of Fig. 8.3 charts the value of the pound in the period surrounding the crisis. In the months prior to the crisis, the pound gains in value. Two unanticipated negative shocks to the government's public

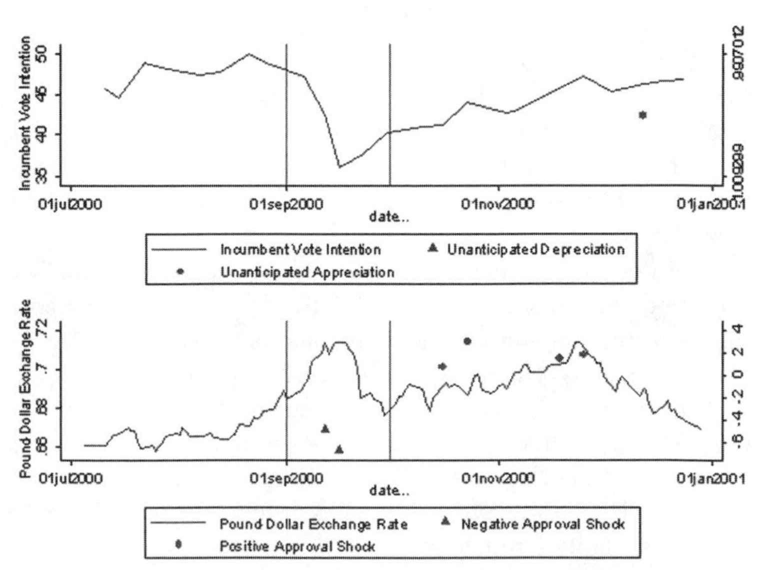

Figure 8.3. Public opinion and exchange rate behavior during the 2000 petrol crisis.

standing early in September, however, led to a depreciation, helping to push down the value of the pound by 3.4 percent. But the government's quick recovery in the polls helped quell the depreciation and volatility. As the government's popularity rebounded, again indicating that a Labour victory in the next election was a certainty, the pound's slide abruptly stopped and, over time, began to appreciate.

CONCLUSION

As in the previous chapters, the results confirm that the expectations of economic agents condition the impact of political processes on market behavior. Only unanticipated information – or news – causes agents to update their beliefs and alter their choices. To measure the arrival of political news, we compute one-step ahead forecasts of the government's public support and compare them with realized values. While predictable change in public support for the incumbent did not affect market behavior, the arrival of new information causes currency traders to modify their behavior. A negative public opinion shock, when the government's support falls unexpectedly, results in a depreciation of the pound.

But many political processes are not exogenous to market behavior. Political outcomes like the public's support of the incumbent government depend, in part, on the performance of the economy. The short duration of the political events analyzed in the preceding chapters – cabinet formations and election night returns – allowed us to assume that market behavior did not affect political processes. Analyzing the evolution of vote intention over time, however, requires an explicit consideration of the endogeneity between markets and politics.

Taking our cue from the finance literature, we assumed the citizens used all available information when making their political evaluations. These agents will adjust their political behavior only when confronted with unanticipated information about market behavior. Thus, market outcomes will change the government's public support only when they are unexpected. The results confirm the argument. Predictable every-day movements of the exchange rate have no substantive effect on the government's popularity. Unanticipated depreciations, however, hurt the incumbent's standing. By accounting for both agents' rational expectations and the endogeneity of political and market outcomes, we can establish that political processes and market outcomes interact in a systematic fashion.

It remains a challenge to unpack the mechanisms that link currency, market behavior and public opinion: exactly why do unanticipated depreciations hurt the government's public standing? A depreciation, for instance, may result in a loss of government credibility. Or it may signal that market actors view the government's policy management as incompetent. Finally, depreciations have distributional consequences that may affect how different sectors and sub-groups of the population evaluate the government. Exploring these different mechanisms represents fertile ground for future research.

9

Conclusion: Political Predictability and Financial Market Behavior

The predictability of political outcomes conditions how markets respond to political events. Where democratic political events have less predictable outcomes, market returns are depressed and volatility increases. In contrast, where market actors can easily forecast the political outcome, returns do not exhibit any unusual behavior. Across currency, stock, and, to a lesser degree, bonds, we demonstrated empirical support for this proposition using a variety of techniques in a number of markets (spot, forward, and futures). The predictability of outcomes can help explain the variation of market responses to political events.

Further, prior beliefs about an eventual outcome condition how political developments affect market behavior. Where new information confirms expectations, market actors do not adjust their portfolios. But when news causes market actors to update their beliefs, markets actors do reallocate their portfolios, and overall market behavior changes. By investigating information arrival in separate political events, we find empirical support for this argument as well.

In some sense, these conclusions are not controversial. Indeed, anecdotal evidence from the financial news media confirms these arguments almost everyday: Markets are "cautious" in the run-up to a particular election. The "market" is taking a "wait-and-see attitude" towards the new government. Market actors "widely anticipated the cabinet dissolution" and did not move in response to the "expected announcement."

Prior academic investigations, however, have been less successful in finding systematic evidence that markets respond to politics in this manner. While some research does conclude that political predictability affects market behavior, other studies cannot support these empirical findings. Still other studies evaluate how government partisanship, electoral timing, electoral institutions, the balance of legislative and executive power, the policy process, the institutional status of the central bank, and the capacity of the bureaucracy affect market behavior. These studies offer no clear results. Overall, a survey of the academic literature leaves the impression that market responses to political events follow no coherent pattern.

What, then, makes our findings so consistent? First, we based our investigation on *both* the finance and political science literatures. The finance literature tells us not only that information matters to market actors when they reallocate their portfolios, but *how* that information matters. Despite recent challenges to the efficient markets hypothesis, its underlying message that markets quickly incorporate available information provides a valuable starting point. The finance literature also underscores the importance of prior beliefs and expectations. Only new information – information that is unanticipated – is likely to move markets. Moreover, recent research in behavioral finance also demonstrates that market actors develop expectations based on information outside the market.

The political science literature, in turn, gives us insight into the type of information available to market actors and how they use that information to forecast political outcomes. Political scientists have developed increasingly sophisticated models of political processes that formalize the strategic behavior of political actors. These models allow them to predict outcomes based on different starting values of relevant variables – for instance, poll results, the distribution of legislative seats, party positions, the electoral clock, etc. We contend that astute political observers make similar, if less formal, calculations as they forecast the outcomes of political events. Consequently, these models can serve as a proxy measure for the information available to market actors. While still an indirect measure of the political/policy expectations of market actors, these models provide a better estimate of the information available to market actors than traditional (dummy variable) measures of government partisanship and electoral timing.

Drawing on these two literatures, we are able to design appropriate empirical tests – tests that more accurately reflect how markets behave, tests that emphasize the political information relevant to market actors, tests that are more likely to be consistent with theoretical intuitions about the relationship between politics and markets.

We also pursue a methodological strategy to evaluate market behavior that is consistent with approaches in financial economics. We first draw on fundamental models of market behavior – the efficient markets hypothesis, arbitrage pricing theory, rational expectations theory – to provide a baseline for our expectations. Second, the size and technological sophistication of these asset markets implies that prices in these markets adjust quickly to the arrival of new information. Therefore, we work at the lowest level of temporal aggregation possible given the data constraints. Third, we employ both large-*n* cross-national analysis as well as case studies of individual political events. Only by combining both strategies can we fully evaluate the impact of political information on market behavior. These methodological strategies help insure that we capture the influence of politics on asset markets and also guard against making conclusions based on a single empirical method, a single research design, or a single level of aggregation.

MARKETS AND DEMOCRACY

In recent years, many political economists and popular commentators have argued that the presence of ever wider and deeper asset markets poses new challenges to democratic principles. These arguments contend that owners of mobile (financial) capital increasingly possess the ability to shift their portfolios out of markets if they are dissatisfied with the local policy environment. To attract investment, therefore, politicians must adopt a "market-friendly" mix of institutional arrangements and policy commitments, making policy choices less reflective of voter desires and more responsive to the (implicit) policy demands of financial capital. Citizens, in turn, have little choice but to accept these new policies, thwarting their true policy preferences and breeding public dissatisfaction with democracy.

The posited role of asset markets in constraining democracy involves a long and complex chain of causal mechanisms. Each link in this causal chain requires theoretical development and empirical scrutiny before political economists can reach firm conclusions about the relationship between markets and democratic performance. In this book, we have focused on one particular link: how markets respond to democratic political events. The results demonstrate that markets are calm during political events that have predictable short-term outcomes. What do these results suggest about the relationship between asset markets and democracy? We offer some cautious speculation about how our work connects with these larger debates about asset markets, policy, institutions, and democracy.

ASSET MARKET BEHAVIOR AND DEMOCRATIC INSTITUTIONS

Our results suggest that market and political reforms in the industrial democracies over the past twenty years may be designed to break the linkages between financial market behavior and democratic political outcomes.

We have demonstrated that policy uncertainty surrounding political outcomes increases market volatility, which can inhibit trade and investment. Increased economic openness and more widespread asset ownership may have increased the economic costs of political competition, making high levels of democratic political uncertainty simply too costly to sustain. Owners of assets, therefore, have an incentive to demand reforms that (1) limit political uncertainty and (2) reduce their exposure to politically-induced financial market volatility.

In turn, politicians have found themselves increasingly vulnerable to financial market volatility. Financial market turbulence can negatively affect the ability of politicians to retain office by hurting approval ratings or increasing the costs of borrowing. Politicians, therefore, have incentives to supply institutional reforms that (1) limit their susceptibility to the negative political consequences of financial market volatility and (2) increase political predictability to prevent financial market volatility.

The intersection of interests between the demanders of institutional reform (i.e., asset owners) and the suppliers of reform (i.e., politicians) is consistent with the pattern of institutional reforms we observe in the industrial democracies over the past 20 years (Table 9.1). For instance, most industrial democracies have adopted central bank institutions to make central bankers more independent of direct political control (e.g., Bernhard 2002; Bernhard and Leblang 2002b). An independent central bank helps to ensure policy stability and predictability and could, therefore, mitigate some of the financial costs associated with political uncertainty.

In the European Union, member states have adopted a single currency. As our results demonstrate, currency market volatility has not only economic costs, but direct political costs for governments. The possibility of speculative exchange market pressure and devaluations within the EMS, therefore, presented a potential hazard for member state governments. Speculators could destroy not just the currency peg, but also the reputations and public standing of incumbent politicians! The single currency insulates politicians from the negative consequences of market

Table 9.1. *Institutional reform in the industrial democracies since 1979*

Country	Year	Reform to electoral system, central bank, exchange rate
Australia	1983	Adopt floating exchange rate
Austria	1996	Join European monetary system, post-Maastricht
Belgium	1979	Join European monetary system
	1991	Sign Maastricht treaty
	1993	Grant Central Bank more independence
Canada		
Denmark	1979	Join European monetary system
	1991	Sign Maastricht treaty (eventually opt-out of euro)
Finland	1996	Join European monetary system, post-Maastricht
	1998	Grant Central Bank independence
France	1979	Join European monetary system
	1991	Sign Maastricht treaty
	1993	Grant Central Bank independence
Germany	1979	Join European monetary system
	1991	Sign Maastricht treaty
Ireland	1979	Join European monetary system
	1991	Sign Maastricht treaty
	1998	Grant Central Bank independence
Italy	1979	Join European monetary system
	1981	Grant Central Bank more independence (divorce)
	1991	Sign Maastricht treaty
	1992	Leave European monetary system
	1992	Grant Central Bank independence
	1994	Electoral system reform
	1996	Return to European monetary system
Japan	1993	Electoral system reform
	1998	Grant Central Bank independence
New Zealand	1985	Adopt floating exchange rate
	1990	Grant Central Bank independence
	1992	Electoral system reform
Netherlands	1979	Join European monetary system
	1991	Sign Maastricht treaty
Norway	1992	Adopt floating exchange rate
	1994	Adopt fixed exchange rate*

(*continued*)

Table 9.1. *(continued)*

Country	Year	Reform to electoral system, central bank, exchange rate
Sweden	1996	Join European monetary system, post-Maastricht
	1998	Grant Central Bank independence
United Kingdom	1990	Join European monetary system
	1992	Leave European monetary system
	1997	Grant Central Bank independence

* In 1994, Norway decided to manage the krone vis-à-vis the ECU. While the monetary policy guidelines stated that the monetary policy would be aimed at keeping the krone stable against the ECU, no commitment was made to defend a specific parity.

turmoil by removing the possibility of currency speculation between member states.

Several industrial democracies have also experimented with electoral reform. Italy, New Zealand, and Japan, for instance, recently adopted new, mixed-member electoral systems, designed to make political competition in these countries more predictable and stable while still allowing for meaningful partisan choice. These relatively-disproportionate proportional electoral systems are likely to produce large centrist parties – the type of parties that enjoy a "strong" position in the process of coalition formation. By making politics more predictable, these reforms should reduce the frequency and depth of abnormal returns observed during periods of political competition.

The occurrence of these institutional reforms is far too contingent to be attributed solely to the impact of larger and more volatile capital markets. But it is worth noting that our results indicate that these reforms are remarkably *consistent* with the interests of asset owners. As asset ownership has spread in the industrial democracies, the lower returns generated by political uncertainty impose greater and more widespread costs. These costs are likely to grow with demographic trends in the industrial democracies, particularly an aging population that will rely on their investments for income and place a heavier fiscal burden on the state (OECD 2002; Poterba 2004). These economic costs have political ramifications: while a variety of shocks have precipitated reforms, the interests of asset owners constitute one of the important background conditions influencing patterns of institutional reform.

Stretching the implications of our research even further, the relationship between political predictability and asset markets suggests a rationale for the coincidence of two global trends: increased financial integration and the widespread adoption of democratic institutions (e.g., Bates 2001). Although we operate in the context of established democracies, our results indicate that asset owners prefer political predictability. Where asset owners can easily forecast political outcomes (and, in turn, policy choices), they are better able to adjust their portfolios.

While democratic political processes entail some risk, democracies are far more transparent and open than authoritarian regimes. Under a democracy, asset owners have information about the policy environment – information they need to make better investment decisions. Further, political outcomes and policy choices are more predictable under a democracy with competing political agendas, diverse representation, and meaningful accountability.

Increased levels of financial integration give asset owners even more options for investment. The global competition for this capital, therefore, provides politicians with incentives to reform their systems, to adopt democratic institutions which will, in turn, attract investment. The power of global capital, therefore, can help reinforce the trend of democratization.

ASSET MARKETS AND THE QUALITY OF DEMOCRACY

While asset market behavior may provide incentives for the adoption of certain types of democratic institutions, its impact on the quality of democracy remains an open question. Some political economists contend that the mobility of investment capital severely limits the choices available to voters since politicians must adopt pro-market policies to attract and retain capital. Even though formal democratic practices exist, significant political choices do not.

This view, in our opinion, is a rather strong position. Market actors do prefer predictable short-term outcomes. But there is nothing inherent about short-term predictability that threatens the quality of democracy. Certainly, sustainable democracy requires a type of long-term distributive uncertainty, where today's policy losers can reasonably expect to be tomorrow's winners. But those long-term expectations can be formed in a variety of institutional arrangements, some of which enhance the short-term predictability of outcomes.

The impact of financial market integration on the quality of democracy depends, in part, on the behavior of political leaders. Even if financial markets constrain what parties can accomplish in office, parties still have incentives to differentiate themselves from their competitors in order to attract votes. If their ability to deliver outcomes in some issue areas is limited, they can emphasize different sets of issues, offering new alternatives and policy bundles for voters. In some cases, innovative policy appeals may create new options for voters, allowing them to vote on issues that were ignored or de-emphasized in the previous policy space of political competition. Financial integration, therefore, does not necessarily thwart democracy – voters may still have choices. But these are likely to be different sets of choices, reflecting changes in the nature of political discourse and the underlying issue dimensions of party competition.

LINKING MARKETS AND DEMOCRACY

Our results do not represent the last word on these issues. Instead, we hope our work inspires others to take up the theoretical, analytical, and empirical challenges necessary to link markets and democracy. As a way of conclusion, we highlight a number of those research tasks.

First, we need more theoretical and empirical work on the microfoundations of investor behavior to evaluate how political information influences markets. Recent research in behavioral finance implies that traders become informed about politics in a variety of ways and to varying degrees. Do they pay direct attention to political information?[1] Do they tease out political information from price movements? How do their prior beliefs influence how they interpret this information? What determines those prior beliefs? Traders also make their decisions continuously rather than at discrete intervals, raising issues concerning the dynamics of learning and information processing surrounding political events.[2]

As we have argued, we believe that political science can provide insight into the political information available to market actors. We have relied on formal models of political processes to provide proxy measures of market beliefs, making the implicit assumption that economic actors have rational expectations about political processes. Yet other research in political science focuses on how citizens become informed about political processes. The voting behavior literature, for instance, suggests that voters rely on elite cues or information short-cuts when casting their ballots.

[1] After conducting interviews with traders, Mosley (2003) concludes that they do not pay close attention to political news in making investment decisions.

[2] Important contributions to our understanding of dynamic behavior in markets include Ljungqvist and Sargent (2000), Evans and Honkapohja (2001), and Duffie (2001). Granato and Wong (2005) apply similar models to political environments.

Do investors use similar tools to evaluate potential political outcomes? Public opinion surveys regularly report that citizens are poorly informed about candidate positions or even basic political facts. Do investors have a more accurate picture of the political process? Addressing these issues may not only help us understand how investors shift their portfolios in response to political events, but it also may explain whether and how investors vote differently than "average" citizens. Connecting the behavioral literatures across political science and finance, therefore, represents a potentially fertile research frontier.

Second, we need a better understanding of whether information about political processes has fundamentally different market effects than economic information, as some authors have claimed. That is, what type of decisions do investors make based on their evaluation of potential political outcomes? Do political events cause investors to shift their portfolios in ways that differ from decisions taken in the face of new economic information? For instance, our results show that less predictable political events tend to depress expected returns from equity investments but have no discernible impact on the performance of ten year government bonds. Where is the money going? Do investors perceive that equities and bonds are not substitutes? Are they shifting their assets across borders?[3]

The wide range of opportunities available to investors makes it even more difficult to uncover the impact of political events. Investors can shift their portfolios across markets and across borders; they can also move their holdings within markets. For instance, investors can alter their equity holdings, moving to particular stocks that are likely to be favored by different political outcomes (see, for instance, McGillivray 2003). Further, investors may shift the temporal domain of their investments, moving between assets that have long-term value and those that mature in the near-term as political events approach.

Concrete answers to these questions require disaggregated data on specific investment transactions – data that are not publicly available or

[3] Theoretical models and empirical evidence agree that asset owners have a significant "home bias" when it comes to the choice of investment instruments (for instance, French and Poterba 1991; Lewis 1999). One explanation for this bias centers on asymmetric information: they have better information about domestic stocks than foreign stocks. This leads to a portfolio comprised of more domestic than foreign stocks (Frankel and Schmukler 1997). Investors also presumably have a better sense of the domestic political environment.

widespread.[4] Determining how political events affect portfolio allocation, however, is a necessary step in calculating the distributional consequences of market behavior and the economic costs of democratic uncertainty.

A third research frontier taps into how market behavior can provide information about political processes. A number of "boutique" markets – e.g., the Iowa electronic market,[5] British betting parlors – already use investment behavior to predict electoral outcomes. Given the accuracy of those markets, it seems reasonable to expect that the behavior of asset prices could forecast political results: when an election will be called, whether a cabinet will be dissolved, who will be elected, etc. For instance, we expect that the term structure of government bonds will yield clues about how long investors anticipate a cabinet government to last in office. Other assets may also help predict different political outcomes.

The political information embedded in market behavior also has uses beyond telling the future. Herron (2000) employs the price of government bonds prior to the 1992 British general election to generate a measure of partisanship based on market expectations. He is thus able to quantify the expected policy differences between the Labour and Conservative parties. Uncovering political information from market behavior, therefore, may have dividends not just for forecasting outcomes, but also for providing measures of political variables in other models of political processes.

Fourth, the distributional consequences of asset market behavior are still not well-understood. Who benefits from abnormal returns? Who loses from excessive market volatility? How does market behavior ripple through the economy to affect not only growth but also equality? Without a more detailed map of these distributional implications, it is difficult to specify fully the costs of democratic uncertainty on market behavior.

Finally, much work remains to be done on how market behavior affects political processes: to what extent do politicians respond to the evolution of asset prices? Many arguments about the relationship between capital mobility and democracy are built on the assumption that politicians adjust their policies in anticipation of market reactions, simply forgoing any proposal that is likely to spark a sharp market reaction. Of course, it is difficult to observe this strategic inaction. Instead, we need a deeper

[4] We are aware of a small daily data set of cross-border equity flows to emerging countries compiled by State Street Corporation. This data has been employed in studies by Griffin, Nardari, and Stulz (2002) and Portes and Rey (2005).

[5] http://www.biz.uiowa.edu/iem/

understanding of how politicians view asset markets and use asset market behavior to shape policy choices. That is, politicians may employ the performance of asset prices as another barometer of their policy performance, just as they would consider opinion polls. To evaluate this possibility, we need to learn how politicians interpret asset market behavior. How much do politicians care about anticipated changes in asset prices? Are they likely to shift their own behavior only in the face of large, unexpected price shifts? How might politicians seek to manipulate market outcomes to further their own agenda? Just as more research is needed on how markets respond to politics, we also need more information about how politicians respond to markets.

The relationship between democracy and markets represents a traditional, fundamental concern, not just for political economists but also for citizens. With the globalization of economic activity, these essential questions have a renewed urgency. Unfortunately, the enormity of the question has too often led social scientists to make claims about the "big picture" without fully evaluating how each piece of the puzzle fits together. Based on imperfect or faulty assumptions, these answers are often untested, incomplete, or flawed.

Nevertheless, we believe that social scientists are now in a better position to tackle these issues. A renewed emphasis on multidisciplinary and cross-disciplinary research has made it possible to combine theories and analytical tools from across different fields. Data sources are richer, more detailed, and more widely available. New methods and research tools exist to analyze this data. These developments have improved our capacity to investigate the specific mechanisms that link politics and economics without losing sight of the larger research question. By carefully exploring the specific connections between financial integration, political processes, and institutional reform, we believe that the social scientific community will improve our understanding of the relationship between democracy and capitalism.

References

Alesina, A., De Broeck, M., Prati, A. and Tabellini, G. (1992). Default risk on government debt in OECD countries. *Economic Policy*, **15**, 427–51.

Alesina, A., Grilli, V. and Milesi-Ferretti, G. M. (1994). The political economy of capital controls. In *Capital Mobility: the Impact on Consumption, Investment, and Growth*, eds. L. Leiderman and A. Razin. Cambridge: Cambridge University Press.

Alesina, A. and Rosenthal, H. (1995). *Partisan Politics, Divided Government, and the Economy*. New York: Cambridge University Press.

Alesina, A. and Roubini, N. (1997). *Political Cycles and the Macroeconomy*. Cambridge: MIT Press.

Alesina, A., Roubini, N. and Cohen, G. (1993). Electoral business cycles in industrial democracies. *European Journal of Political Economy*, **23**, 1–25.

Alesina, A. and Sachs, J. (1988). Political parties and the business cycle in the United States: 1948–1984. *Journal of Money, Credit, and Banking*, **20**(1), 63–82.

Alexander, C. (2001). *Market Models: A Guide to Financial Data Analysis*. New York: John Wiley & Sons.

Aliber, R. Z. (1973). The interest rate parity theorem: a reinterpretation. *Journal of Political Economy*, **81**, 1451–9.

Allison, P. (1984). *Event History Analysis*. Beverly Hills: Sage Publications.

Alt, J. and Chrystal, K. A. (1983). *Political Economics*. Berkeley: University of California Press.

Alt, J. and King, G. (1994). Transfers of governmental power: the meaning of time dependence. *Comparative Political Studies*, **27**(2), 190–210.

Alt, J. (1979). *The Politics of Economic Decline*. New York: Cambridge University Press.

Ammer, J. and Mei, J. (1996). Measuring international economic linkages with stock market data. *Journal of Finance*, **51**, 1743–64.

Andrews, D. (1994). Capital mobility and state autonomy: toward a structural theory of international monetary relations. *International Studies Quarterly*, **38**, 193–218.

Bachman, D. (1992). The effect of political risk on the forward exchange bias: the case of elections. *Journal of International Money and Finance*, **11**, 208–19.

Bailey, R. (2005). *The Economics of Financial Markets*. Cambridge: Cambridge University Press.

Baillie, R. T. and McMahon, P. C. (1989). *The Foreign Exchange Market: Theory and Econometric Evidence*. New York: Cambridge University Press.

Ballie, R. and Bollerslev, T. (1989). The message in daily exchange rates: a conditional-variance tale. *Journal of Business and Economic Statistics*, **7**, 297–305.

Baillie, R., Bollerslev, T. and Mikkelsen, H. (1996). Fractionally integrated generalized autoregressive conditional heteroskedasticity. *Journal of Econometrics*, **74**, 3–30.

Barberis, N. and Thaler, R. (2002). A survey of behavioral finance. *National Bureau of Economic Research Working Paper 9222*.

Barr, D. G. and Priestley, R. (2002). *Expected Returns, Risk and the Integration of International Bond Markets*, Manuscript, Imperial College, London.

Barro, R. and Gordon, D. (1983). Rules, discretion, and reputation in a model of monetary policy. *Journal of Monetary Economics*, **12**, 101–21.

Bates, R. (2001). *Prosperity and Violence: The Political Economy of Development*. New York: W.W. Norton and Company.

Beck, N. (1991). Comparing dynamic specifications: the case of presidential approval. *Political Analysis*, **3**, 51–88.

Beck, N. (1997). *Modeling Space and Time: The Event History Approach*, Manuscript.

Beck, N., Katz, J. and Tucker, R. (1998). Beyond ordinary logit: taking time seriously in binary time-series-cross-section models. *American Journal of Political Science*, **42**(4), 1260–1288.

Bera, A. and Higgins, M. K. (1993). A survey of ARCH models: properties, estimation, and testing. *Journal of Economic Surveys*, **7**, 305–66.

Berk, R. (1990). A primer on robust regression. In *Modern Methods of Data Analysis*, eds. J. Fox and J. S. Long. Thousand Oaks, CA: Sage Press.

Bernhard, W. (2001). *Exchange Rate Stability and Political Accountability in the European Monetary System*, Typescript, University of Illinois at Urbana-Champaign.

Bernhard, W. (2002). *Banking on Reform: Political Parties and Central Bank Independence in the Industrial Democracies*. Ann Arbor: University of Michigan Press.

Bernhard, W. and Leblang, D. (2002a). Political processes and foreign exchange markets: the forward exchange rate bias. *American Journal of Political Science*, **46**(2), 316–33.

Bernhard, W. and Leblang, D. (2002b). Political parties and monetary commitments. *International Organization*, **56**(4), 803–30.

Bernhard, W. and Leblang, D. (2006). Polls and pounds: political expectations and exchange rate volatility in Britain. *Quarterly Journal of Political Science*, **1**(1), 26–61.

Bernoth, K., von Hagen, J. and Schuknecht, L. (2004). Sovereign risk premia in the European government bond market. *European Central Bank, Working Paper 369 (June)*.

Bernstein, W. (2004). *The Birth of Plenty: How the Prosperity of the Modern World was Created*. New York: McGraw-Hill.

Black, F. (1972). Capital market equilibrium with restricted borrowing. *Journal of Business*, **45**, 444–54.

Block, F. (1977). The ruling class does not rule: notes on the Marxist theory of the state. *Socialist Revolution*, **33**, 6–28.

Blomberg, S. B. and Hess, G. (1996). Politics and foreign exchange rate forecasts. *Research Working Paper 96–02*, Federal Reserve Bank of Kansas City.

Bollerslev, T. (1986). Generalized autoregressive conditional heteroskedasticity. *Journal of Econometrics*, **31**, 307–27.

Bollerslev, T. (1990). Modeling the coherence in short-run nominal exchange rates: a multivariate generalized arch model. *Review of Economics and Statistics*, **72**, 498–505.

Bollerslev, T., Chou, R. Y. and Kroner, K. F. (1992). ARCH modeling in finance. *Journal of Econometrics*, **52**, 5–59.

Bollerslev, T. and Mikkelsen, H. (1996). Modeling and pricing long-memory in stock market volatility. *Journal of Econometrics*, **73**, 151–84.

Bollerslev, T. and Rossi, P. (1996). Introduction. In *Modeling Stock Market Volatility: Bridging the Gap to Continuous Time*, ed. P. Rossi. San Diego, CA: The Academic Press.

Bossaerts, P. (2002). *The Paradox of Asset Pricing*. Princeton: Princeton University Press.

Box-Steffensmeier, J. and Smith, R. M. (1996). The dynamics of aggregate partisanship. *American Political Science Review*, **90**(3), 352–371.

Boyer, B. H., Gibson, M. S. and Loretan, M. (1997). Pitfalls in tests for changes in correlations. *International Finance Discussion Papers 597*, Board of Governors of the Federal Reserve System.

Brace, P. and Hinckley, B. (1991). The structure of presidential approval. *Journal of Politics*, **53**(4), 993–1017.

Brace, P. and Hinckley, B. (1992). *Follow the Leader: Opinion Polls and Modern Presidencies*. New York: Basic Books.

Bracker, K., Docking, D. S. and Koch, P. (1999). Economic determinants of evolution in international stock market integration. *Journal of Empirical Finance*, **6**, 1–27.

Branson, R. and Henderson, D. (1985). The specification and influence of asset markets. In *Handbook of International Economics*, Volume II, eds. R. Jones and P. Kenen. Amsterdam: North Holland.

Brehm, J. and Gronke, P. (1994). *Modeling volatile approval: a modified ARCH approach to presidential approval ratings*. Paper presented at APSA, New York.

Brennan, R. and Prediger, D. (1981). Coefficient kappa: some uses, misuses, and alternatives. *Educational and Psychological Measurement*, **41**, 687–699.

Britton, A. (1991). *Macroeconomic Policy in Britain 1974–1987*. New York: Cambridge University Press.

Brooks, C. (2002). *Introductory Econometrics for Finance*. New York: Cambridge University Press.

Brooks, R. and del Negro, M. (2002). The Rise in Comovement Across National Stock Markets: Market Integration or Global Bubble? *IMF Working Paper WP/02/147*.

Brown, S. and Warner, J. (1980). Measuring security price performance. *Journal of Financial Economics*, **8**, 205–258.

Brown, S. and Warner, J. (1985). Using daily stock returns: the case of event studies. *Journal of Financial Economics*, **14**, 3–31.

Budge, I. and Kingemann, H.-D. (2001). Finally! Comparative over-time mapping of party policy movement. In *Mapping Policy Preferences: Estimates for Parties, Electors and Governments 1945–1998*, ed. Budge et al. New York: Oxford University Press, pp. 19–50.

Budge, I., Kingemann, H.-D., Volkens, A., Bara, J. and Tanenbaum, E. (2001). *Mapping Policy Preferences: Estimates for Parties, Electors, and Governments 1945–1998*. New York: Oxford University Press.

Butler, D. and Butler, G. (2000). *Twentieth-Century British Political Facts 1900–2000*, 8th edition. New York: St. Martin's Press.

Cameron, C. (2000). *Veto Bargaining: Presidents and the Politics of Negative Power*. New York: Cambridge University Press.

Cameron, D. (1984). Social democracy, corporatism, labour quiescence and the representation of economic interest in advanced capitalist society. In *Order and Conflict in Contemporary Capitalism*, ed. J. H. Goldthorpe. Oxford: Clarendon Press.

Campbell, J. Y. (2002). Consumption-based asset pricing. In *Handbook of the Economics of Finance*, eds. G. Constantinides, M. Harris and R. M. Stulz. Amsterdam: North Holland.

Campbell, J. Y., Lo, A. W. and MacKinlay, A. C. (1997). *The Econometrics of Financial Markets*. Princeton: Princeton University Press.

Campbell, J. Y. and Shiller, R. J. (1987). Cointegration and tests of present value models. *Journal of Political Economy*, **95**, 1062–88.

Campbell, J. Y. and Shiller, R. J. (1991). Yield spreads and interest rate movements: a bird's eye view. *The Review of Economic Studies*, **58**, 495–514.

Canova, F. and de Nicolo, G. (2003). The equity premium and the risk-free rate: an investigation across time and countries. *IMF Staff Papers*, **50**, 222–249.

Castles, F. and Mair, P. (1984). Left-right political scales: some expert judgments. *European Journal of Political Research*, **12**, 83–8.

Cavaglia, S., Brithgman, C. and Aked, M. (2000). The increasing importance of industry factors. *Financial Analysts Journal*, **56**, 41–56.

Charemza, W. W. and Deadman, D. F. (1992). *New Directions in Econometric Practice*. Aldershot, England: Edward Elgar.

Chen, N.-F. (1983). Some empirical tests of the theory of arbitrage pricing. *The Journal of Finance*, **38**, 1393–1414.

Chen, N.-F. (1991). Financial investment opportunities and the macroeconomy. *Journal of Finance*, **46**, 529–554.

Chen, N.-F., Roll, R. and Ross, S. A. (1986). Economic forces and the stock market. *Journal of Business*, **59**, 383–403.

Cheung, Y.-W. and Lai, K. (1998). *Macroeconomic Determinants of Long-Term Stock Market Comovements Among Major EMS Countries*, Manuscript, Department of Economics, University of California, Santa Cruz.

Christodoulakis, N. and Kalyvitis, S. (1997). Efficiency testing revisited: a foreign exchange market with Bayesian learning. *Journal of International Money and Finance*, **16**, 367–85.

Clark, P. (1973). A subordinated stochastic process model with finite variance for speculative prices. *Econometrica*, **41**, 135–55.

Clarke, H., Ho, K. and Stewart, M. (2000). Major's lessor (not minor) effects: Prime Ministerial approval and governing party support in Britain since 1979. *Electoral Studies*, **19**, 255–273.

Clarke, H. and Stewart, M. (1995). Economic evaluations, prime ministerial approval and governing party support: rival models reconsidered. *British Journal of Political Science*, **25**, 145–170.

Clarke, H. D., Stewart, M. C. and Whiteley, P. F. (1998). New models for new labour: the political economy of labour party support, January 1992–April 1997. *American Political Science Review*, **92**(3), 559–575.

Cobham, D., ed. (1994). *European Monetary Upheavals*. Manchester: Manchester University Press.

Cochrane, J. H. (2001). *Asset Pricing*. Princeton: Princeton University Press.

Codogno, L., Favero, C. and Missale, A. (2003). Yield Spreads on EMU Government Bonds. *Economic Policy*, **18**, 503–532.

Copeland, L. and Jones, S. (2001). Default probabilities of European sovereign debt: market-based estimates. *Applied Economic Letters*, **8**, 321–24.

Corsetti, G., Pericoli, M. and Sbracia, M. (2002). Some Contagion, Some Interdependence: More Pitfalls in Tests of Financial Contagion. *Working Paper*, Department of Economics, Yale University.

Cox, G. (1987). Electoral equilibria under alternative voting institutions. *American Journal of Political Science*, **31**, 82–108.

Cox, G. (1989). Undominated candidate strategies under alternative voting rules. *Mathematical Modelling*, **12**, 451–60.

Cukierman, A., Webb, S. B. and Neyapti, B. (1992). Measuring the independence of central banks and its effect on policy outcomes. *World Bank Economic Review*, **6**(3), 353–98.

Cuthbertson, K. (1996). *Quantitative Financial Economics: Stocks, Bonds and Foreign Exchange*. New York: John Wiley and Sons.

Dacorogna, M. M., Gencay, R., Muller, U. A., Olsen, R. B. and Pictet, O. (2001). *An Introduction to High Frequency Finance*. New York: Academic Press.

DeBoef, S. (2000). Modeling equilibrium relationships: error correction models with strongly autoregressive data. *Political Analysis*, **9**, 78–94.

DeVries, C. (1992). Stylized facts of nominal exchange rate returns. In *Handbook of International Macroeconomics*, ed. F. van der Ploeg. London: Blackwell.

Diebold, F. X., Lee, J.-H. and Weinbach, G. C. (1994). Regime-switching with time varying transition probabilities. In *Nonstationary Time Series Analysis and Cointegration*, ed. C. Hargreaves. Oxford: Oxford University Press, pp. 283–302.

Diebold, F. and Nerlove, M. (1989). The dynamics of exchange rate volatility: a multivariate latent factor ARCH model. *Journal of Applied Econometrics*, **4**, 1–21.

Domowitz, I. and Hakkio, C. (1985). Conditional variance and the risk premium in the foreign exchange market. *Journal of International Economics*, **19**, 47–66.

Dooley, M. P. and Isard, P. (1980). Capital controls, political risk, and deviations from interest-rate parity. *Journal of Political Economy*, **88**, 370–84.

Downs, A. (1957). *An Economic Theory of Democracy*. Boston: Addison-Wesley.

Drazen, A. (2000). *Political Economy in Macroeconomics.* Princeton: Princeton University Press.

Duffie, D. (2001). *Dynamic Asset Pricing Theory*, 3rd edition. Princeton: Princeton University Press.

Eichengreen, B. and Mody, A. (2004). Do collective action clauses raise borrowing costs. *The Economic Journal*, **114**, 247–64.

Eichengreen, B., Rose, A. and Wyplosz, C. (1995). Exchange market mayhem: the antecedents and aftermath of speculative attacks. *Economic Policy*, **21**, 249–312.

Elton, E. J., Gruber, M. J., Brown, S. J. and Goetzmann, W. N. (2003). *Modern Portfolio Theory and Investment Analysis*, 6th edition. New York: John Wiley and Sons.

Enders, W. (2004). *Applied Econometric Time Series*, 2nd edition. New York: John Wiley and Sons.

Engel, C. (1994). Can the Markov-switching model forecast exchange rates? *Journal of International Economics*, **36**, 151–165.

Engel, C. (1996). The forward discount anomaly and the risk premium: a survey of recent evidence. *Journal of Empirical Finance* (June), 123–91.

Engle, R. (1982). Autoregressive conditional heteroscedasticity with estimates of the variance of United Kingdom inflation. *Econometrica*, **50**, 987–1007.

Engle, R. (1984). Wald, likelihood ratio, and Lagrange multiplier tests in econometrics. In *Handbook of Econometrics*, Vol. 2, eds. Z. Griliches and M. Intriligator. Amsterdam: North-Holland.

Engle, R. (1996). The econometrics of ultra-high frequency data. *NBER Paper 5816*.

Engle, R. F., Lilien, D. M. and Robins, R. P. (1987). Estimating time varying risk premia in the term structure: the ARCH-M model. *Econometrica*, **55**, 391–408.

Epps, T. and Epps, M. (1976). The stochastic dependence of security price changes and transactions volumes: implications for the mixture-of-distributions hypothesis. *Econometrica*, **44**, 305–25.

Evans, G. and Honkapohja, S. (2001). *Learning and Expectations in Macroeconomics.* Princeton, NJ: Princeton University Press.

Fama, E. (1970). Efficient capital markets: a review of theory and empirical work. *Journal of Finance*, **25**, 383–417.

Fama, E. (1984). Forward and spot exchange rates. *Journal of Monetary Economics*, **14**, 319–338.

Fama, E. (1991). Efficient capital markets II. *Journal of Finance*, **46**, 1575–1618.

Fama, E. L., Jensen, F. M. and Roll, R. (1969). The adjustment of stock prices to new information. *International Economics Review*, **10**, 1–21.

Fama, E. F. and French, K. R. (1993). Common risk factors in the returns on stocks and bonds. *Journal of Finance*, **47**, 426–465.

Fama, E. and MacBeth, J. (1973). Risk, return and equilibrium: empirical tests. *Journal of Political Economy*, **71**, 607–636.

Farrell, D. M. (2001). *Electoral Systems: A Comparative Introduction.* New York: Palgrave.

Fiorina, M. (1981). *Retrospective Voting in American National Elections.* New Haven: Yale University Press.

Flandreau, M., Cacheux, L. and Zumer, F. (1998). Stability without a pact? Lessons from the European gold standard. 1880–1914. *Economic Policy*, **26**, 117–62.

Forbes, K. J. and Chinn, M. D. (2003). A decomposition of global linkages in financial markets over time, *Working Paper 4413–03*. MIT Sloan School of Management.

Forbes, K. J. and Chinn, M. D. (2004). A decomposition of global linkages in financial markets over time. *Review of Economics and Statistics*, **86**, 705–722.

Forbes, J. and Rigobon, R. (2002). No contagion, only interdependence: measuring stock market co-movements. *Journal of Finance*, **999**, 900–909.

Foster, F. D. and Vishwanathan, S. (1995). Can speculative trading explain the volume–volatility relation? *Journal of Business and Economic Statistics*, October, 379–396.

Frankel, J. and Mussa, M. (1985). Asset markets, exchange rates and the balance of payments. In *Handbook of International Economics*, Volume II, eds. R. Jones and P. Kenen. Amsterdam: North Holland.

Frankel, J. A. and Engel, C. M. (1984). Do asset demand functions optimize over the mean and variance of real returns? A six currency test. *Journal of International Economics*, **17**, 309–323.

Frankel, J. A. and Schmukler, S. L. (1997). Country funds and asymmetric information. Center for International and Development Economics Research (CIDER) *Working Papers C97-087*. University of California at Berkeley.

Franklin, C. (2001). *Pre-Election Polls in Nation and State: a Dynamic Bayesian Hierarchical Model.* Presented at the 2001 Annual Meeting of the American Political Science Association, San Francisco.

Franses, P. H. and van Dijk, D. (2000). *Non-Linear Time Series Models in Empirical Finance*. New York: Cambridge University Press.

Franzese, R. (2002). Electoral and partisan cycles in economic policies and outcomes. *Annual Review of Political Science*, **5**, 369–421.

Freeman, J. R., Hays, J. C. and Stix, H. (1999). *The Electoral Information Hypothesis Revisited*, Manuscript, University of Michigan.

Freeman, J. R., Hays, J. C. and Stix, H. (2000). Democracy and markets: the case of exchange rates. *American Journal of Political Science*, **44**(3), 449–468.

French, K. and Poterba, J. (1991). Investor diversification and international equity markets. *American Economic Review*, **81**, 222–226.

Frieden, J. (1991). Invested interests: the politics of national economic policies in a world of global finance. *International Organization*, **45**, 425–451.

Frieden, J. (1999). *Sectoral Interests and European Monetary Integration: An Empirical Assessment*, Typescript, Harvard University.

Friedman, M. (1953). The case for flexible exchange rates. In *Essays in Positive Economics*. Chicago: University of Chicago Press.

Froot, K. and Frankel, J. (1989). Forward discount bias: is it an exchange risk premium? *Quarterly Journal of Economics*, **104**, 139–161.

Froot, K. and Frankel, J. (1990). Anomalies: foreign exchange. *Journal of Economic Perspectives*, **4**, 179–192.

Gallant, A. R, Rossi, P. E. and Tauchen, G. (1992). Stock prices and volume. *Review of Financial Studies*, **5**, 199–242.

Garcia, R. (1998). Asymptotic null distribution of the likelihood ratio test in a Markov-switching model. *International Economic Review*, **39**, 763–788.

Garrett, G. (1992). The political consequences of Thatcherism. *Political Behavior*, **14**, 361–382.

Garrett, G. (1995). Capital mobility, trade, and the domestic politics of economic policy. *International Organization*, **49**(4), 657–687.

Gartner, M. and Wellershoff, K. W. (1995). Is there an election cycle in stock market returns? *International Review of Economics and Finance*, **4**, 387–410.

Gemmill, G. (1992). Political risk and market efficiency: tests based on British stock and options markets in the 1987 election. *Journal of Banking and Finance*, **16**, 211–31.

Gemmill, G. (1995). Stockmarket behavior and information in British elections. *Working Paper*, City University Business School.

Gerber, A. and Green, D. (1998). Rational learning and partisan attitudes. *American Journal of Political Science*, **42**, 794–818.

Glosten, L. R., Jaganathan, R. and Runkle, D. E. (1993). On the relation between the expected value and the volatility of the nominal excess return on stocks. *The Journal of Finance*, **48**, 1779–1801.

Goodman, J. and Pauly, L. B. (1993). The obsolescence of capital controls? Economic management in an age of global markets. *World Politics*, **46**, 50–82.

Granato, J. (1996). The effect of policy-maker reputation and credibility on public expectations: an application to macroeconomic policy changes. *Journal of Theoretical Politics*, **8**(4), 449–70.

Granato, J. and Wong, M. C. S. (2005). *The Role of Policymakers in Business Cycle Fluctuations*. New York: Cambridge University Press.

Green, D. and Gerber, A. (2000). *Samplemiser* 4.0.

Green, D., Gerber, A. and DeBoef, S. (1999). Tracking opinion over time: a method for reducing sampling error. *Public Opinion Quarterly*, **63**, 178–192.

Green, D., Palmquist, B. and Schickler, E. (2002). *Partisan Hearts and Minds*. New Haven, CT: Yale University Press.

Greene, W. (2003). *Econometric Analysis*, 5th edition. New Jersey: Prentice Hall.

Griffin, J. M. and Karolyi, G. A. (1998). Another look at the role of the industrial structure of markets for international diversification strategies. *Journal of Financial Economics*, **59**, 351–73.

Griffin, J. M., Nardari, F. and Stulz, R. M. (2002). Daily cross-border equity flows: published or pulled? *Ohio State University: Dice Working Paper No. 2002–6*.

Grilli, V., Masciandaro, D. and Tabellini, G. (1991). Political and monetary institutions and public finance policies in the industrialized democracies. *Economic Policy*, **10**(October), 342–92.

Gros, D. and Thygesen, N. (1998). *European Monetary Integration: from the European Monetary System to European Monetary Union*, 2nd edition. New York: Longman Press.

Gujarati, D. (2003). *Basic Econometrics*, 4th edition. New York: McGraw-Hill.

Haggard, S. and McCubbins, M., eds. (2001). *Presidents, Parliaments and Policy*. Cambridge: Cambridge University Press.

Hall, P. (1986). *Governing the Economy: the Politics of State Intervention in Britain and France*. New York: Oxford University Press.

Hallerberg, M. (2004). *Domestic Budgets in a United Europe: Fiscal Governance from the End of Bretton Woods to EMU*. Ithaca, NY: Cornell University Press.

Hallerberg, M. and von Hagen, J. (1998). Electoral institutions, cabinet negotiations, and budget deficits within the European Union. In *Fiscal Institutions and Fiscal Performance*, eds. J. Poterba and J. von Hagen, pp. 209–32. Chicago: University of Chicago Press.

Hallwood, C. P. and MacDonald, R. (1994). *International Money and Finance*, 2nd edition. Oxford: Basil Blackwell.

Hamilton, J. D. (1989). A new approach to the economic analysis of nonstationary time series and the business cycle. *Econometrica*, **57**, 357–384.

Hamilton, J. D. (1994). *Time Series Analysis*. Princeton University Press: Princeton.

Hamilton, J. D. and Susmel, R. (1994). Autoregressive conditional heteroskedasticity and changes in regime. *Journal of Econometrics*, **64**, 307–333.

Hansen, B. E. (1992). The likelihood ratio test under non-standard conditions: testing the Markov switching model of GNP. *Journal of Applied Econometrics*, **7**, S61–S82.

Hansen, B. E. (2001). *The New Econometrics of Structural Change: Dating Changes in U.S. Labor Productivity*. Typescript, University of Wisconsin.

Hansen, L. (1982). Large sample properties of generalized method of moments estimators. *Econometrica*, **50**, 1029–1054.

Hansen, L. and Hodrick, R. (1980). Forward exchange rates as optimal predictors of future spot rates: an econometric analysis. *Journal of Political Economy*, **88**, 829–53.

Hanushek, E. A. (1974). Efficient estimators for regressing regression coefficients. *The American Statistician*, **28**, 66–67.

Harvey, C., Solnik, B. and Zhou, G. (1994). *What determines expected international asset returns? NBER Working Paper.*

Hausman, J. (1978). Specification tests in econometrics. *Econometrica*, **46**, 1251–1271.

Heckman, J. (1979). Sample selection bias as a specification error. *Econometrica*, **47**, 153–161.

Helleiner, E. (1994). *States and the Reemerging of Global Finance: From Bretton Woods to the 1990s*. Ithaca, NY: Cornell University Press.

Herron, M. (2000). Estimating the economic impact of political party competition in the 1992 British election. *American Journal of Political Science*, **44**(3), 326–337.

Herron, M., Lavin, J., Cram, D. and Silver, J. (1999). Measurement of political effects in the U.S. economy: a study of the 1992 presidential election. *Economics and Politics*, **11**, 51–81.

Heston, S. L. and Rouwenhorst, K. G. (1994). Does industrial structure explain the benefits of international diversification? *The Journal of Finance*, **36**, 3–27.

Treasury, H. M. (2003). *EMU and the Cost of Capital*. London: Bank of England.

Hibbs, D. A. (1987). *The Political Economy of Industrial Democracies*. Harvard Univ. Press: Cambridge, Mass.

Hodrick, R. J. (1987). *The Empirical Evidence on the Efficiency of Forward and Futures Foreign Exchange Markets*. London: Harwood Academic Publishers.

Howison, S. and Lamper, D. (2000). Trading volume in models of financial derivatives, *Working Paper*, Center for Industrial and Applied Mathematics, University of Oxford.

Huber, J. (1996a). *Rationalizing Parliament: Legislative Institutions and Party Politics in France*. New York: Cambridge University Press.

Huber, J. (1996b). The vote of confidence in parliamentary democracies. *American Political Science Review*, **90**(2), 269–282.

Huber, J. and Gabel, M. (2000). Putting parties in their place: inferring party left-right ideological positions. *American Journal of Political Science*, **44**(1), 94–103.

Ilmanen, A. (1996). When do bond markets reward investors for interest rate risk? *Journal of Portfolio Management*, Winter.

Ito, T. (1986). Capital controls and covered interest parity between the Yen and the Dollar. *Economic Studies Quarterly*, **37**, 223–40.

Jackson, S. (1995). *Re-thinking equilibrium presidential approval: Markov-switching error correction*, Presented at the Annual Meeting of the Political Methodology Section, Bloomington, IN.

Jacobs, L. R. and Shapiro, R. Y. (2000). *Politicians Don't Pander: Political Manipulation and the Loss of Democratic Responsiveness.* Chicago: University of Chicago Press.

Jones, P. and Hudson, J. (1996). The quality of political leadership: a case study of John Major. *British Journal of Political Science*, **26**(2), 229–244.

Jorion, P. (1992). Term premiums and the integration of the Eurocurrency markets. *Journal of International Money and Finance*, **11**, 17–39.

Jowell, R., Hedges, B., Lynn, P., Farrant, G. and Heath, A. (1993). The 1992 British election: the failure of the polls. *Public Opinion Quarterly*, **57**(Summer), 238–263.

Karolyi, G. A. and Stulz, R. M. (2002). Are financial assets priced locally or globally? In *Handbook of the Economics of Finance*, eds. G. Constantinides, M. Harris and R. M. Stulz. North Holland.

Karpoff, J. (1987). The relation between price changes and trading volume: a survey. *Journal of Financial and Quantitative Analysis*, **22**, 109–126.

Kavanaugh, D. (1987). *Thatcherism and British Politics: The End of Consensus?* New York: Oxford University Press.

Kennedy, P. (1998). *A Guide to Econometrics*, 4th edition. Cambridge, MA: MIT Press.

Kim, C.-J., Morley, J. C. and Nelson, C. R. (2002). *Is there a Positive Relationship Between Stock Market Volatility and the Equity Premium?* Manuscript, Washington University, St. Louis.

King, A., ed. with Wybrow, R. J. (2001). *British Public Opinion: 1937–2000, The Gallup Polls.* London: Politico's Publishing.

King, G., Alt, J., Burns, N. and Laver, M. (1990). A unified model of cabinet dissolution in parliamentary democracies. *American Journal of Political Science*, **34**(3), 846–71.

King, G. and Zeng, L. (2001). Logistic regression in rare events data. *Political Analysis*, **9**, 137–63.

King, M., Sentant, E. and Wadhawani, S. (1994). Volatility and links between stock markets. *Econometrica*, **62**, 901–933.

King, R. G. and Kurmann, A. (2002). Expectations and the term structure of interest rates: evidence and implications. *Federal Reserve Bank of Richmond Economic Quarterly*, **88**, 49–95.

Kirk, R. E. (1995). *Experimental Design: Procedures for the Behavioral Sciences.* Pacific Grove, CA: Brooks-Cole.

Kmenta, J. (1986). *Elements of Econometrics*, 2nd edition. New York: Macmillan.

Kose, M. A., Otrok, C. and Whiteman, C. (2003). *Understanding the Evolution of World Business Cycles*, Manuscript, International Monetary Fund.

Kothari, S. P. and Shanken, J. (1992). Stock return variation and excess dividends: a time-series and cross-sectional analysis. *Journal of Financial Economics*, **31**, 177–210.

Koutmos, G. and Theodossiou, P. (1994). Time-series properties and predictability of Greek exchange rates. *Managerial and Decision Economics*, **15**, 159–67.

Krasker, W. (1980). The 'peso problem' in testing the efficiency of forward exchange markets. *Journal of International Economics*, **6**, 269–276.

Krehbiel, K. (1998). *Pivotal Politics*. University of Chicago Press.

Kydland, F. and Prescott, E. (1977). Rules rather than discretion: the inconsistency of optimal plans. *Journal of Political Economy*, **85**, 473–91.

Lamoureux, C. and Lastrapes, W. (1990). Heteroskedasticity in stock return data: volume versus GARCH effects. *Journal of Finance*, **45**, 221–9.

Laux, P. and Ng, L. (1993). The sources of GARCH: empirical evidence from an intraday returns model incorporating systematic and unique risks. *Journal of International Money and Finance*, **12**, 543–60.

Laver, M. (2001). *Estimating the Policy Positions of Political Actors*. New York: Routledge.

Laver, M. and Budge, I., eds. (1991). *Party and Coalition Policy in Western Europe*. New York: Cambridge University Press.

Laver, M. and Schofield, N. (1998). *Multiparty Government: The Politics of Coalition in Europe*. Ann Arbor: University of Michigan Press.

Laver, M. and Shepsle, K. (1996). *Making and Breaking Governments*. Cambridge: Cambridge University Press.

Leblang, D. and Bernhard, W. (2000). The politics of speculative attacks in industrial democracies. *International Organization*, **54**(2), 291–324.

Leblang, D. and Bernhard, W. (2006). Parliamentary politics and foreign exchange markets: the world according to GARCH. *International Studies Quarterly* (March) **50**(1): 69–92.

Leblang, D. and Mukherjee, B. (2004). Presidential elections and the stock market: comparing Markov-switching and fractionally integrated GARCH models. *Political Analysis*, Summer.

Leblang, D. and Mukherjee, B. (2005). Government partisanship, elections and the stock market: examining American and British stock returns, 1930–2000. *American Journal of Political Science* (October) **49**, 781–803.

Lemmen, J. and Goodhart, C. (1999). Government bond markets: a panel data econometric analysis. *Eastern Economic Journal*, **25**, 77–107.

Lewis, K. (1995). Puzzles in international financial markets. In *Handbook of International Economics*, Volume III, eds. G. Grossman and K. Rogoff. Elsevier Science.

Lewis, K. K. (1999). Trying to explain home bias in equities and consumption. *Journal of Economic Literature*, **37**, 571–608.

Lewis-Beck, M. (1988). *Economics and Elections: The Major Western Democracies*. Ann Arbor: University of Michigan Press.

Lewis-Beck, M., Norpoth, H. and Lafay, J.-D., eds. (1991). *Economics and Politics: The Calculus of Support*. Ann Arbor: University of Michigan Press.

Li, L. (2002). *Macroeconomic Factors and the Correlation of Stock and Bond Returns*, Manuscript, Department of Economics, Yale University.

Lijphart, A. (1984a). Measures of cabinet durability: a conceptual and empirical evaluation. *Comparative Political Studies*, **17**(2), 265–79.

Lijphart, A. (1984b). *Democracies*. New Haven: Yale University Press.

Lijphart, A. (1999). *Patterns of Democracy: Government Forms and Performance in Thirty-Six Countries*. New Haven: Yale University Press.

Lin, T. and Roberts, B. (2001). *Markets and politics: the 2000 Taiwanese election*. Paper presented at the Annual Meeting of the Midwest Political Science Association, Chicago, Illinois.

Lindblom, C. (1977). *Politics and Markets: The World's Political Economic Systems*. New York: Basic Books.

Lintner, J. (1965). Security prices, risk and maximal gains from diversification. *Journal of Finance*, **20**, 587–615.

Ljungqvist, L. and Sargent, T. (2000). *Recursive Macroeconomic Theory*. Cambridge, MA: MIT Press.

Lobo, B. and Tufte, D. (1998). Exchange rate volatility: does politics matter? *Journal of Macroeconomics*, **20**, 351–65.

Longin, F. and Solnik, B. (2001). Extreme correlation of international equity markets. *Journal of Finance*, **56**, 649–675.

Lonning, I. M. (2000). Default premia on European government debt. *Weltwirtschaftliches Archiv*, **136**, 259–283.

Lumsdaine, R. L. (1991). *Asymptotic Properties of the Maximum Likelihood Estimator in GARCH (1,1) and IGARCH (1,1) Models*, Manuscript, Department of Economics, Princeton University.

Lupia, A. and Strom, K. (1995). Coalition termination and the strategic timing of legislative elections. *American Political Science Review*, **89**, 648–65.

MacDonald, R. and Taylor, M. P. (1991). Testing efficiency in the interwar foreign exchange market: a multiple time series approach. *Weltwirschaftliches Archiv*, **127**, 500–523.

Mackuen, M., Erikson, R. and Stimson, J. A. (1989). Macropartisanship. *American Political Science Review*, **83**, 1125–1142.

Mackuen, M., Erikson, R. and Stimson, J. A. (1995). Dynamic representation. *American Political Science Review*, **89**(4), 543–565.

Malkiel, B. (2003). The efficient market hypothesis and its critics. *Journal of Economic Perspectives*, **17**, 59–82.

Mandelbrot, B. and Taylor, H. (1967). On the distribution of stock price differences. *Operations Research*, **15**, 1057–62.

Mark, N. (1985). On time varying risk premia in the foreign exchange market. *Journal of Monetary Economics*, **16**, 3–18.

Markovitz, H. (1959). *Portfolio Selection: Efficient Diversification of Investments*. New York: John Wiley & Sons.

Marston, R. C. (1995). *International Financial Integration: A Study of Interest Differentials between the Major Industrial Countries*. Cambridge: Cambridge University Press.

Martin, L. (2000). *Public Opinion Shocks and Cabinet Termination*, Typescript, Florida State University.

McBrady, M. (2003). *What Explains Industrial Country Sovereign Spreads?* Manuscript: Darden Graduate School of Business, University of Virginia.

McCarty, N., Poole, K. and Rosenthal, H. (2002). *Polarized Politics in the Transfer State*, Manuscript, Princeton University.

McGillivray, F. (2003). *Coalition Formation and Stock Price Volatility*, Manuscript, New York University.

McKinnon, R. (1962). Optimum currency areas. *American Economic Review*, **53**, 717–24.

Meese, R. (1990). Currency fluctuations in the post-Bretton Woods era. *Journal of Economic Perspectives*, **4**, 117–34.

Meese, R. and Rogoff, K. (1983). Empirical exchange rate models of the seventies: do they fit out-of-sample? *Journal of International Economics*, 3–24.

Meese, R. and Rogoff, K. (1987). Was it real? The exchange rate-interest differential relation over the modern floating-rate era. *Journal of Finance*, 933–48.

Mehra, R. and Prescott, E. (1985). The equity premium puzzle. *Journal of Monetary Economics*, **15**, 145–61.

Mehra, R. and Prescott, E. (2003). The equity premium in retrospect. National Bureau of Economic Research. *Working Paper W9525*.

Melvin, M. and Yin, X. (2000). Public information arrival, exchange rate volatility, and quote frequency. *The Economic Journal*, **110**, 644–661.

Mincer, J. and Zarnowitz, V. (1969). The evaluation of economic forecasts. In *Economic Forecasts and Expectations*, ed. J. Mincer. New York: National Bureau of Research.

Monroe, B. (2001). *Bias and Responsiveness in Multiparty Representation*, Typescript, Michigan State University.

Mosley, L. (2002). *Global Capital Markets and National Governments*, Cambridge: Cambridge University Press.

Mulgan, R. (1994). *Politics in New Zealand*. Auckland: Auckland University Press.

Mundell, R. (1961). A theory of optimal currency areas. *American Economic Review*, **51**, 509–17.

Mussa, M. (1984). The theory of exchange rate determination. In *Exchange Rate Theory and Policy*, eds. J. Bilson and R. Marston. Chicago, Il: University of Chicago Press.

Nadeau, R., Niemi, R. and Amato, T. (1996). Prospective and comparative or retrospective and individual? Party leaders and party support in Great Britain. *British Journal of Political Science*, **26**(2), 245–258.

Nadeau, R., Niemi, R. and Amato, T. (2000). Elite economic forecasts, economic news, mass economic expectations, and voting intentions in Great Britain. *European Journal of Political Research*, **38**, 135–170.

Neal, L. (1990). *The Rise of Financial Capitalism: International Capital Markets in the Age of Reason*. New York: Cambridge University Press.

Nelson, D. B. (1991). Conditional heteroskedasticity in asset returns: a new approach. *Econometrica*, **59**, 347–70.

Newey, W. K. and West, K. D. (1987). A simple, positive semi-definite heteroskedasticity and autocorrelation consistent covariance matrix. *Econometrica*, **55**, 703–8.

Norpoth, H. (1991). The popularity of the Thatcher government: a matter of war and economy. In *Economics and Politics*, eds. H. Norpoth, M. Lewis-Beck and J.-D. Lafay. Ann Arbor: University of Michigan Press.

North, D. (1981). *Structure and Change in Economic History*. New York: W.W. Norton and Company.

Obstfeld, M. and Stockman, A. (1985). Exchange rate dynamics. In *Handbook of International Economics*, Volume II, eds. R. Jones and P. Kenen. Amsterdam: North Holland.

Obstfeld, M. and Taylor, A. M. (2004). *Global Capital Markets: Integration, Crisis, and Growth*. Cambridge: Cambridge University Press.

OECD (2002). Increases in Investment in the 1990s: the role of output, cost of capital and finance. *Financial Market Trends*, **83**, 121–42.

O'Hara, M. (1995). *Market Microstructure Theory*. London: Blackwell Publishing.

Oxley L. and McAleer, M. (1993). Econometric issues in macroeconomic models with generated regressors. *Journal of Economic Surveys*, **7**, 1–40.

Pagan, A. R. and Schwert, G. W. (1990). Alternative models of stock volatility. *Journal of Econometrics*, **45**, 267–290.

Patterson, K. (2000). *An Introduction to Applied Econometrics*. New York: St. Martin's Press.

Perron P. (1989). The great crash, the oil price shock, and the unit root hypothesis. *Econometrica*, **57**, 1361–1402.

Persson, T. and Tabellini, G. (2002). *Political Economics: Explaining Economic Policy*. Cambridge, MA: MIT Press.

Portes, R. and Rey, H. (2005). The determinants of cross-border equity flows. *Journal of International Economics*, **65**, 269–296.

Poterba, J. (2004). The impact of population aging on financial markets. *NBER Working Papers 10851*, National Bureau of Economic Research, Inc.

Powell, G. B. (1982). *Contemporary Democracies*. Cambridge: Harvard University Press.

Powell, G. B. (2000). *Elections as Instruments of Democracy*. New Haven: Yale University Press.

Quinn, D. P. (1997). The correlates of change in international financial regulation. *American Political Science Review*, **91**(September), 531–551.

Quinn, D. and Inclan, C. (1997). The origins of financial openness: a study of current and capital account liberalization. *American Journal of Political Science*, **41**(3), 771–813.

Quinn, D. P. and Woolley, J. T. (2001). Democracy and national economic performance: the preference for stability. *American Journal of Political Science*, **45**(July), 634–657.

Rae, D. (1971). *The Political Consequences of Electoral Laws*. New Haven: Yale University Press.

Rajan, R. G. and Zingales, L. (2003). *Saving Capitalism from the Capitalists*. New York: Crown Books.

Riker, W. (1962). *The Theory of Political Coalitions*. New Haven: Yale University Press.

Roberts, B. (1994). *The Industrial Organization of the 1992 US Presidential Election.* Paper Presented at the Annual Meeting of the Midwest Political Science Association, Chicago, Illinois.

Rogoff, K. (1990). Equilibrium political budget cycles. *American Economic Review*, **80**, 21–36.

Roll, R. (1977). A critique of the asset pricing theory's tests: part I. *Journal of Financial Economics*, **4**, 129–176.

Roll, R. (1992). Industrial structure and the comparative behavior of international stock market indices. *Journal of Finance*, **47**, 3–41.

Roll, R. and Yan, S. (1998). *An Explanation of the Forward Premium 'Puzzle'*, Manuscript, Los Angeles: The Anderson School at UCLA.

Ross, S. A. (1976). The Arbitrage Theory of Capital Asset Pricing. *Journal of Economic Theory*, **13**, 341–360.

Roubini, N. and Sachs, J. (1989a). Government spending and budget deficits in the industrial countries. *Economic Policy*, **8**, 99–132.

Roubini, N. and Sachs, J. (1989b) Political and economic determinants of budget deficits in the industrial democracies. *European Economic Review*, **33**, 903–38.

Sanders, D. (1999). Conservative incompetence, labour responsibility and the feel-good factor: why the economy failed to save the Conservatives in 1997. *Electoral Studies*, **18**, 251–270.

Sanders, D. (2000). The real economy and the perceived economy in popularity functions: how much do voters need to know? *Electoral Studies*, **19**, 275–294.

Sanders, D., Marsh, D. and Ward, H. (1993). The electoral impact of press coverage of the British economy. 1979–87. *British Journal of Political Science*, **23**(2), 175–210.

Scharpf, F. (1987). *Crisis and Choice in European Social Democracy.* Ithaca: Cornell University Press.

Schofield, N. (1992). *Political Competition in Multiparty Coalition Governments*, Typescript, Washington University.

Sharpe, W (1964). Capital asset prices: a theory of market equilibrium under conditions of risk. *Journal of Finance*, **19**, 425–42.

Sharpe, W. (1970). *Portfolio Theory and Capital Markets.* New York: McGraw-Hill.

Shepsle, K. (1991). *Models of Multiparty Electoral Competition.* Chur: Harwood Academic Publishers.

Shiller, R. (1979). The volatility of long-term interest rates and expectations models of the term structure. *Journal of Political Economy*, **87**, 1190–1219.

Shiller, R. (1990). The term structure of interest rates. In *Handbook of Monetary Economics*, Volume I, eds. B. M. Friedman and F. H. Hahn. New York: Elsevier Science Publishers.

Shleifer, A. (2000). *Inefficient Markets: An Introduction to Behavioral Finance.* Cambridge: Cambridge University Press.

Smith, A. (2000). *Election Timing in Majoritarian Parliaments*, Typescript, Yale University.

Smith, A. (2004). *Election Timing.* New York: Cambridge University Press.

Sola, M. and Timmerman, A. (1994). *Fitting the Moments: A Comparison of ARCH and Regime-Switching Models for Daily Stock Returns.* London Business School DP, pp. 6–94.

Solnik, B. (2000). *International Investments*, 4th edition. New York: Pearson Addison Wesley.

Stein, E. and Streb, W. (1998). Elections and the timing of devaluations. *Working Paper*, Inter-American Development Bank, Washington, DC.

Stewart, M. C. and Clarke, H. D. (1992). The (un) importance of party leaders: leader images and party choice in the 1987 British election. *The Journal of Politics*, **54**(2), 447–470.

Strange, S. (1996). *Retreat of the State: The Diffusion of Power in the World Economy.* New York: Cambridge University Press.

Strom, K. and Leipart, J. (1993). Policy, institutions, and coalition avoidance: Norwegian governments. 1945–1990. *American Political Science Review*, **87**(4), 870–887.

Tabellini, G. and Alesina, A. (1990). Voting on the Budget Deficit. *American Economic Association, American Economic Review*, **80**(1), 37–49.

Tauchen, G. and Pitts, M. (1983). The price variability-volume relationship in speculative markets. *Econometrica*, **51**, 485–506.

Tavelli, H., Tullio, G. and Spinelli, F. (1998). The evolution of European Central Bank independence: an updating of the Masciandaro and Spinelli index. *Scottish Journal of Political Economy*, **45**(3), 341–44.

Taylor, M. (1995). The economics of exchange rates. *Journal of Economic Literature*, **33**, 13–47.

Thaler, R. H. (1992). *The winner's curse: Paradoxes and anomalies of economic life.* Princeton: Princeton University Press.

Theodossiou, P. (1994). The stochastic properties of major Canadian exchange rates. *The Financial Review*, **29**, 193–221.

Timmerman, A. G. (1996). Excess volatility and predictability of stock prices in autoregressive models with learning. *Review of Economic Studies*, **63**, 523–557.

Tobin, J. (1969). A general equilibrium approach to monetary theory. *Journal of Money, Credit and Banking*, **1**, 15–29.

Tsay, R. (2002). *Analysis of Financial Time Series.* New York: John Wiley and Sons.

Tsebelis, G. (2002). *Veto Players: How Political Institutions Work.* Princeton, NJ: Princeton University Press.

Turner, C. M., Startz, R. and Nelson, C. R. (1989). A Markov model of heteroskedasticity, risk and learning in the stock market. *Journal of Financial Economics*, **25**, 3–22.

Van Norden, S. and Huntley, S. (1997). Regime-switching in stock-market returns. *Applied Financial Economics*, **7**, 177–191.

Warwick, P. (1994). *Government Survival in Parliamentary Democracies.* New York: Cambridge University Press.

Westerfield, R. (1977). The distribution of common stock price changes: an application of transactions time and subordinated stochastic models. *Journal of Financial and Quantitative Analysis*, **12**, 743–65.

Wlezien, C. (2001). On forecasting the presidential vote. *PS: Political Science and Politics*, **34**, 25–31.

Wlezien, C. and Erikson, R. (2001). Campaign effects in theory and practice. *American Politics Research*, **29**, 419–36.

Wooldridge, J. (2002). *Econometric Analysis of Cross Section and Panel Data*. Cambridge, MA: MIT Press.

Zakoian, J. M. (1990). *Threshold Hetereoskedastic Models*, Manuscript, CREST, INSEE, Paris.

Zakoian, J. M. (1994). Threshold heteroskedastic models. *Journal of Economic Dynamics and Control*, **18**, 931–44.

Zivot, E. and Andrews, D. W. K. (1992). Further evidence on the great crash, the oil price shock, and the unit-root hypothesis. *Journal of Business and Economic Studies*, **10**, 251–270.

Index